GW00992776

fishing in Ireland

THE COMPLETE GUIDE

fishing in Ireland

THE COMPLETE GUIDE

Dick Warner • Kevin Linnane
• Peter R. Brown

Appletree Press, Belfast.

First published in Northern Ireland by
The Appletree Press Ltd
7 James Street South
Belfast BT2 8DL
1980
Reprinted June 1980

ISBN 0 904651 32 0

CONTENTS

FOREWORD

The first fish I ever caught in Ireland, and that was more than 25 years ago, came on a hot and drowsy July afternoon on Lough Corrib. It shouldn't have been the first: all morning long I'd waited for a breeze to come up so that I could dap the Harry—the daddy-long-legs—for a big brown trout. But the breeze never came, I was never a purist, and fishing close up to the lily pads that somnolent afternoon, I caught perch after perch after perch . . .

The lattermost fish that Ireland gave me—never say the last—was a bass from the high surf on Brandon Bay in the Dingle Peninsula of Kerry, just a few months ago. And, between that first struggling little perch and that bass pulling the surf rod over hard from somewhere beyond the third breaker, have come more fish than I could count, though some I still remember: the 10¼ lbs trout from Lough Mask that I beseiged for a week, the three pike, over 20 lbs each, that came from Lough Allen on successive days and won me a bet, struck months before, in a downtown bar in New York.

Catches, too, draughts of great cod, pollack and coalfish from the Black Rock outside of Belmullet in Co. Mayo, the five salmon that a few of us took from the Bandon river in Co. Cork in a couple of hours, causing the old Earl, who'd given us permission for the whole day's fishing, to cut off somewhat abruptly at lunch time . . .

The other sort of day, when it was too hot or too cold, too stormy or too calm, too bright or too dull, comes along in Ireland as it does everywhere else. But what a fishing country it is! And what good fishing friends you make there, what sights you see, what you'll have forever to talk about. This new and expert guide helps you relish and delight in all that Ireland can offer in its lakes, rivers and oceans. For that, its authors deserve the best of rewards—plenty of fishing time for themselves—now that their task is over.

Clive Gammon
Manhattan, 1980

Pike fishing, River Erne, Co. Cavan

ACKNOWLEDGEMENTS

The authors and publisher gratefully acknowledge the assistance of the following in the preparation of this book:

The Inland Fisheries Trust, for permission to reproduce maps and diagrams; the Northern Ireland Tourist Board and Bord Failte, for permission to reproduce photographs; and the Irish Specimen Fish Committee, for permission to reproduce the table of Irish Record Fish and Schedule of Specimen Weights.

Peter R. Brown would like to thank Philip E. Leonard, of the N.I. Dept. of Agriculture (Fisheries Division), for his kind assistance with the Northern Ireland chapter of the Game Fishing section; and Dick Warner would like to thank the following individual anglers for their advice on coarse fishing: Vincent Baker, Barry Brill, Gordon Dickison, John Donohue, Hugh Gough, James Keaveney, Damien Maddock, and Victor Refausse.

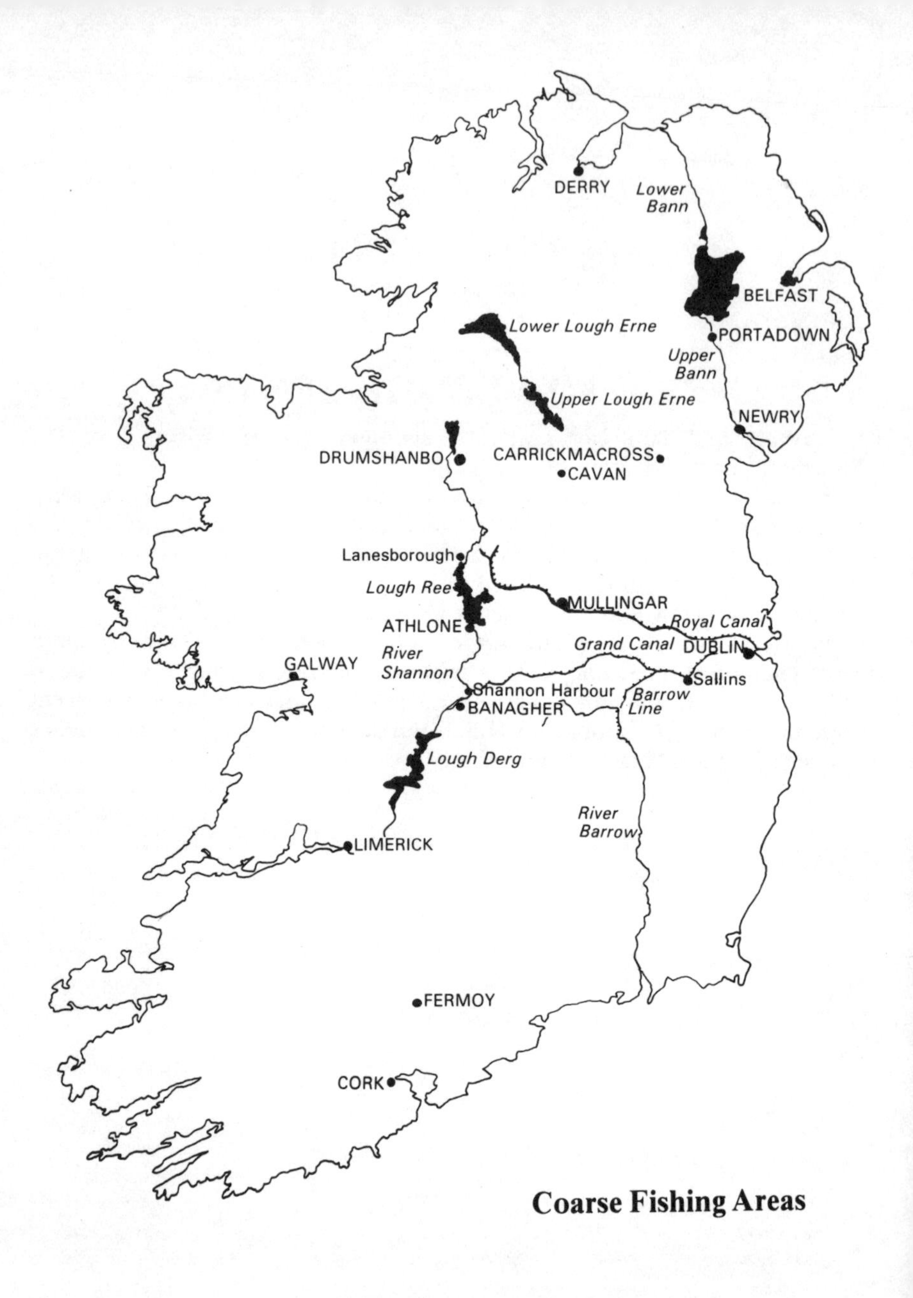

Coarse Fishing Areas

COARSE FISHING
Dick Warner

INTRODUCTION

Coarse fish are freshwater fish which are not members of the salmon and trout family. Ireland has a lot to offer the coarse fisherman but the tourist literature describing the country as an "Angler's Paradise" where monstrous fish give themselves up from every puddle and ditch must be regarded with suspicion. To do well, you need detailed information on what to do and where to do it.

This book is not particularly concerned with fishing methods. Hundreds of others have been written on coarse fishing techniques and they can easily be consulted. In this section, I will try to tell you where you can go at various times of the year to have a reasonable chance of catching different species of fish. But before going into details, it might be a good idea to look at some of the general characteristics of Irish coarse fishing and to examine some ways in which the special conditions of this country may require the angler to depart from normal coarse angling methods, which have mostly been developed in other countries.

Ireland has a mild damp climate and a lot of water containing coarse fish. Some of this water suffers from pollution, mainly sewage, agricultural effluent and the side effects of turf cutting. Fortunately, however, a lot of it remains unaffected. The population of the country is small and the percentage of this population seriously interested in coarse fishing is minute, probably numbering hundreds rather than thousands, although it is growing rapidly. Political troubles in Northern Ireland and economic problems all over the world have affected the tourist boom of the 1960s which brought us so many foreign anglers. Moreover, angling is almost unregulated by restrictions, laws and close seasons in the Republic and only slightly more so in Northern Ireland.

All this means that the coarse angler in Ireland is faced with an almost bewildering choice of well-stocked, very clear water, much of which receives little or no angling pressure. This is not as good as it might sound, for contrary to popular belief and to the situations in game or sea angling, virgin coarse fishing is difficult. Coarse fish, by and large, do not feed naturally on anglers' baits. They are educated to do so by the frequent introduction of bait and groundbait and by the fact that the fish are normally returned alive after being caught.

The vast majority of Irish rudd, however, have never seen a piece of bread and it may take them some time to realise it is edible! The same could not be said of the rudd in the hard-fished waters of eastern England, where many of the rudd fishing techniques we use were developed.

Irish coarse fish are generally not tackle-shy, but often tend to be less tolerant of the sight and sound of human beings. They also tend to be larger on average than fish in Britain or the Continent and they often live in waters which have never seen a weed-drag and which abound in natural snags. The waters are generally much less opaque than those of countries where there is greater industrial population density and inland waterway traffic.

The intelligent angler can draw the obvious conclusions from these facts. When fishing for the non-predatory species, he will usually do better if he seeks out areas where there are signs of angling pressure, as there is then a chance that some groundbait has been put in. In general, he should also give more consideration to natural baits such as worms than to the artificial ones like bread. He should fish rather stronger line and larger hooks than the textbooks recommend, and he should take special care not to scare the fish by being clumsy.

These factors don't apply to pike, although methods of pike fishing do vary slightly in Ireland. The three principal methods are live-baiting, dead-baiting and the use of artificial lures. Live-baiting is banned by law in the Republic; it can only be used in the North. Although great advances in the use of static deadbaits for pike have been made in England over the last ten years, I personally believe that it is a method which works best on waters where there is a fair degree of angling pressure on the prey species and where pike are conditioned to picking up small fish that have been damaged or killed by anglers. In such areas of Ireland, static dead-baiting works excellently. In virgin waters, I have always had better results with a spun or trolled artificial or dead-bait.

Another problem arising from the fact that coarse fishing is very much a minority sport in Ireland is that bait and tackle are not as generally available as in Britain or on the Continent. As a rule of thumb it can be taken that maggots and proprietary dried groundbait are nearly always available in Dublin and Belfast, apart from a few months in the middle of winter, and are sometimes available in the more popular provincial angling centres.

Bloodworms are never sold. Bread is of course universally available and a tactful approach to a large bakery or an animal feedstuffs supplier can usually produce stale bread, crumb, bran, flake-maize or sausage rusk. Worms can be dug and sometimes small boys can be bribed to do the work. Specialist tackle is a bit of a hit or miss affair. Some shops stock quite a good selection, while others will just have basic stuff more suited to sea and game angling. If you are stuck, use the classified telephone directory and ask around. Basically, however, the visitor is advised to bring good quantities of tackle with him; apart from his own needs, if he makes contact with any of the local anglers, a gift of good quality soft shot or decent hooks will be very welcome in exchange for some local knowledge. Another useful piece of gear is a small portable boat. Many lakes and rivers are completely ringed by reeds or lilies and it is much easier to get out beyond them in a boat than to try and cut them down. If you don't have your own boat, they can be hired at some centres.

There is a small but growing number of coarse angling clubs; a list may be found in the appendix of useful addresses at the end of this section. They are very helpful when it comes to advising visitors and are well worth contacting. Most of the clubs organise matches which are usually open to outsiders. Visitors to Ireland should note that a year-round calendar of competitions has been developed in recent years, with a number of big money matches during the

WHEN TO FISH

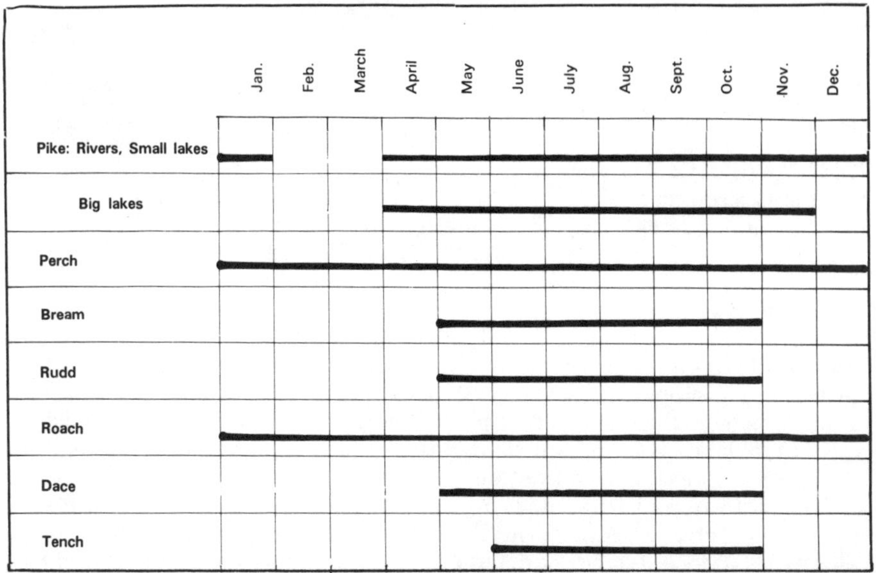

English Close Season in April and May. Details can be obtained from the National Federations or Tourist Boards (see appendix). Apart from the Tourist Boards in the North and the South, which provide information which is comprehensive but sometimes inaccurate and unrealistic, detailed angling information is available from the state bodies controlling inland fisheries in both parts of Ireland—the Inland Fisheries Trust Inc. in the Republic and the Department of Agriculture and Fisheries in Northern Ireland. Their information tends to be less comprehensive but more accurate; the addresses are also in the appendix.

Lists of record fish and specimen fish (fish which are unusually large, but not of record-breaking size, for which a badge is awarded) are kept by the Irish Specimen Fish Committee (see appendix). Anglers wishing to claim specimens and records should apply to the Committee for its rules and should bear in mind that in most cases the body of the fish must be examined by the Committee to establish its authenticity.

Foreign coarse anglers planning to visit Ireland should note that they can expect to catch fish all the year round, as there are no close seasons for coarse fish in Ireland. However, the warmer months produce better fishing for all species, with the possible exception of pike. There is also less likelihood of floods.

Before going on to describe a selection of venues in detail, it might be as well to describe the species of fish that are available. Ireland has a comparatively small variety of species and large areas of country in the south-west, the northwest and in the mountains that ring the coast have no coarse fish at all. But Ireland is a small country and there are very few places where an angler is much more than half an hour's drive from excellent fishing.

RUDD (Scardinius Erythrophthalmus) are probably the most characteristic species of Irish coarse fish. They are widely distributed in canals, ponds, lakes and the slower moving stretches of rivers. Rudd can be difficult to identify since they bear some resemblance to the roach and also because they hybridise readily with bream.

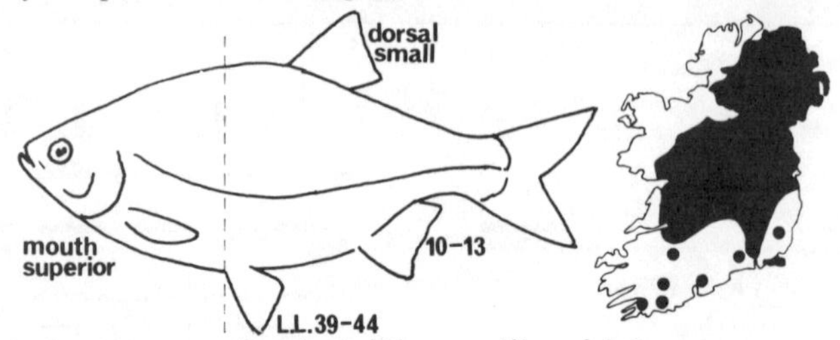

A mature rudd is golden-bronze coloured, whereas roach are silver. It has redder fins than those of roach, and a redder eye. The two best methods of telling the species apart are the position of the dorsal fin and the shape of the mouth. The dorsal fin is set behind the pelvic fins in the rudd and directly above them in the roach. The mouth is turned up in the rudd and turned down in the roach. The whole thing is further complicated by the fact that rudd are often called roach in parts of Ireland. Hybrids are more difficult to recognise and are dealt with separately under their own heading.

The best bait for small rudd is probably maggots. Bread in its various forms is excellent for the larger fish in areas where they have become accustomed to it. Worms are supposed to be good, but I've never had much luck with them. Rudd can also be caught on artificial flies. Anglers not used to fishing for rudd should bear in mind that, more than any other coarse fish, they are surface and mid-water feeders and bait should be presented accordingly. However, if the angler is being bothered by shoals of small fish, a bigger bait shotted to fall rapidly below the shoal often picks up much larger fish.

The Irish record rudd is 3 lbs 1 oz (1.428 kg) and the specimen is 2 lbs 4 ozs (1.012 kg). Any competent and dedicated angler putting in a week's fishing on a good rudd water could reasonably expect several fish over a pound (0.5 kg). Rudd can be caught all the year round but the warmer the weather, the easier it becomes. Rudd shoals have a reputation, particularly among match fishermen, for being difficult to hold with groundbait. I have never found this to be so if the swim is fed intelligently. I think the problem may arise because rudd are quite shy and habitually swim near the surface, so that it becomes easy to scare them off with careless movements or noises—which would include fist-sized lumps of mashed bread.

COMMON BREAM (Abramis Brama) are almost as widely distributed as rudd, and are found in similar types of water, although at most times of the year they prefer the deeper parts of rivers and lakes. Unlike rudd they feed almost entirely on the bottom. They are difficult to confuse with any other fish except hybrids. In

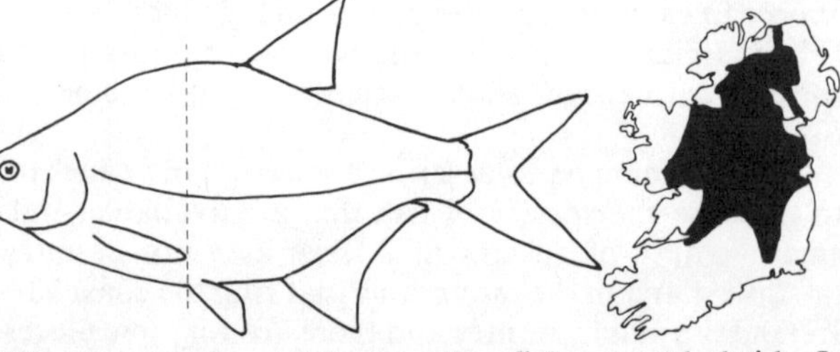

some parts of the country small, shiny fish can be caught which are known locally as "silver bream". These are not the true silver bream (Blicca Bjoerkna) but "skimmer" or immature common bream.

Bream are found throughout Europe, so there should be no need to go into details of angling methods or baits. One thing, however, that the foreign angler should bear in mind is that Irish bream are often very large and frequently swim in immense shoals. This means that ten or twenty pounds (4.5–9.0 kg) of groundbait can be consumed in minutes. To be successful, baiting up and feeding a swim may have to be done on a gargantuan scale.

The Irish record bream weighted 11 lbs 12 ozs (5.336) and the specimen weight is 7 lbs 8 ozs (3.424 kg). A swim which is producing well on, say, the Shannon can be expected to produce up to 100 lbs (45 kg) in a day and 200 lbs (90 kg) is not out of the question if you're a hard worker. Very large bream are more difficult, but there are venues mentioned in the text which are certainly capable of producing double-figure fish if they are fished hard and well round the clock. Most Irish bream fishing is carried out in summer; winter fishing is quite possible, but it must be regarded as pioneering at this stage in the development of Irish coarse fishing.

HYBRIDS is the name commonly given in Ireland to rudd/bream crosses, although roach and bream also hybridise in the Erne system. Hybrids cause considerable problems of identification to Irish anglers and can be confusing for foreign anglers who often have not come across them before. They grow large and many fishermen have thought that they had broken the Irish rudd record, only to learn that what they had caught was just a good-sized hybrid.

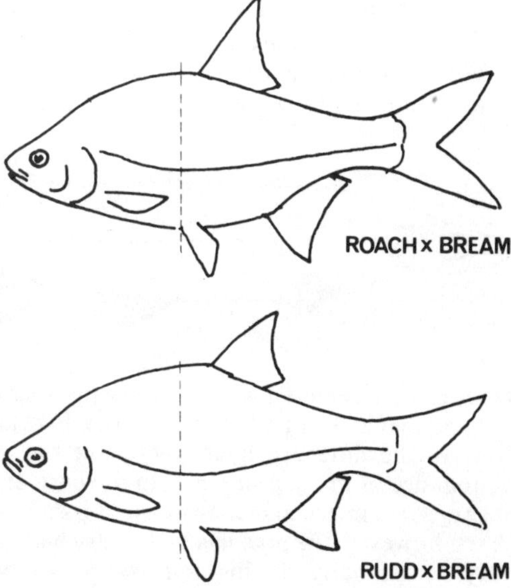

For quick identification, the two things to look at are the colour of the fins and the shape of the mouth. If you catch a rudd which has brown or blackish coloured fins instead of bright orangey-red ones, or a bream which has any reddish tint to its fins, the chances are that it is a hybrid. The same applies to a rudd which seems to have a mouth shaped like a bream's or vice versa. In the final analysis, it may require the services of a trained ichthyologist to give an absolute ruling, which is why the Irish Specimen Fish Committee must see the body of a fish before it can adjudicate a specimen or record claim. Hybrids have their own category in the record list and are a very common and sporting fish. The record is 5 lbs 13½ ozs (2.678 kg) and the specimen weight is 3 lbs (1.4 kg). 2 lbs (0.9 kg) fish are not at all unusual.

Although the mainstream of scientific opinion tends to hold that all hybrids are sterile, which means they must all be fifty per cent rudd and fifty per cent bream, my observations are that they tend to take up the behaviour patterns of one or other of the parent fish rather than develop their own habits.

However, hybrids more commonly follow the example of rudd. They are noticeably better fighters than either of the parent species and reach good weights, which is why Irish coarse anglers spend quite a lot of time fishing for them.

The smaller fish tend to move in shoals, commonly mixed with rudd, and sometimes with bream. The larger hybrids have a tendency, particularly in the Grand Canal, to travel in small groups of from two to ten fish which are made up only of hybrids. In warmer weather these small groups of fish will cruise the canal in mid-water, over the summer-length weeds, and are very easily scared. On summer evenings, they often feed heavily on floating flies and can be fished for with dry flies, floating crusts or casters fished 'on the drop' on very light tackle. Alternatively, a clear spot in the weeds can be baited up and if the hybrids move on to it and get their heads down, they can be caught by laying-on.

I am convinced that we have a lot to learn about hybrids, both about their biology and how to catch them. The vast majority of them are caught by anglers fishing for either rudd or bream, so the same tackle and baits should be used. Any water which holds both the parent species can be expected to hold bybrids as well, particularly if the population density of the fish is fairly heavy.

PIKE (Esox Lucius) are certainly the most popular of our coarse fish species

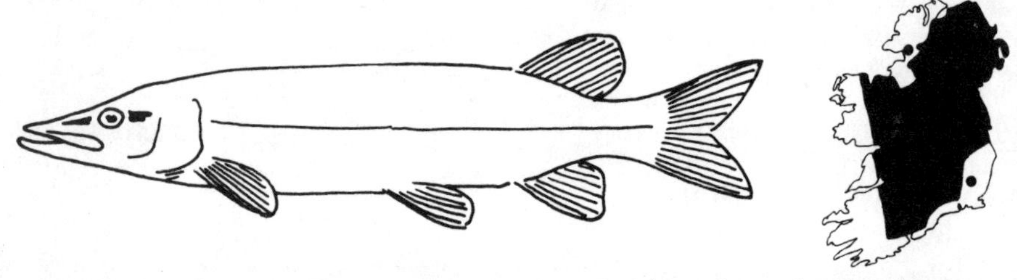

among Irish anglers and a growing number of visitors from the Continent are coming to this country to fish for them. Pike are found throughout the temperate zone in the northern hemisphere but the amount of suitable water and the abundance of prey species has, in the past, ensured a greater number and larger average size in Ireland than is usual throughout most of their range. In recent years, however, the pike has had a very bad time in Ireland. Although it is eaten only occasionally in this country, it is a very popular fish food in certain countries of eastern and western Europe. Modern transport techniques led to the development of commercial pike fisheries in Ireland and many tons a year were exported to European markets. Moreover, the establishment of the Inland Fisheries Trust in the 1950's also led to the extermination of thousands and thousands of pike, since the Trust was given a brief to promote fishing for trout, upon which pike prey. But it could be pointed out that pike were only removed from a small number of waters.

Today, the outlook is a bit brighter. A law was passed in 1977 which virtually banned commercial fishing for pike, restricted the number of rods an angler could use at any one time to two, although he may now have more than two with him, and banned live-baiting to prevent the spread of roach around the country.

The constitution of the Inland Fisheries Trust was changed over twenty years ago to incorporate coarse fishing development, so there is now a much more enlightened view of the value and importance of pike in a fishery. Anglers should welcome this trend, obey the new laws and return the pike carefully to the water unless they want to keep a reasonable number for eating.

The Irish rod-caught record pike from a river is 42 lbs (18.9 kg) and from a lake, 38 lbs 2 ozs (17.656 kg). The specimen weights are 20 lbs (9 kg) from a river and 30 lbs (14 kg) from a lake. However, much bigger fish than this have been taken commercially, and a fish of 53 lbs (24.4 kg) was taken on rod and line in Lough Conn in 1920. This fish held the Irish record for many years, although the present Committee considers the evidence for its existence inadequate. It must, however, be regarded as the best authenticated fish over 50 lbs (23 kg) to have been caught in the British Isles.

The pike is easy to recognise and the techniques for its capture are well-known internationally, so there should be no need to go into them here, apart from repeating that live-baiting is only permitted in Northern Ireland and suggesting that the value of static dead-baits may be limited. Frogs are a popular bait among resident anglers. Most pike fishing in Ireland is done in the autumn and winter. The reasons for this are probably the persistence of the Victorian fallacy that pike are only 'in season' in the winter and the fact that many pike anglers are really trout fishermen looking for occupation on winter weekends. Pike feed all the year round, and can be caught all the year round, although a case can be made for laying off in February and March, when they are spawning, or in summer when some pike waters can be difficult to fish because of the weed growth. Pike are very widely distributed and will be found in many waters not specifically mentioned in the text of this book; anglers should ask locally. A pike of over 10 lbs (4.5 kg) should be within the grasp of most competent anglers.

To give an idea of their distribution, the Inland Fisheries Trust recently carried out a census on the match stretch of the Barrow Branch of the Grand Canal just outside Athy. They found a fish of between ten and twenty pounds (4.5–9.0 kg) for every four hundred yards (365 metres) of the Canal on average and one fish of over twenty pounds (9.0 kg). Very big fish are a matter of luck, local knowledge and persistence.

PERCH (Perca fluviatilis) are also very widely distributed both internationally and in Ireland. They are easy to identify and fishing methods here do not differ significantly from those in use elsewhere. However, Ireland cannot be considered an outstanding country for perch fishing because the fish are generally very small. The Irish record is 5 lbs 8 ozs (2.524 kg)

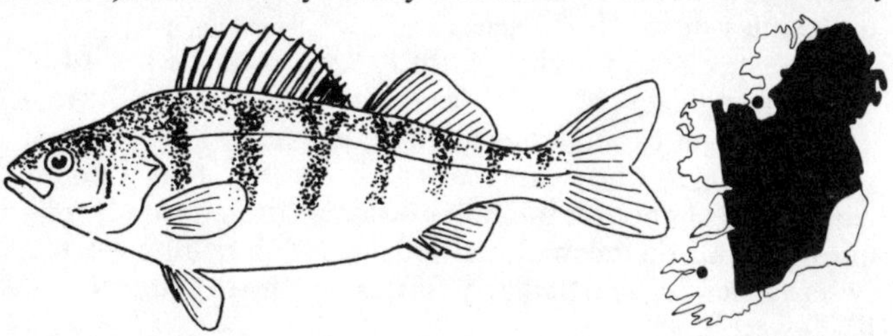

and the specimen weight is 3 lbs (1.4 kg), but the average run of fish in the majority of waters is under half a pound (0.25 kg).

There are one or two known venues where larger perch can be taken and these are mentioned in the text; undoubtedly there are more to be discovered. In the meantime, Irish perch fishing must be regarded as something of a mystery.

ROACH (Rutilus Rutilus) are not widely distributed in Ireland, and many so-called roach are in fact rudd. They are not a native fish, and the first ones were introduced in the last century to the River Blackwater in Munster, where they flourished but did not spread. Today the Blackwater must be regarded as one of the world's top roach rivers.

Some time in the late fifties or early sixties, a second introduction was made into the lower end of the River Erne system in Northern Ireland. At first this was successful and good catches were made around Omagh. Then things began to go wrong. There was a roach population explosion and they spread into every corner of this extensive system of rivers and lakes, right up to the source in Lough Gowna in the Republic. As they continued breeding, other species of fish began to disappear, until roach, bream and pike were the only fish to turn up consistently in the system. With the waters becoming overcrowded, the average size dropped. Today much of the system produces only thousands of stunted fish weighing around two ounces (56 g). There are, however, some places where better roach can be caught and these are listed in the text.

It should also be said that the Erne system is ecologically unstable at present, but when it reaches climax and settles down, the fishing may be very good indeed. The most worrying aspect of this is that roach have spread out of the Erne system, mainly as a result of anglers transporting them for live bait for pike. They have now started to invade the Shannon system, by far the largest watershed in the country, as well as many of the midland trout lakes and canals. This may mean a very unsettled decade ahead as far as fish populations are concerned and it would be a brave pundit who would predict how things will work out in the end. In the meantime, there is excellent roach fishing to be had at the venues noted in the text.

The specimen weight is 2 lbs (0.9 kg) and the record is 2 lbs 13½ ozs (1.078 kg), although several roach over the record weight have been taken in salmon nets or caught by anglers who did not wish to kill the fish to claim the record. A visiting angler who wants to catch his first two pound (0.9 kg) roach has a reasonable chance on the Blackwater. A three-pounder (1.4 kg) is not out of the question. All the normal methods of roach fishing work; quiver-tipping with a swim-feeder is particularly effective in the deeper, faster swims of the Blackwater.

DACE (Leuciscus Leuciscus) are even more restricted in their distribution than roach. They are only found in the Munster Blackwater, where they were introduced at the same time as the roach. They grow to a very good weight and fishing for them in the streamy swims on the middle reaches of the river is very enjoyable.

The specimen weight is 1 lb (0.5 kg) and the record is 1 lb 2 ozs (0.556) but this must be regarded as one of the most vulnerable of the Irish records. Any angler who loves and understands dace fishing, and who is prepared to put in a couple of weeks in the summer around Mallow or Fermoy must have a very good chance of breaking the record. Few anglers in Ireland fish specifically for dace.

As there are no chub in Ireland, the identification of dace presents no problems. Methods of angling for them are just as the text books say, although it must be remembered that the Blackwater is a much bigger river than the classic English dace stream. They can also be caught on the artificial fly. Unlike roach, which can give good sport all the year round, dace are primarily a summer fish, although this may be simply because no-one has yet bothered to work out how and where to fish for them in the Blackwater during the winter months.

TENCH (Tinca Tinca) is also a fish that was introduced to Ireland, but this

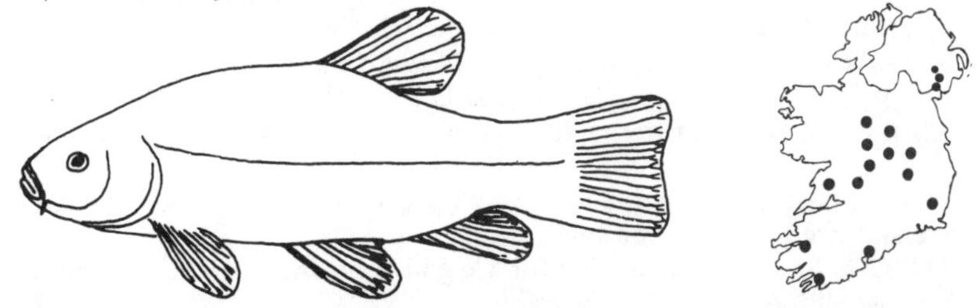

happened a long time ago, probably in the Middle Ages. For a long time they had a very restricted distribution, but during the last twenty years they have been introduced all over the country. Tench take some time to settle down after being moved, but are now thoroughly established at several venues mentioned in the text and provide top quality fishing.

The record is 7 lbs 13¼ ozs (3.571 kg) and the specimen weight is 6 lbs (2.7 kg). Many waters produce good averages, and it is rare to catch a female fish under 3 lbs (1.4 kg) or a male under 2 lbs (0.9 kg). A few waters have even higher averages, where a female under 5 lbs (2.5 kg) is an oddity. Irish tench will take worms, bunches of maggots or bread and show unpredictable preferences for one or the other. They are traditionally fish of the summer and in the waters they inhabit this means a lot of weeds. An angler will need some kind of weed-cutting implement in all but the best-known and most fished areas and should use relatively strong tackle. Otherwise Irish tench fishing follows text book patterns, although our fish don't seem to be quite so shy or difficult as some of the foreign writers find theirs.

CARP (Cyprinus Carpio) are found in Ireland, but this country cannot be considered to have great carp fishing. They are found only in a few waters at present, and many of these are private. However, carp are being introduced widely and the picture may change in the future. The record is only 18 lbs 12 ozs (8.536 kg), compared to the British record of 44 lbs (19.8 kg). The specimen weight is 10 lbs (4.5 kg). The carp record will probably be broken in the near future by a fish from the Lough in Cork, but it will be some years before our fishing begins to approach in quality that available in the south of England or certain continental countries.

Techniques are the same as those practised in other countries, except that Irish carp are not as 'sophisticated' as some of their foreign cousins and so it is probably adequate to use the more old-fashioned baits rather than modern particles and high protein compounds. .

EELS (Anguilla anguilla) are plentiful in Ireland and can be a nuisance to

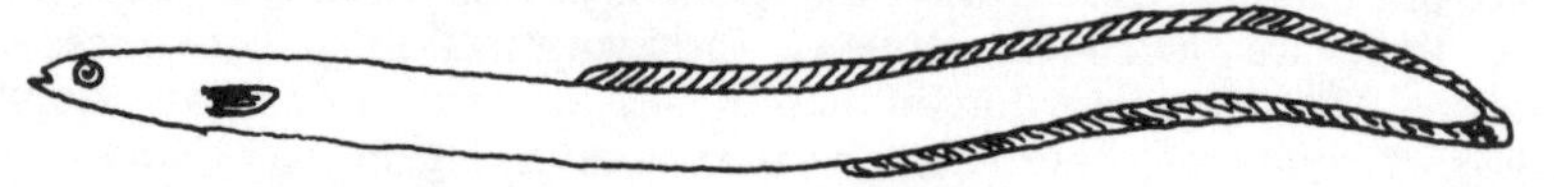

anglers after other fish. In fact, for this reason, bream anglers in certain parts of the country—Cavan and Monaghan in particular—never put maggots or worms in their groundbait. The eel record is 6 lbs 15 ozs (3.125 kg) and the specimen weight is 3 lbs (1.4 kg). The average eel is much smaller than this, seldom exceeding a pound and a half (0.75 kg). Anglers interested in larger fish must seek out the few waters which grow them to very large sizes. By and large, this will involve pioneering, as very few of these waters are known, apart from the Lough in Cork and a few ponds near Dublin. But the large fish undoubtedly do exist, and any angler prepared to devote a lot of time and expertise to using the specialist eel-fishing techniques developed in other countries could probably revise the specimen and record weights dramatically. The usual baits for eels in Ireland are lobworms or small dead rudd.

OTHER FISH species angled for are gudgeon, which are not widely distributed but which grow to a relatively large size in the Barrow/Nore system, shad, minnows and loach.

Minnows and loach are really only of interest as bait, with minnows being widely distributed and loach more localised. Allis and Thwaite shad are found in Ireland, but the only ones angled for to a reasonable degree are Thwaite shad, and these are only caught consistently in one place, St Mullins on the River Barrow, when they come up to spawn in May and June. This unusual and sporting fish is normally taken on small spinners. The only other fish that the coarse angler is likely to encounter are trout and salmon, which may take baits intended for their humbler cousins, or flounder and mullet, which are really sea fish, but are commonly taken on coarse fishing tackle in rivers.

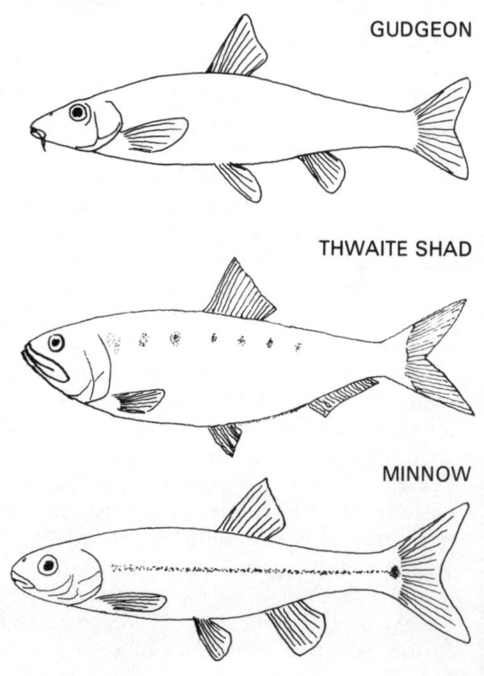

Having discussed the fish and the methods of catching them, it's time to get on with the real purpose of this section, which is to tell you exactly where to go to put the theory into practice.

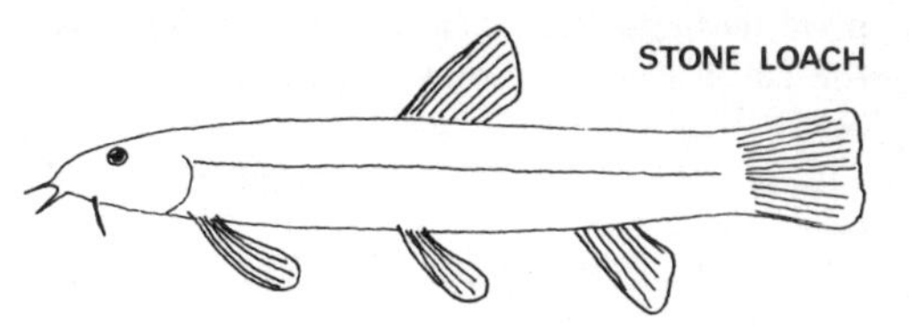
STONE LOACH

1. GRAND & ROYAL CANALS, MULLINGAR LAKES & LIFFEY

The Main line of the Grand Canal runs from Dublin westwards to the Shannon. It is maintained for navigation, but commercial traffic ceased in 1960. The Inland Waterways Association of Ireland publishes a guide to the waterway which may be useful to anglers. The Irish Ordnance Survey publishes excellent ½ inch to the mile maps. Sheet sixteen deals with the eastern half of the canal and sheet fifteen with the western. The canal has fish throughout its length, even in Dublin, where stretches which were polluted in the past have recently been restocked. But some stretches of the canal are very much better than others and moving even twenty yards (18.2 metres) along the bank can make the difference between a sprinkling of small perch and a really good net. The following venues are known to produce quality fishing.

GOLLIERSTOWN

At Gollierstown, the canal runs through a rock cutting and is narrow and deep with trees and bushes growing out of the banks. There is a bridge but no road and a number of flooded limestone quarries on both banks. The lack of a road makes access difficult; you either come by boat or walk nearly a mile (1.6 km) along the north bank from the 12th lock at the Lucan road bridge. This pilgrimage is made by many young Dublin anglers who cycle or take the bus from the city.

The quarry ponds are fished for pike, mainly in the two to six pounds range (0.9–2.7 kg), small rudd and bream. It is less well-known that there are numbers of perch up to and over a pound (0.5 kg), which is far above the average for the canal, along the stretch where it runs through the cutting.

13TH LOCK

This lock is not far from Celbridge and can be reached by driving along the towpath on the south bank, either from Aylmer Bridge to the east or from Henry Bridge to the west. There are pike and perch, mainly small, throughout this stretch of the canal. There is also a small population of large trout, as well as a shoal of good bream and very large hybrids below the lock; its headquarters is the basin about three hundred yards (274 metres) below (east) of it. These fish are shy. About three hundred yards (274 metres) above the lock on the south bank, there is a farmhouse with a number of ponds round it. These are actually flooded quarry workings; fishing in these ponds is by permission of the farmer only and produces small rudd (ideal pike baits), pike of a better average size than those in the canal and specimen eels.

SALLINS (Map 1)

This stretch of the canal can be approached either from the village of Sallins by a rather bumpy towpath on the northern bank, or by a more complicated route on a better road on the southern bank. The canal can be crossed by a road bridge in Sallins or a pedestrian underpass at the Leinster Aqueduct and fishes equally well from either bank.

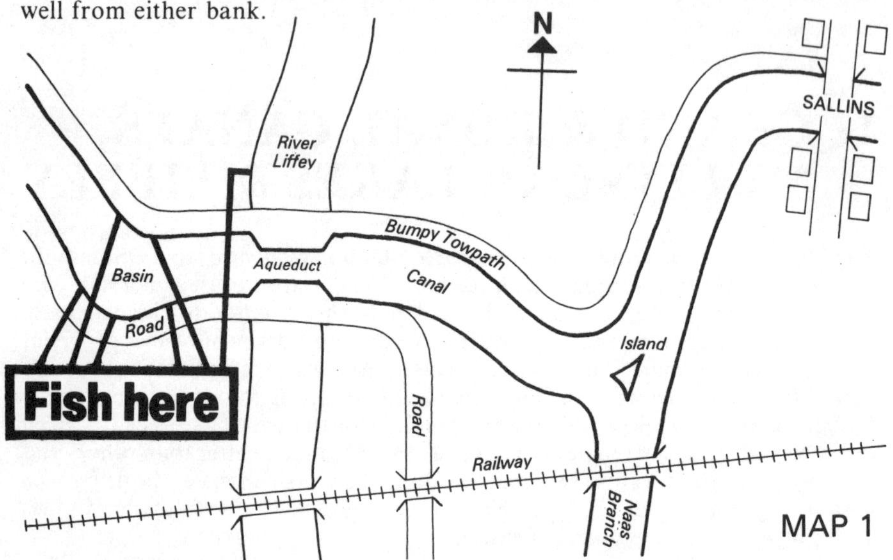

The best swims are in the basin immediately to the west of the aqueduct. The basin contains moderate rudd and perch and a shoal of good bream in the 4 lbs (1.8 kg) range. It is occasionally visited by tench. Depth will be around four feet (1.2 metres) and laying on with bread or maggots takes the bream. The rudd and perch respond best to a single maggot fished on the drop and some loose feed. The river below the aqueduct can produce bigger perch on a legered lob. The canal is well protected from the wind and there are possible swims further west if those in the basin have been taken. It fishes best in warm weather. The Naas branch of the canal, marked on the sketch map, contains fish but is difficult, being clear, shallow and weedy.

DIGBY BRIDGE

This bridge is at the sixteenth lock and is a convenient access point to a stretch of canal of over a mile (1.6 km) in length which has excellent fishing. The stretch has all the usual Grand Canal species (bream, rudd, pike, perch, tench, eels and hybrids) and has in addition been stocked with carp. However, it is best known for its excellent tench fishing in the warmer months of the year. The most popular swims for tench are immediately above and below the sixteenth lock and above (west of) the seventeenth lock for a distance of about five hundred yards (457 metres). The best bream swim is just below the sixteenth lock or midway between the sixteenth and seventeenth.

There is good access from the road and parking space. The stretch above the seventeenth lock is very heavily weeded and well-sheltered from the wind by the trees. Normally, several swims are cleared of weed by anglers from the nearby Prosperous Angling Club. The stretches each side of the sixteenth lock are rather more exposed and do not weed up quite so heavily. The tench have a good average size. They are almost invariably caught by float-fishing on the bottom and a line of about four pounds (1.8 kg) breaking strain and a hook about size ten is usual. Commonest bait is probably a bunch of maggots, though there are occasions when worms, bread or a combination of these can be very effective.

COCK BRIDGE

This bridge is above the 'tench stretch' and is noted for a good shoal of bream which patrols the canal above and below the bridge.

LOWTOWN (Map 2)

Lowtown is at the junction of the main line of the Grand Canal and the Barrow Line, which is dealt with in a later chapter. It is a popular mooring for canal craft and the important Milltown Feeder joins the summit level near here. The water is exceptionally clear, particularly in the summit level, and there can be quite a bit of boat traffic in summer. There is a road bridge at Robertstown and you can drive along the towpath on the north bank from there to Lowtown. There is another bridge at Lowtown at the nineteenth lock, Main Line, and a footbridge over the Barrow Line at its junction with the Main Line.

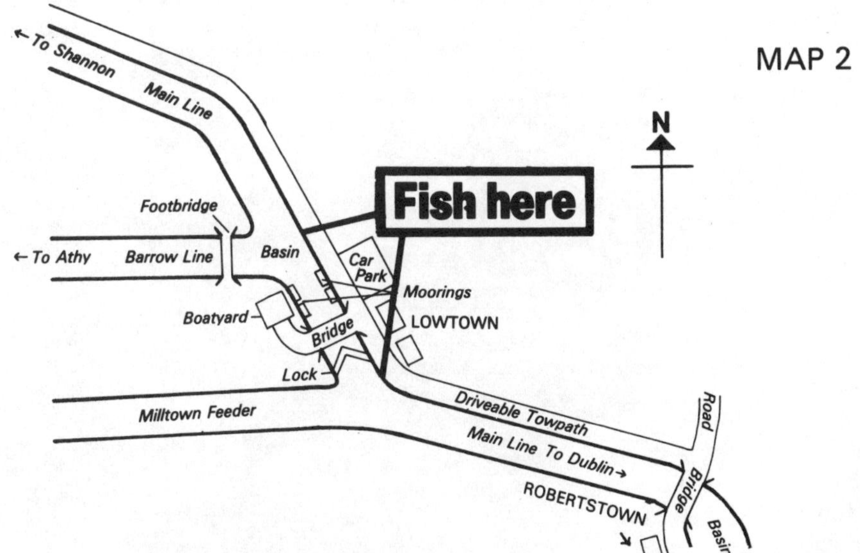

There is excellent fishing for rudd and hybrids in this area, both in the Main Line and the feeder. A good swim is in the basin where the Barrow Line joins the Main Line, just below the car park in Lowtown. Fish bread flake on the drop and use a fairly fine, bread-based groundbait. The fish are mainly in the eight to twelve ounce (22–34 g) range, although there are bream and hybrids up to five pounds (2.3 kg). Summer evenings are best, although this stretch can be fished

The Grand Canal at Robertstown, Co. Kildare

all the year round. Good fishing can also be had in the basin immediately above the lock, although weeds and the exceptional clarity of the water can make this a bit difficult.

ALLENWOOD (Map 3)
There is a match stretch pegged from just below Shee Bridge, outside Allenwood, down towards Ticknevin. There is good road access on the north bank for about half a mile (0.8 km) below Shee Bridge and from Hamilton's Bridge to a point opposite the Lullymore factory. East of Hamilton's Bridge to a point just short of Shee Bridge there is road access to the south bank. The fishing here is principally for bream, rudd and hybrids. The most productive pegs on this stretch are probably at the Lullymore factory and a stretch just to the west of Shee Bridge. The clear water brought in by the Milltown Feeder at Lowtown gives way to much darker, peatier conditions further west as the Bog of Allen is approached.

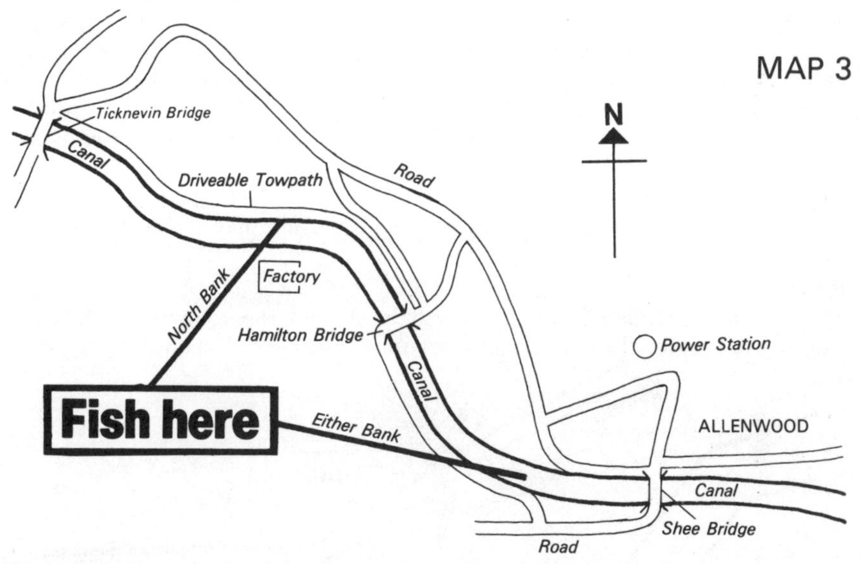

TICKNEVIN
The lock at Ticknevin is the last before the 18 mile (28.9 km) level across the Bog of Allen. It is a spot noted for bream and the productive swims are immediately below (west) the lock and about half a mile (0.8 km) to the west of it. There are recent reports that roach have been introduced at the lock.

Access is by a bumpy towpath on the south bank or by road from the south.

EDENDERRY BRANCH
There is a short branch line of the canal into the town of Edenderry. It is still open and provides quite good fishing. Bream can be caught in a depth of about five feet (1.52 metres) in the canal harbour in the town.

RHODE BRIDGE
A shoal of small but willing bream can often be contacted right at the bridge.

THE RED GIRLS
West of Toberdaly Bridge, there is a rough towpath on the north bank down towards the Bord na Mona light railway bridge. From here down to Kileen Bridge, there is fishing for good rudd and average bream. This stretch of bank was named 'The Red Girls' by bargemen in the old days in honour of a family with a flock of beautiful red-headed daughters who lived along here. Unfortunately they seem to be extinct.

DAINGEAN
Fish east of the village; access is best on the north bank. The best swims are on the bend. Average bream.

THE 24TH LOCK
The 24th lock is a couple of miles (3.2 km) east of Tullamore. It is the headquarters of a firm called Celtic Canal Cruisers which hires out boats.

To find the lock, turn off the main Dublin/Tullamore road at the signpost for the cruiser company and follow the signs until you come to their headquarters and moorings, which are just above the lock. The fishing is principally for rudd, bream and hybrids. The swims are just above the lock, along the boat moorings. It is very easy to fill a net here with small fish or 'flirters', particularly wher using maggots as a bait. The trick is to get a larger bait down through the small fry to the three pound (1.4 kg) bream and hybrids which also live in the swim.

TULLAMORE
Bream to four pounds (1.8 kg) can be caught in the canal harbour right in the town.

RAHAN (Map 4)
The village of Rahan is on the north bank and the road from Rahan to Tullamore crosses the canal over Corcoran's Bridge and then hugs the south

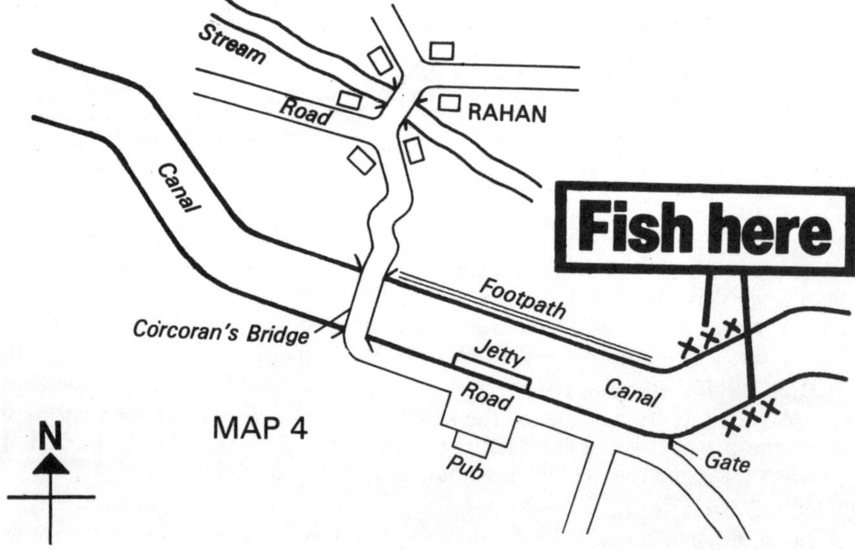

bank for about half a mile (0.8 km). In the course of this stretch there is a boat mooring jetty and an excellent pub. (It is worth mentioning that a considerable bonus to the dedicated canal angler is the many pubs which border the canal and date from the days when it was the sole route by which the products of Arthur Guinness' Dublin brewery travelled to slake the thirsts of the west of Ireland). This stretch offers the angler the normal Grand Canal bill of fare, including an excellent shoal of bream. Where the canal leaves the line of the road at the eastern end of the stretch, it widens slightly. This has proved a most productive swim, fishing equally well from either side.

31ST LOCK

About two miles (3.21 km) west of the Rahan stretch are the 30th and 31st locks, which are only a short distance apart. The 30th lock can be reached by driving along the towpath on either the north or the south bank from the Rahan direction. There is a bridge at this lock and to get further west, towards Pollagh, you have to stick to the south bank. There is excellent fishing for rudd, bream and hybrids; there are no records of specimen fish from the area, but several nets weighing over one hundred pounds (45 kg) have been taken.

The best swims are on the south bank in front of the house about midway between the two rocks, on either bank just below the 31st lock and about threequarters of a mile (1.2 km) further west where there is a bend in the canal and a disused quarry. The swim just below the 31st lock is the one to try if the water temperature is high and the level is low, as the fish may be oxygen-starved under these conditions and locks have an oxygenating influence.

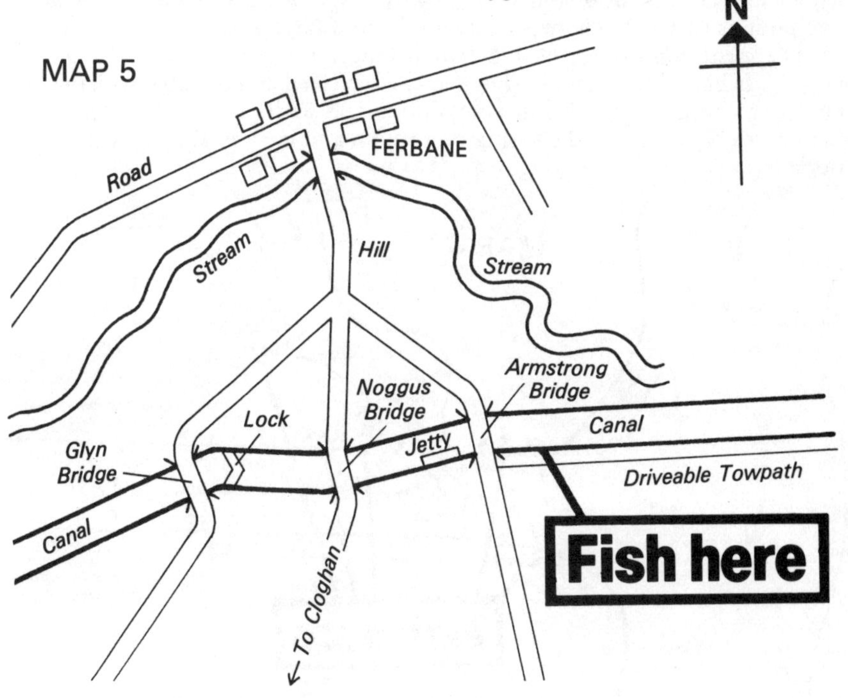

FERBANE (Map 5)

There is also an excellent swim at Ferbane, just east of Armstrong Bridge on the south bank. The towpath is suitable for driving. The fish here seem to be of above average size. It has produced bream to six pounds (2.7 kg), which is very large for the canal, although the average run is somewhere between one and three pounds (0.5–1.4 kg).

The rudd are a good size too and give good sport to casters in the summer months as well as to the more normal baits of maggots and bread. Despite the larger size of fish, there is no need to fish heavy tackle here. In fact, there is nowhere on the canal where one needs to use a line stronger than 3 lbs (1.4 kg) breaking strain unless the quarry is pike or tench in very weedy swims.

BELMONT

To find the swim, start at the cross-roads in the village of Belmont. Take the Cloghan road to the south. After about five hundred yards (457 metres) it crosses the River Brosna. About two hundred yards (182 metres) further on, turn right down a track and park by the derelict mill. You then climb over a gate and find yourself on a footpath along the canal bank; to your left is the road bridge and lock. To your right, about seventy yards (64 metres) away, the canal bends. You fish to your right up to and including the bend where the canal gets a little wider and a little deeper (up to five feet—1.52 metres), although the lock-keepers have difficulty in maintaining this level in the summer if there is a lot of boat traffic in and out of Shannon Harbour.

The fish consist of small rudd and hybrids and quite a few skimmer bream with a shoal of decent bream averaging over two pounds (0.9 kg) and reaching five pounds (2.3 kg). There are small pike and large eels.

The great importance of this swim is that it is protected on both sides by a very dense belt of trees and bushes and can be fished comfortably with fine float tackle or a swingtip in gale force conditions. It is worth noting if you are fishing the nearby Shannon in the spring or autumn and have problems with gales or floods.

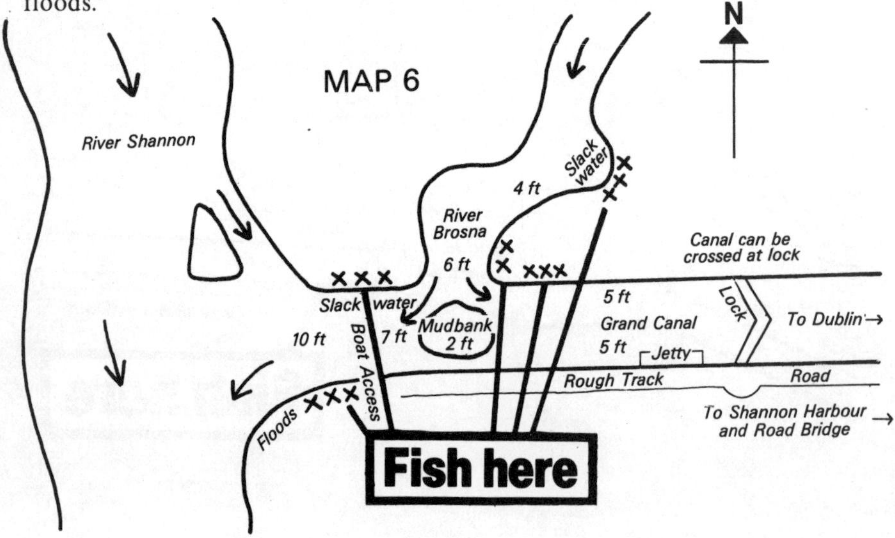

SHANNON HARBOUR (Map 6)

The village of Shannon Harbour (which is often confused with the nearby village of Shannon Bridge) is situated just to the east of the point where the Grand Canal, the River Shannon and the River Brosna meet. This confluence provides excellent and varied fishing all the year round and under all conditions, except when the River Brosna, which has been canalised for drainage purposes, is in flood.

There are bream to over five pounds (2.3 kg), hybrids over three pounds (1.4 kg) and rudd to two pounds (0.9 kg). The most popular bait is maggots, followed by redworms, particularly if the water in the Brosna is coloured, and bread on warm summer evenings. The moving water can be trotted with a float or fished with a swim-feeder; the slacks are normally fished with a swing-tip but float addicts will do as well laying on for bream or taking rudd on the drop. The swim on the north bank between the mouth of the Brosna and the Shannon can only, for practical purposes, be reached by boat and there are none for hire locally. Depth and current direction under normal summer conditions are given on the sketch map.

THE ROYAL CANAL

The Royal Canal, like the Grand, connects Dublin to the Shannon, but does so by a more northerly route. Unlike the Grand, it has been closed for navigation for the past twenty years, although some stretches have recently been opened by amateur enthusiasts. Some levels are now totally dry and others are so overgrown as to be impossible for angling.

Apart from the stretches in the heart of Dublin, all parts of the canal where there is a reasonable depth of clear water all the year round contain fish, although in many cases the only species present appears to be perch and they are not very big. Pike and rudd are also widely distributed in the canal and there are quite a few tench as well as some bream and hybrids.

The waterway is not fished anything like as much as the Grand Canal and there are certainly parts of it which have excellent fishing, particularly for rudd. They remain to be discovered. The fishing in the known venues such as those mentioned below is challenging and unusual—the swims are just holes in the weed, often no more than six feet (1.8 metres) in diameter, the water is clear, only about three feet (0.91 metres) deep and the angler is often only twenty feet (6.09 metres) from his bait. Hooking a large tench under these conditions is quite difficult, but very exciting. The rudd are best stalked rather in the manner of a chalk-stream trout angler and then fished for with a free-lined piece of breadflake or worm or maggot presented under a very small self-cocking float. In fact a fly rod is a useful addition to the holdall on the Royal.

ENFIELD

If you're coming from Dublin, turn left off the main Mullingar road in the middle of the double bridge over the railway and canal onto the towpath. Drive along the towpath for about a mile (1.6 km) until you come to a gate across it. You can park here. Climb the gate and almost immediately you will come across half a dozen obvious tench swims. The method is laying on as light as you dare, and the usual bait a bunch of maggots. Dawn and dusk on summer days are the most successful times, although it will fish throughout the twenty four hours. In good light you can actually see the tench swimming out of the weeds into the swim, which is very exciting. Polaroid glasses are a help. Continuing on along the towpath to where the canal takes a bend to the left, a shoal of rudd to about two pounds (0.9 kg) can often be seen swimming near the surface on sunny days. There are also some good pike, but no bream. At the time of going to press, the local club is developing swims in this area.

HILL OF DOWN

Driving from Dublin in the direction of Mullingar, you turn right just after passing Callaghy's supermarket, which is on the right soon after you have gone through Moyvalley. Keep on this road, ignoring left turns, until you come to a T-Junction with the bridge over the canal and the red rail bridge on your right. This is called Blackshade Bridge. Turn right across the bridges and park on the left. There is a gate onto the canal bank. Walk half a mile (0.8 km) west along the bank towards the Hill of Down until you reach the bushes and small trees. Start fishing for tench, rudd and possible bream.

MULLINGAR AREA

Stretches of the canal both east and west of Mullingar are known to produce large rudd and some tench. Ballynacarrigy to the west of the town and Thomastown to the east have fishing. The clear shallow stretches are sometimes fished at night during the summer for both tench and rudd. Floating crust has been used successfully for rudd.

THE MULLINGAR LAKES

The Royal Canal passes through Mullingar, so this is a convenient point to assess the coarse fishing available in the many lakes in the area. There are three big limestone lakes, Loughs Owel, Derravarragh and Ennell. Of these, Ennell is quite badly polluted with sewage from the town of Mullingar and Owel and Derravarragh are mainly noted for trout fishing. However, all three lakes contain reasonable pike and perch, some of which grow very large. The pike and perch fishing is mainly done in winter and is almost entirely from boats, which can be hired in the area. Inquire at local hotels, or tourist information offices. The normal methods used are spinning and trolling. The lakes are large and it is best to ask locally what areas of them have produced fish recently or to try and engage the services of a boatman with the boat.

There are a number of smaller lakes in the area which are of interest exclusively to the coarse fisherman and which provide angling for tench, bream, rudd, hybrids and eels, all of which reach specimen size. There are too many of these lakes for them all to be described here but the venues detailed below are all reliable big fish waters.

LOUGH ANALLA (Map 7)

Lough Analla is situated just off the main Mullingar-Delvin road and is about seven miles (11.2 km) from Mullingar and three miles (4.82 km) from Delvin. The fishing is for tench and rudd with pike and perch of secondary interest. Bread is the most successful bait, followed by maggots and worms; the lake has produced many specimen rudd and at least two specimen tench in recent years. The most productive swims are along the south shore near where the River Deel flows out of the lake. It is best to fish ten to fifteen yards (9.1–13.7 metres) out in a depth of eight or nine feet (2.4–2.7 metres) in normal summer levels. Bank access is available all round the lake, although it's boggy in wet weather, and the

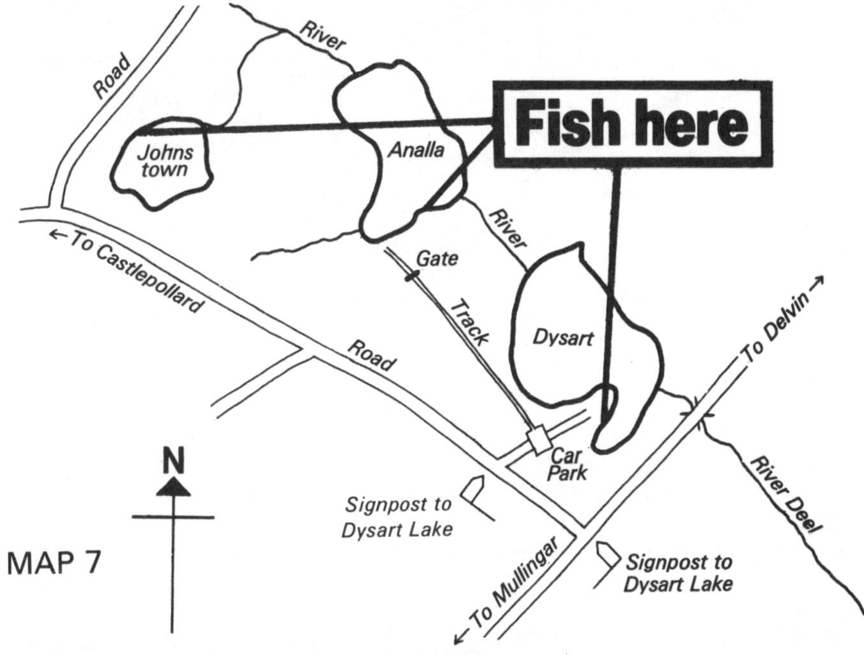

maximum depth is about fifteen feet (4.57 metres).

LOUGH DYSART (Map 7)

Lough Dysart is right beside Analla and connected to it by the River Deel. It has the same species but is of a rather different character, being more uneven in depth and having blacker, muddier water. The tench are also darker in colouring. The best swims are on the little peninsula on the south west shore where there is room for about eight anglers. You fish about three rod-lengths out in a depth of eight to ten feet (2.4–3.0 metres). There is good shelter from the wind and float-fishing is a popular method. There is access from the bank all round the lake.

JOHNSTOWN LAKE (Map 7)

Johnstown lake is the third and smallest of this group. It offers similar fishing and access; swims are on the west shore.

BALLINAFID LAKE (Map 8)

Ballinafid lake differs from the previous ones in that it also contains bream, and very big ones too. It is about four miles (6.43 km) from Mullingar on the Mullingar-Longford road; the access is directly opposite a pub called 'The Covert'. It is a small boggy lake between Lough Owel and the road and cannot be fished from the bank. However, there are two large stands on the road side of the lake which can accommodate up to eight anglers at a time. Depth is fairly uniform—eight to ten feet (2.4–3.0 metres) ten yards (9.1 metres) out from the stands with a maximum depth of around fourteen feet (4.26 metres) towards the other end of the lake. Boats can be hired at the pub. Bread has accounted for most of the big bream.

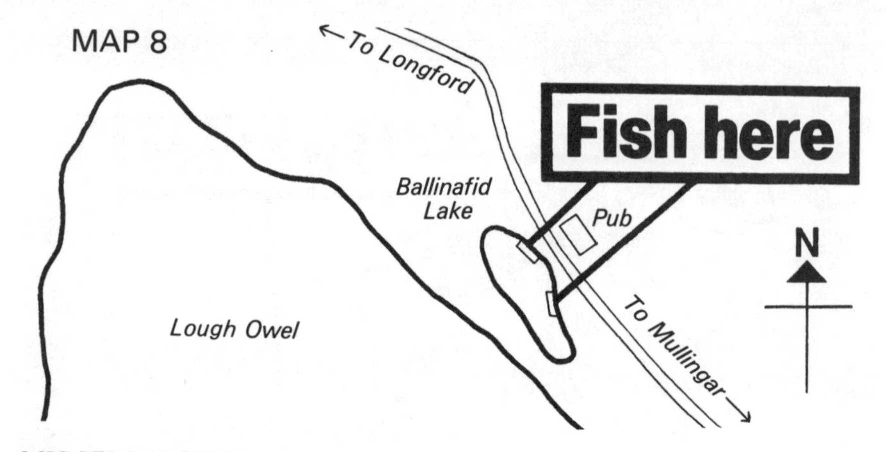

MISCELLANEOUS

There are many other small lakes and ponds in the Mullingar area: most have good rudd fishing, many have tench and some have good bream. It is worth mentioning McEvoy's Lough, Brittas Lake, Lough Drin and Slevins Lake, which, as well as holding bream, have produced specimen eels to legered lob worms.

THE LIFFEY

The Liffey rises near Sally Gap in the Wicklow mountains and fairly early on in its course is dammed to form the huge Poulaphouca reservoir. It then swings in a big loop through Co. Kildare and reaches the sea at Dublin as a river of some size.

It has a small run of salmon and the limestone stretches in Co. Kildare have excellent trout fishing; because of this most of the fishing is preserved. The river also has quite good pike and perch fishing throughout its length, excellent rudd fishing in the lower reaches and some bream and hybrids. There are rumours that roach and tench have been unofficially stocked. Increased interest in coarse angling by young people in Dublin probably means that the Liffey will receive more attention in future and that the lower reaches could develop as an important coarse fishery.

At present, the difficulty is that there is practically no free fishing. A coarse angler can join a game fishing club such as Dublin Trout Anglers which will give him the right to fish considerable stretches of the Liffey and on Poulaphouca. Alternatively, he can use the fact that the game fishermen generally have no objection to bona fide coarse anglers and actively encourage them on some parts of the fishery if they will guarantee to kill the coarse fish they catch—this is a matter of common sense. An angler float-fishing bread for rudd will seldom be turned away; an angler spinning through a 'fly-only' stretch of prime trout water is likely to get a less sympathetic reaction, even if he says he was spinning for perch. The following venues are known to produce fish.

LEIXLIP

There is a dam and a small reservoir here. There are pike, perch, bream, hybrids and eels, but the principal interest is rudd to specimen size.

To fish the reservoir, take the road which leads from Lucan to Celbridge and before you get to Celbridge, turn right at a crossroads which is signposted to a meat processing plant. Follow this road until you come to a bridge over the Liffey, stop there and use the gate on the right hand side just before the bridge. The reservoir is shallow and clear and the rudd shoals patrol the margins about ten yards (9.1 metres) out. A carpet of ground bait should be laid to hold the wandering fish and light float tackle with all the weight immediately below the float is the method. Reasonable rudd fishing can also be had in the river itself below the reservoir. In this case, access is in Leixlip village itself by walking upstream from the road bridge. The fishing on the reservoir is preserved and Dublin Trout Anglers have rights. As far as I can gather, there is free fishing in Leixlip village.

POULAPHOUCA-BLESSINGTON (Map 9)

Poulaphouca reservoir contains trout, pike and perch. It is an enormous acid water in the Wicklow mountains with two principal feeders, the Liffey and the Kings River. When it was first created half a century ago, it provided excellent trout fishing until disease decimated the trout, leaving pike and perch with the upper hand. In recent years, a different disease has been killing pike and the only fish that seem to do really well are the millions of stunted perch it contains. Pike and perch are controlled by angling and netting; trout are stocked regularly. The fishing rights are vested in two trout angling clubs which have no objection to bona fide coarse anglers but ask them not to return coarse fish to the water.

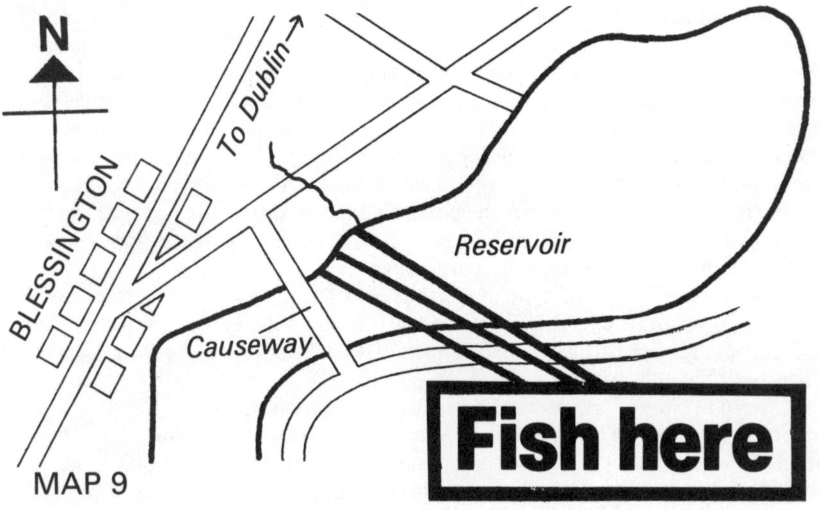

Application must be made to the Electricity Supply Board for a permit to use a boat on the reservoir. The principal interest to coarse anglers is the pike, which still exist in reasonable numbers throughout the lake. Adult pike average four to six pounds (1.8–2.7 kg) with the occasional fish over ten pounds (4.5 kg). Fish over twenty pounds (9.0 kg) have been recorded, but are very rare. The most effective method is probably to spin a plug or spoon, making sure to cover a new piece of water with each cast. Access to a good shore for pike can be had by taking the road from Dublin to Blessington and turning left in the centre of Blessington village. After about a mile (1.6 km) a right turn crosses an arm of the lake on a causeway. Stop here and fish the north west shore.

POULAPHOUCA-VALLEYMOUNT

Probably the best pike fishing on Poulaphouca is the area round the spot where the Kings River flows in south of Valleymount. There is no single convenient access point. The best bet is probably to strike off across country from the road, armed with an Ordnance Survey map. Either side of the river mouth produces fish but the west side is slightly harder to reach and slightly better.

2. THE SHANNON, PRINCIPAL LAKES AND TRIBUTARIES

A guide to coarse fishing on the Shannon compressed into one chapter of a book cannot hope to be comprehensive. It's a huge river, or rather, a huge network of waterways, and parts of it have never been explored by coarse anglers and certainly won't be in the near future.

The river rises out of a hole in the limestone at a place called Derrylahan in Co. Cavan and reaches the sea at Limerick 214 miles (344 km) later. If you add in the tributaries, its length is 1,130 miles (1,818 km) and it drains one fifth of the land area of Ireland. It's the longest river in the British Isles and it passes through a number of very large lakes—Lough Derg is 25 miles long and 10 miles wide (40.2 × 11.2 km). The river is navigable up to quite near its source and most of its course is wide, slow-moving and deep—up to 35 feet (10.7 metres) in the river sections and 200 feet (60.9 metres) in the lakes. It is subject to flooding, particularly in winter. Apart from game fish, it contains pike, perch, bream, rudd, hybrids, tench, eels, pollan and gudgeon. Roach are just starting to spread into the system and there may be some carp.

This chapter will give specific directions for fishing some of the better known venues. Anyone coming to the Shannon for the first time for an angling holiday would be best advised to read through the list and pick a centre which has the characteristics which appeal to him.

But there are many anglers who cruise in boats, come on family holidays or on business who will be confronted by a stretch of water which is not described in detail. The conditions will be strange to them and they may be put off by the very size of the river. For their benefit I will start off with a few very general remarks on how to tackle swims on the Shannon.

Stretches of the river where there is a moderate flow over a muddy bottom and a depth of between six and sixteen feet (1.8–4.9 metres) are quite liable to hold bream. The method to use is legering, normally with a swing-tip although a quiver or a spring-tip may be useful if there is some flood water. The line should be about 5 lbs (2.3 kg) breaking strain and the best terminal tackle is probably a paternoster with a bomb of between half an ounce and an ounce (14–28 g) and a trail of between two and four feet (0.6–1.2 metres), hook size 6 to 10. Most bream on the Shannon are caught in summer on bread but a virgin swim will probably produce better to worms as they are more natural bait. If a boat is available, touch-legering is a very effective method as well. It must be added that bream fishing in unknown waters in the main river is a pretty hit and miss affair unless a reasonable programme of pre-baiting can be organised. As far as ground-baiting is concerned, bear in mind that a shoal of Shannon bream might well contain over a thousand pounds (450 kg) of fish and ten pounds (4.5 kg) of ground bait doesn't go very far.

Rudd can sometimes be seen rolling and feeding on the surface in the main river on summer evenings, usually where there is water of around six feet (1.8 metres) in depth just off a bed of reeds. They can be caught by loose-feeding bread or maggots and trotting down float tackle. Under these conditions, don't fish deeper than two feet (0.6 metres) and hold the float back now and again so that the bait swims up near the surface. But the best place to find rudd, and often other species as well, is one of the many backwaters along the river. They provide very pleasant fishing from a dingy or from the bank with either float tackle or a tip rod. If you are catching rudd at the surface or in mid-water and feeding the swim regularly, push the float up every fifteen or twenty minutes and try a cast on the bottom. Very often you will find that bream, tench or hybrids have moved in on the groundbait that has not been snapped up by the rudd.

Pike are found throughout the river and its lakes and can be caught at all times of the year. Sometimes you'll see a large fish swirling on the water or small fry leaping out in panic—signs of a pike or a large perch. The traditional way of fishing for them on the river and in the lakes is to row steadily along the reedy margins trolling an artificial bait, often a copper or silver spoon three or four inches long (7.6–10.0 cm). In the lakes you want to be trolling near the bottom in ten to fifteen feet (3.04–4.57 metres) of water, although there is evidence that pike are found in much deeper water.

An echo-sounder is an enormous help as it enables an angler to let his lure follow an underwater contour. In the river you'll use a shorter line and row quietly about ten or fifteen feet (3.04–4.57 metres) out from the reeds, keeping an eye out for cruisers so you don't get swamped in their wake. More modern methods of pike fishing work as well, of course. You can fish a static dead-bait in the backwaters, in bays in the reeds or in the weir pools, and this is one of the best methods if you have actually seen a pike. You can also spend very exciting summer afternoons casting a floating plug with light tackle into bays and holes in the weedier swims. The pike will normally be between five and ten pounds (2.3–4.5 kg) but there is always a chance, particularly in the lakes, of a fish between twenty and forty pounds (9.0–18 kg).

Tench are not as widely distributed in the system as rudd, bream or pike and you're not as likely to come across them by chance. Look for a backwater or a bay in one of the lakes or islands which has about six feet (1.8 metres) of water, a muddy bottom and some water lilies. Pre-bait if you possibly can, even if this only means tipping in a bucket of mashed bread and worms the night before and fishing at dawn. Tench and bream often seem to go together in this sort of swim. The best method is probably laying on. The fish tend to be large—up to six pounds (2.7 kg).

Perch and eels are found throughout the system, in all types of water. Perch can be float-fished using small red worms as bait or, particularly in the lakes, can be caught by spinning a very small blade-spinner. They tend to be small. Eels can be caught by legering lobworms or small dead fish. They can be large—up to five pounds (2.3 kg). Fishing is best at night in summer.

The following list of well-known venues starts in the north and proceeds downstream.

DRUMSHANBO (Map 10)

Drumshanbo is the principal centre for fishing in the upper reaches of the river and the first of its large lakes, Lough Allen. All the principal Shannon species are found in the area but the water is peaty and acid. In general the fish are smaller and more sparsely distributed than further south. The one important exception to this generalisation is pike, which can be caught to specimen size in Lough Allen. Pike are fished throughout the lake from boats and there is some good bank fishing around Ballantra Bridge where the river flows out of the lake. There is quite good bream fishing in nearby Lough Scur, with access and car parking from both the south and the north and in Keshcarrigan Lake beside it, which is fished from the north bank. Blackrock Pond, Drumgorman Lake and Lustia Lake have some indifferent tench fishing.

BOYLE WATER

Boyle Water consists of the Boyle river and a number of lakes and short pieces of canal; it lies to the west of the Shannon and joins it just above Carrick-on-Shannon. The principal lake is Lough Key which is in a Forest Park area and very beautiful. Although coarse fishing is available, is it not of the first quality and anglers are advised to concentrate on pike fishing from a boat in the lakes.

CARRICK-ON-SHANNON

Carrick is an important cruiser hire centre on the upper Shannon. The best coarse fishing locally is in a number of small lakes. Lough Scur, which is described under 'Drumshanbo' (above), can be visited. It produces bream to 4½ lbs (2.05 kg). Lough Aduff produces bream to 6 lbs (2.7 kg) and tench to 5 lbs (2.3 kg).

ROOSKY/DROMOD

Roosky is the first spot on the Shannon which is noted for excellent fishing in the river itself. Good fishing for spawning bream can be had in May and June around Pigeon Island just upstream of the village. There is a half mile (0.8 km) of good bank between the bridge and the lock. The river above the lock fishes well from boats. The bream go to 7 lbs (3.2 kg), but the rudd tend to be small. There are also some fishing stands on the east bank in the village. Kilglass Lake, which is five miles away (8 km), has very large bream, rudd and tench. Lough Aduff has good tench and bream (see Carrick-on-Shannon') and there is a small lake outside Dromod which is usually called the 'Bog Lake'; it is noted for tench and bream. Lough Forbes, below Roosky, has an abundance of pike which seldom exceed 10 lbs (4.5 kg).

TERMONBARRY/CLOONDARA

This part of the river is noted for large perch and the best way to fish for them is in the eddies and pools below the weir, from a dinghy. Specimen eels, bream and

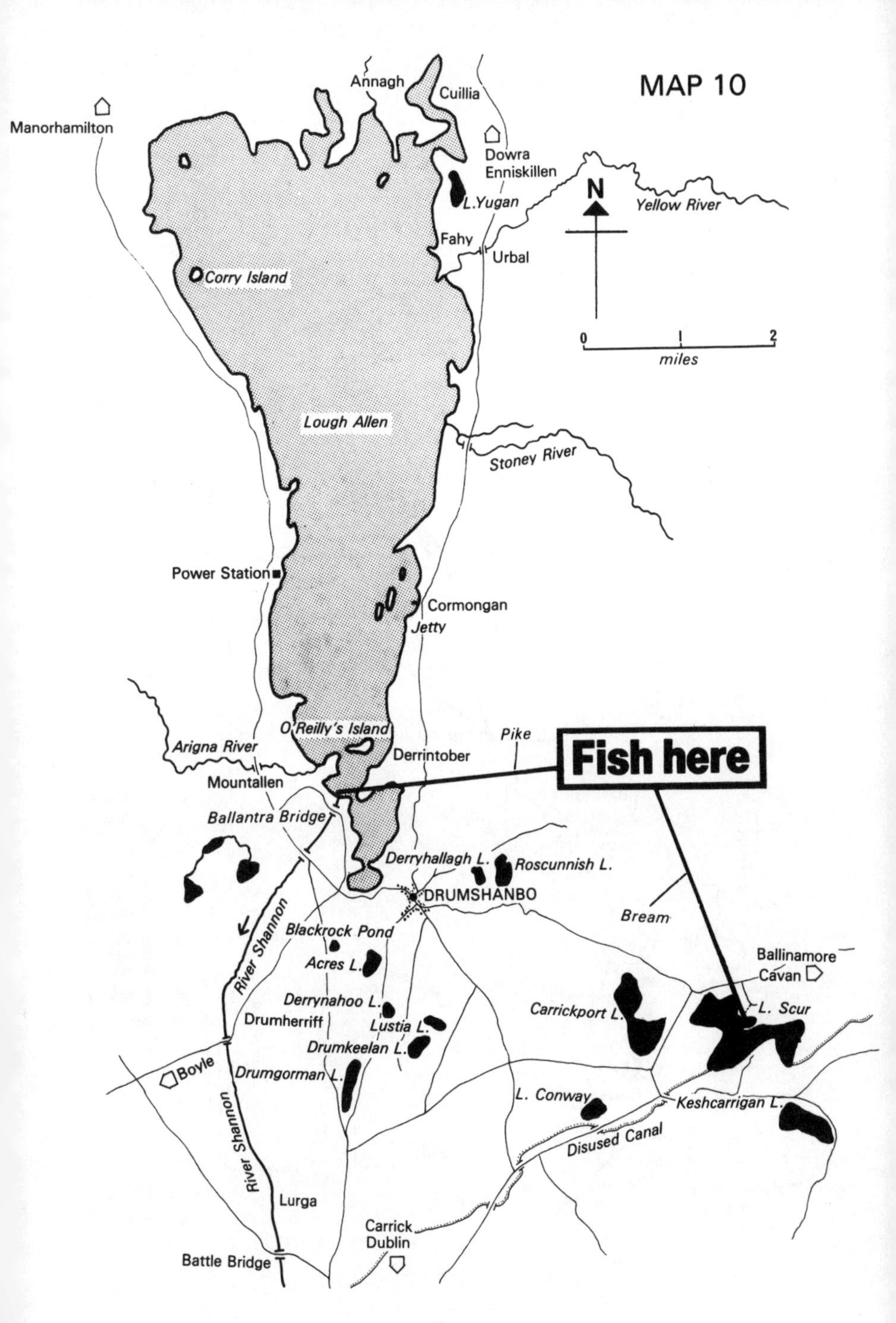
MAP 10
Annagh
Cuillia
Manorhamilton
Dowra
Enniskillen
L.Yugan
N
Yellow River
Fahy
Urbal
Corry Island
0
1
2
miles
Lough Allen
Stoney River
Power Station
Cormongan
Jetty
O'Reilly's Island
Pike
Fish here
Arigna River
Derrintober
Mountallen
Ballantra Bridge
Derryhallagh L.
Roscunnish L.
DRUMSHANBO
Bream
River Shannon
Blackrock Pond
Acres L.
Ballinamore
Cavan
Derrynahoo L.
Carrickport L.
L. Scur
Drumherriff
Lustia L.
Drumkeelan L.
Boyle
Drumgorman L.
L. Conway
Keshcarrigan L.
River Shannon
Disused Canal
Lurga
Carrick
Dublin
Battle Bridge

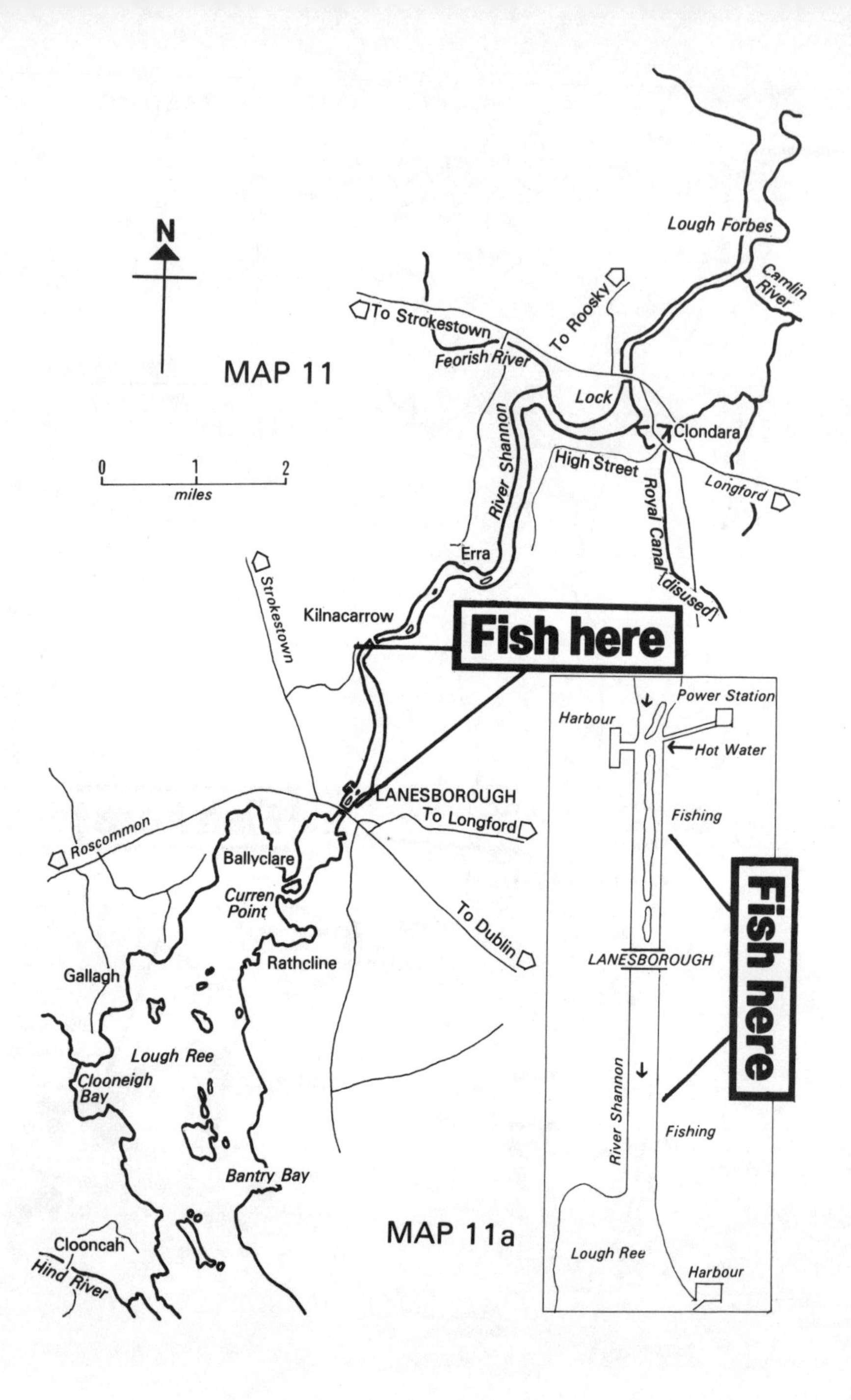

N
MAP 11
0
1
2
miles
Lough Forbes
Camlin River
To Roosky
To Strokestown
Feorish River
Lock
Clondara
High Street
Longford
Royal Canal (disused)
River Shannon
Erra
Strokestown
Kilnacarrow
Fish here
LANESBOROUGH
To Longford
Roscommon
To Dublin
Ballyclare
Curren Point
Rathcline
Gallagh
Lough Ree
Clooneigh Bay
Bantry Bay
Clooncah
Hind River
MAP 11a
Power Station
Harbour
Hot Water
Fishing
Fish here
LANESBOROUGH
River Shannon
Fishing
Lough Ree
Harbour

tench have all come from the centre as well, and the angler who doesn't have a boat will find bank space around and between the two villages. The Royal Canal joins the Shannon here.

LANESBORO (LANESBOROUGH) (Maps 11 and 11a)

This is possibly the best-known coarse angling centre on the Shannon. Every year it produces a very large number of specimen bream and tench and a lesser number of specimen hybrids in the Irish list. But it is important for the stranger to note the nature of the fishing at Lanesboro. It is for spawning fish, only takes place at a certain time of the year, and it is fair to say that it doesn't take place in the beautiful and isolated surroundings which many people prefer for their coarse fishing. Having said that, it is undoubtedly true that it offers probably the most reliable chance in the country of a big tench or bream.

The fishing is from mid-April to mid-June (which coincides with the English close season—one of the reasons why this venue has had so much attention from foreign anglers) and is in a hot-water outflow from a power station just upstream of the town. If the authorities in the Electricity Supply Board switch off the hot water, the fishing tends to go off. The fishing takes the form of either bank fishing along the east bank in the town or from a boat moored at the bottom of the stretch where the river joins Lough Ree, to which the fish return when they have finished spawning. The hot water stretch is quite shallow, usually about three feet (0.9 metres), and towards the end of the fishing period weed growth can present a problem. An angler finding himself in Lanesboro outside the spring period is probably best advised to go to Kilnacarrow upstream of the town where there is bank access and average river fishing.

LOUGH REE (Maps 11 and 11b)

Lough Ree is a large lake, almost an inland sea, which often has rough water. It is full of islands and the shore-line is indented with many reed-fringed bays. It has large quantities of good-sized coarse fish but as an angling proposition it is largely unknown, with the exception of the Inner Lakes, a series of smaller lakes at the south east end which are connected to it by a channel. These are dealt with under a separate heading. Most of the angling done in the main lake is pike trolling carried out along the shores and around the islands. Some pioneers have reported excellent fishing for rudd and tench in bays in the island group around Black Island in the middle of the lake. Angling is not a practical proposition without a boat and the lake can be dangerous for small craft. Marks noted for pike trolling are shores round the north end where the river flows in, Yellow Island at the south end and, for smaller fish, the Cribby Islands on the west shore. There are a number of smaller land-locked lakes along the east shore which offer good fishing, particularly for tench. The principal ones are Ross Lake, Creggan Lake and Dooney's Lake. However, they are reed-fringed and you will have to carry in your own inflatable boat. With so much good fishing in the area with easier access, it is doubtful whether it is worth the trouble.

THE INNER LAKES OF LOUGH REE (Map 11b)

The inner lakes are also boat fishing only and both for these and the main lake an engine is necessary. Boats may be hired from SGS Marine at Ballykeeran or by asking at the tourist office in Athlone.

If you have your own boat you will be able to get it into the water at Coosan

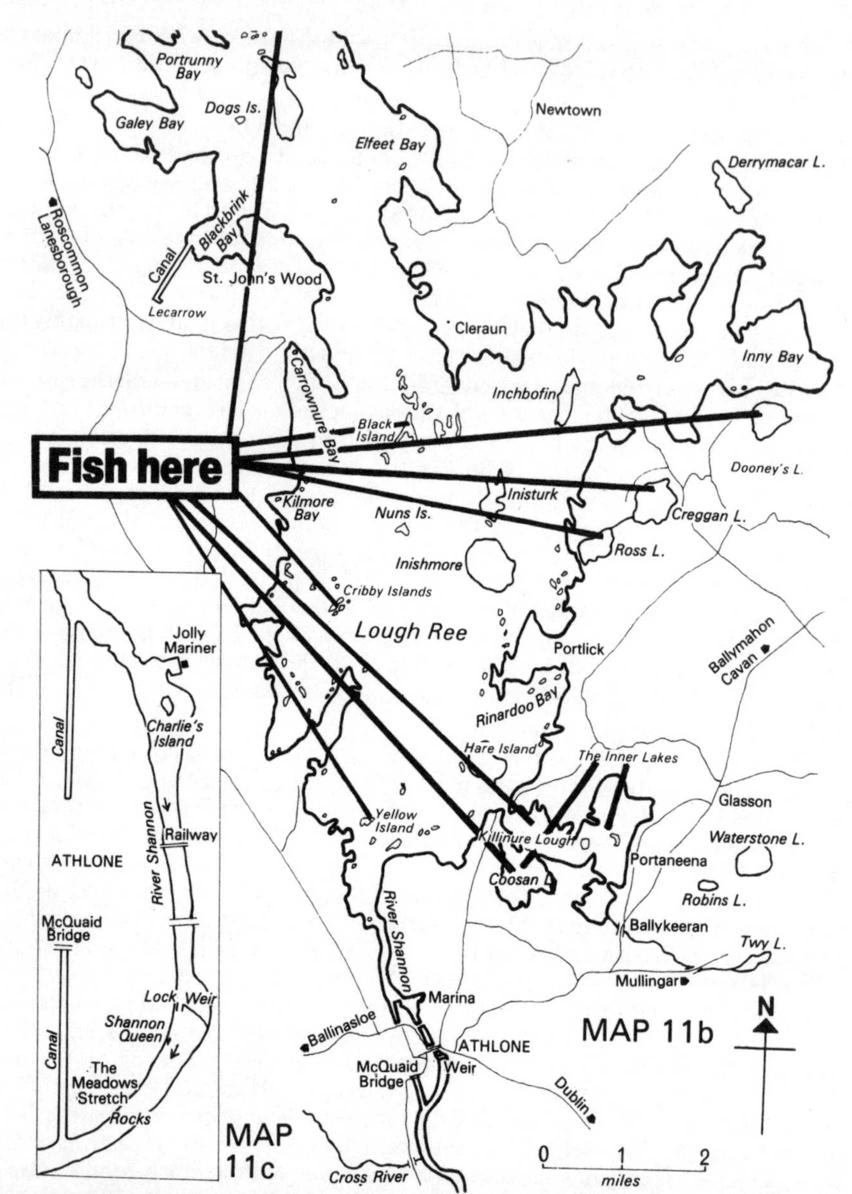

Point. There is quite good pike fishing and excellent fishing for tench, bream, rudd and hybrids, all of which reach specimen weight. Coosan Lough and the channel between it and Killinure Lough have received most attention from anglers. The pike are taken by trolling or by casting plugs in towards the margins; it is much better to troll under oars. The technique for catching the other two species is to take the boat out and select two or three swims with eight to twelve feet (2.4–3.6 metres) of water and some lilies in the vicinity. Don't be afraid to choose swims right up against the reedy margins and concentrate on bays where there is shelter from the wind. These swims should be baited up; leave worms and maggots out of the groundbait in at least one of them, so you can move to it if you have problems with perch or eels. Return and fish the swims every evening and morning as often as you can. Dawn is the best time, particularly for the tench, but you can catch fish at any hour.

ATHLONE (Maps 12 and 11c)

Athlone is an excellent fishing centre with two very different types of pleasure angling in the town itself as well as regular open matches in the summer. Tackle bait and groundbait are available. Specimen hunters should go to the tourist information office and arrange to hire a rowing boat, to be collected at the Jolly Mariner boat club. They can then fish from the anchored boat (get some weights to anchor it with) just above the island opposite the club. This is called Brick Island, but is usually known locally as Charlie's Island after a recluse who used to live on it. The rudd go to just under 3 lbs (1.4 kg), the bream to over 8 lbs (3.6

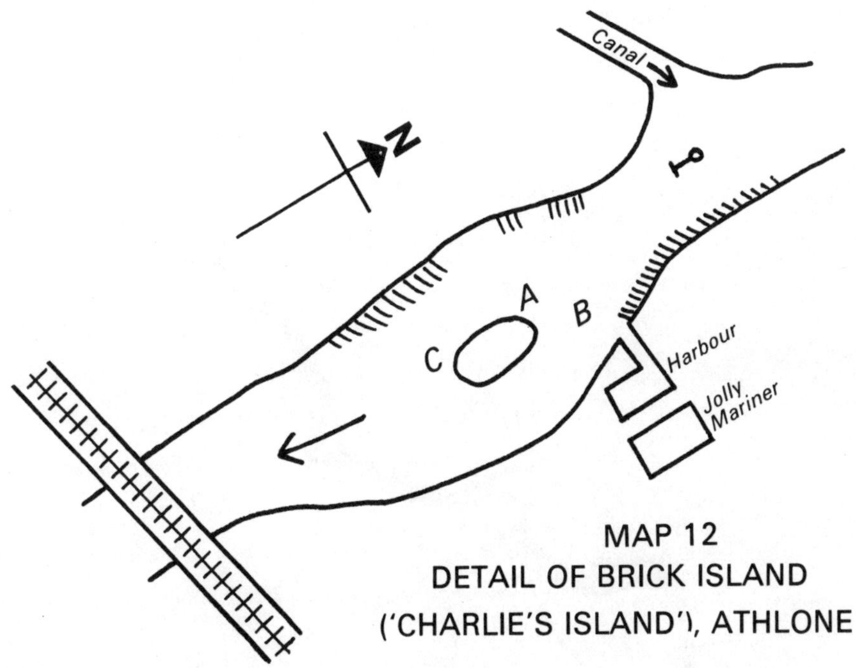

MAP 12
DETAIL OF BRICK ISLAND
('CHARLIE'S ISLAND'), ATHLONE

kg) and the hybrids to over 4½ lbs (2.05 kg). There is the odd large tench and if you are unwise enough to use any bait other than bread, you will discover a myriad of small perch. It is of course summer fishing. The best rudd fishing is at the point marked 'A' on the sketch map and the method is to moor the boat about thirty yards (27 metres) above it, feed in mashed bread and trot a piece of flake on an 8 hook towards the island, fishing it a maximum of two feet (0.6 metres) below the float. Fish from dawn to 9 am and for half an hour before dusk. Rudd can also be caught at the point marked 'C' on the sketch map. The other species are taken at the point marked 'B' on the map by touch-legering bread on a 4 or 6 hook to about 6 lbs (2.7 kg) breaking strain line with a half to one ounce (14–28 g) bomb. If this tackle seems heavy, it is as well to bear in mind that there are strong and devious undercurrents in the water.

Anglers who are more interested in bank fishing for large nets of bream in the 3 to 5½ lbs (1.4–2.5 kg) range should try the Meadows stretch on the west bank

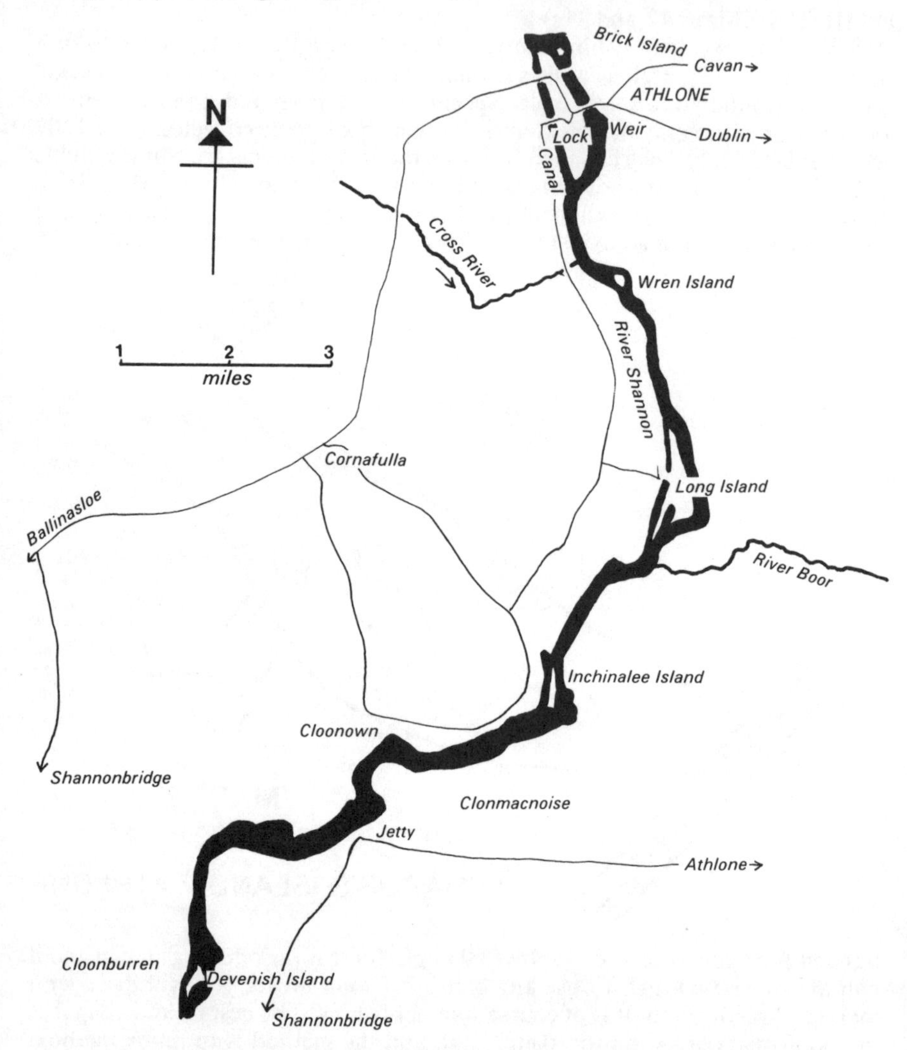

MAP 13

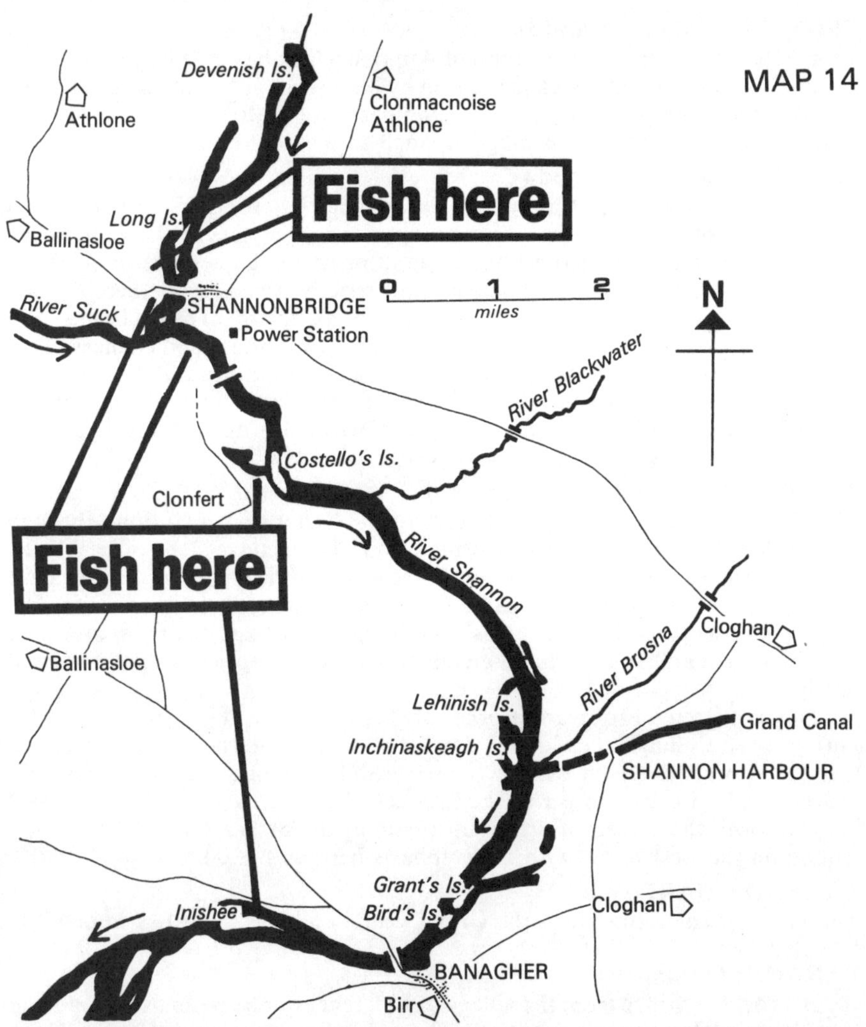

downstream of the town centre. Go to a floating pub/ hotel called the 'Shannon Queen' which is signposted and where the staff make up packets of sandwiches as well as providing liquid refreshments, and park there. The swims are from here downstream for half a mile (0.8 km) to where a canal (which is being developed for angling at the time of writing) joins the river. This is a match stretch and fishes from June through to September. The technique is straightforward legering into from eight to fourteen feet (2.4–4.2 metres) of water with 4 lbs (1.8 kg) line and a paternoster with a ½ oz (14 g) bomb and a hook length twice the lead length. In midsummer, the bait is flake on a 6 to 10 hook. Early and late season worms or maggots are better and the perch problem is not as acute at this time of year. Nets weighing 100 lbs (45 kg) are relatively common and 300 lbs (135 kg) have been achieved by a single angler in a day.

CLONMACNOISE (Map 13)

There is a long stretch of river south of Athlone which has little bank access and has not been developed. Anglers cruising by boat will find excellent rudd fishing at various points alongside the reeds. Clonmacnoise, in the centre of this stretch, is noted for excellent river fishing for small to medium pike.

SHANNONBRIDGE (Map 14)

The River Suck, which is dealt with in the next entry, joins the Shannon here. It is a good centre for all the Shannon species except tench; the rudd reach specimen weight. Boats may be hired and information gathered from Killeen's pub in the village. However, boats are not strictly necessary as there is bank access. The best bream fishing is on the west bank upstream of the bridge. The east bank above the bridge and the west bank below it offer good chances of big rudd. Downstream of Shannonbridge there is a power station and there is access opposite it on the west bank; there are average tench and bream in midsummer but problems with small perch. Further downstream again there is a good backwater on the west bank opposite Costello's Island.

THE RIVER SUCK (Maps 15 and 16)

The River Suck is a fair-sized tributary of the Shannon which flows through Ballinasloe. It is a noted bream fishery and also has excellent pike. All the common Shannon species except tench are present. Parts of the river are swift flowing and offer more to the game fisherman; matches are fished on it. The fishery is rather moody, sometimes producing heavy bags of bream of a high average weight and at other times giving up nothing except a few small rudd and perch.

The best stretch for bream is probably for a distance of just over a mile (1.6 km) between Culliagh and Coreen, downstream of Ballinasloe. Above the town there is also good bream fishing at Derrycahill, if you are prepared to walk nearly a mile (1.6 km) to get to the productive swims. Access is from the east bank in both these cases. Further upstream again, at Walker's, there is good fishing on the west bank, with the emphasis here on the pike.

SHANNON HARBOUR

The venue is the terminus of the Grand Canal and was described in detail in Chapter Two.

BANAGHER (Map 14)

If you cross the bridge from the village of Banagher on the Ballinasloe road and take the first left, you will come to the Green Isle food processing factory. There is good fishing in front of the factory for above average sized fish—the bream go to 8 lbs (3.6 kg) and the rudd to 2½ lbs (1.15 kg). There are big hybrids, too. The factory processes peas, but as far as I know no-one has ever tried using them as bait. Nallers Island near Banagher has tench.

LOUGH DERG

Lough Derg is the largest of the Shannon lakes—a huge sheet of water full of coarse fish, including very large tench and pike, about which very little is known from an angling point of view. At the time of writing, the Inland Fisheries Trust was carrying out an extensive survey of the lake from which, no doubt, a lot of information will be obtained. Hopefully, future editions of this book will be able to be more helpful to anglers wishing to fish Lough Derg.

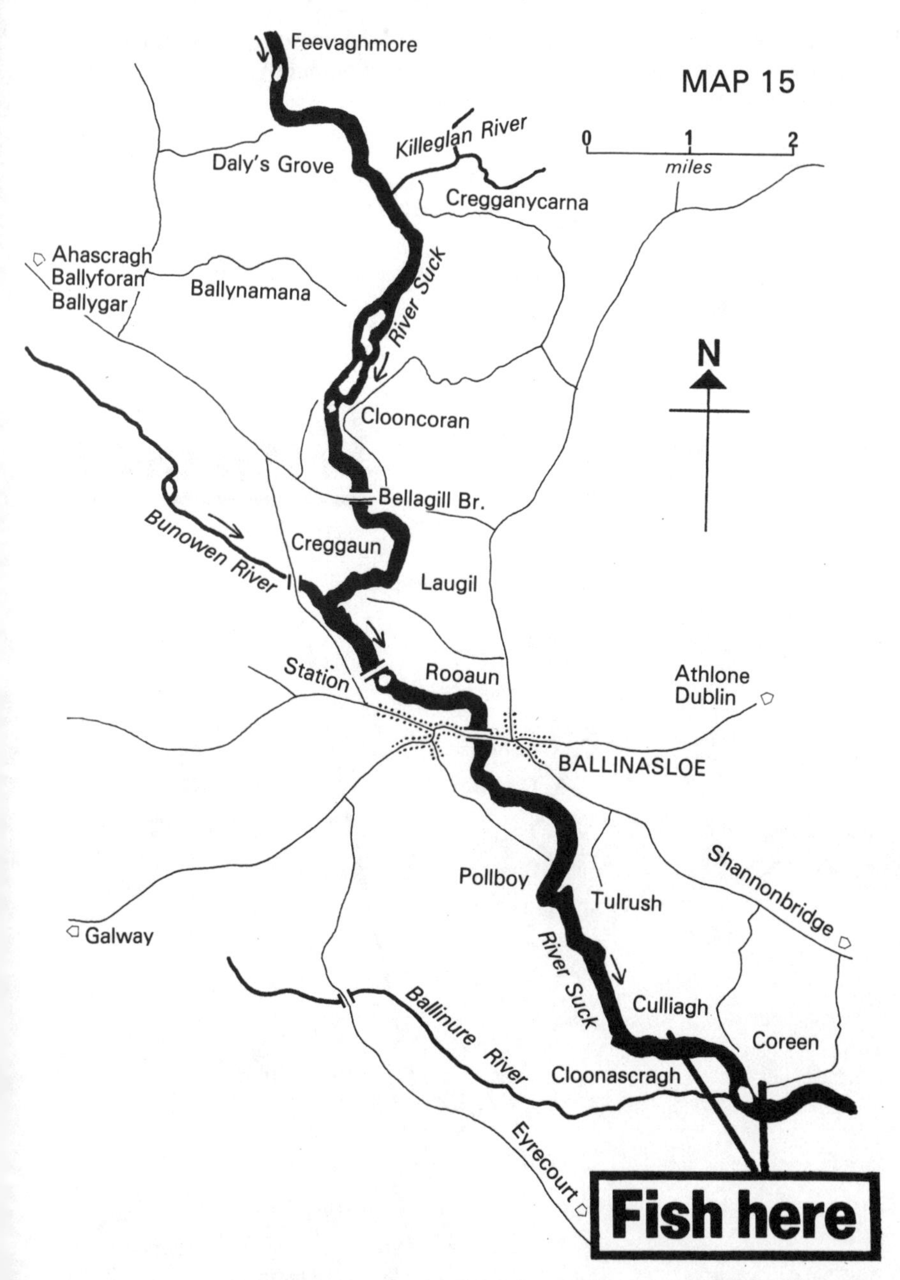

There are three main centres around the lake with accommodation and boat-hiring facilities: Portumna in the north, Scarriff half-way down the west shore, and Killaloe in the south. There are hotels which cater for pike-anglers, mainly visitors from continental Europe who come in winter, and are supplied with boats and knowledgeable boatmen. The fishing is mainly with artificial lures, either spun or trolled.

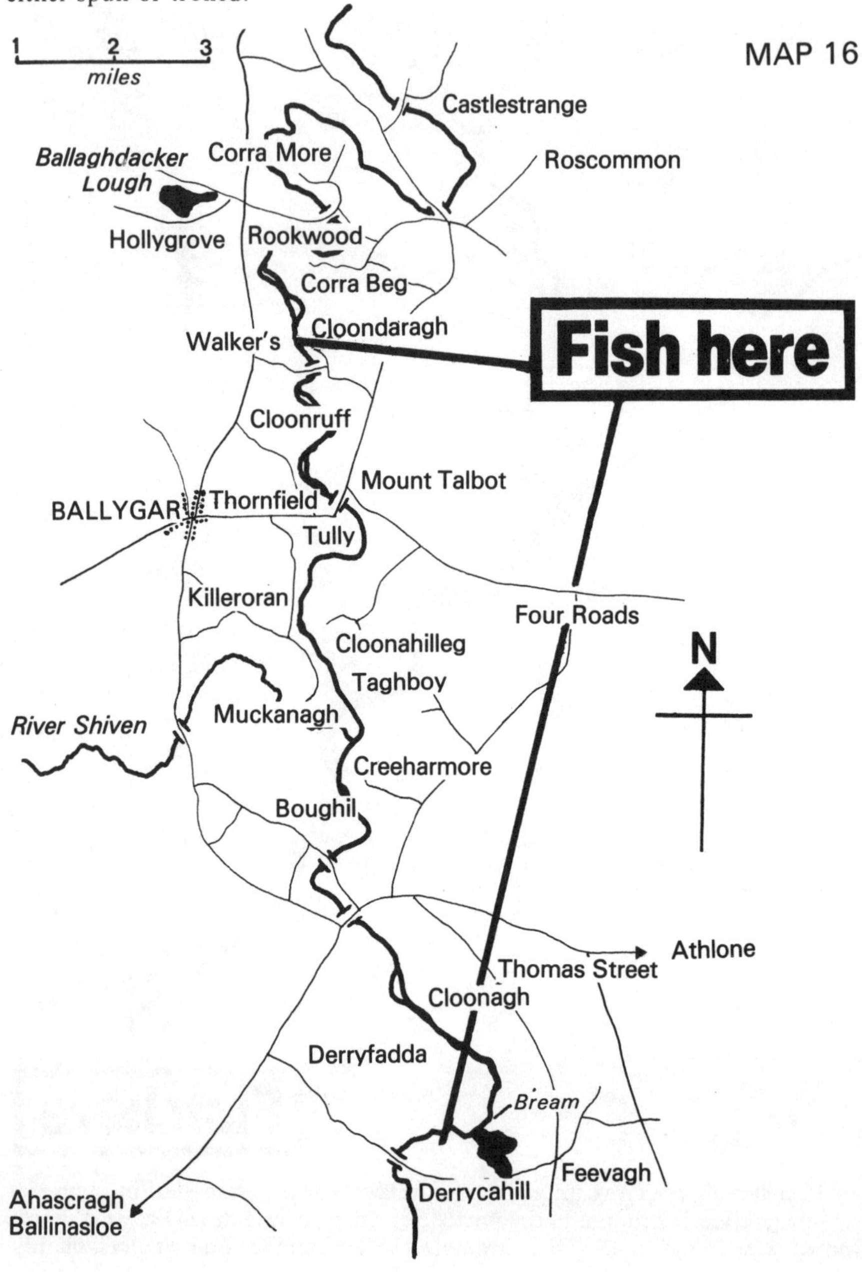

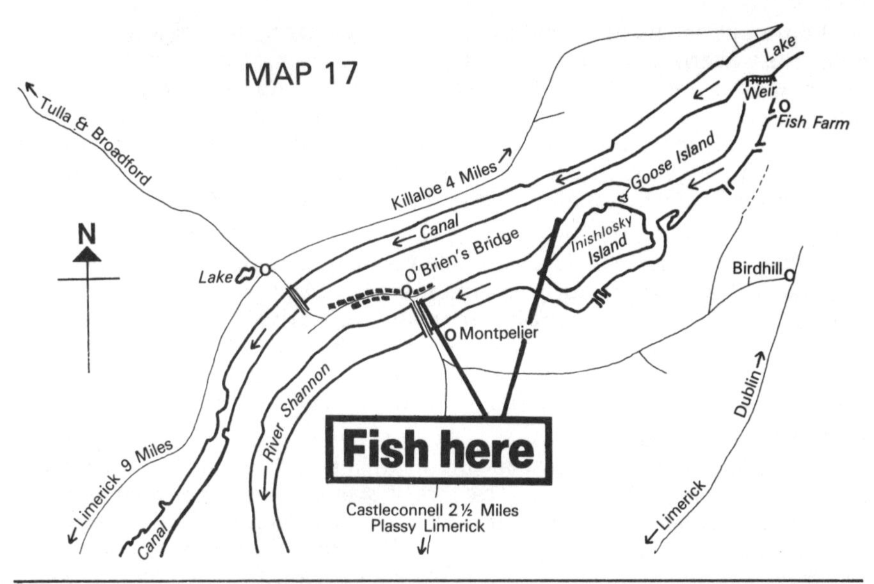
MAP 17
Tulla & Broadford
Killaloe 4 Miles
Lake
Weir
Fish Farm
Goose Island
Canal
O'Brien's Bridge
Inishlosky Island
Lake
Birdhill
Montpelier
N
River Shannon
Dublin
Limerick 9 Miles
Fish here
Canal
Castleconnell 2½ Miles
Plassy Limerick
Limerick

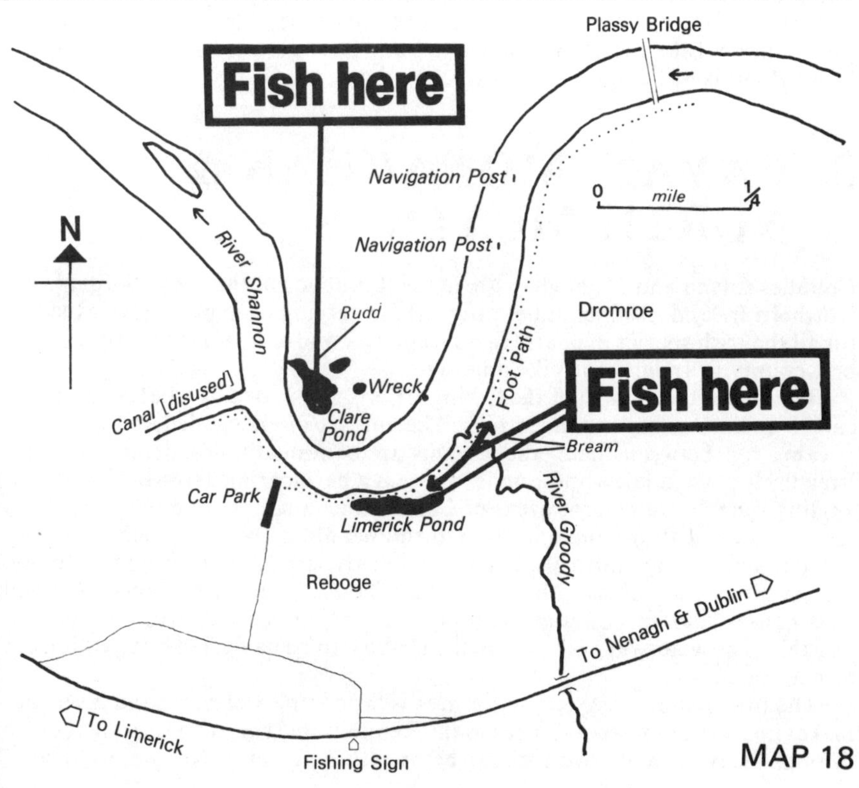
Plassy Bridge
Fish here
Navigation Post
Navigation Post
0 mile 1/4
N
River Shannon
Rudd
Dromroe
Foot Path
Wreck
Fish here
Canal [disused]
Clare Pond
Bream
River Groody
Car Park
Limerick Pond
Reboge
To Nenagh & Dublin
To Limerick
Fishing Sign
MAP 18

Enormous shoals of tench have been seen gathering for spawning in bays along the western shore in late May and early June, but I've never heard of an angler catching one. The other Shannon species are present as well and biologists have taken them in their nets, even the rare pollan, a species of white fish found only in the large lakes of the Shannon. But until more information is available this large inland sea must be regarded as a pike lake and an intriguing prospect for an angling pioneer with a lot of time on his hands.

O'BRIEN'S BRIDGE (Map 17)
The village of O'Brien's Bridge on the lower Shannon offers good bank access and reasonable fishing for all the Shannon species. Depths are considerable—up to nearly forty feet (12.18 metres) in the middle of the river just above the village. There is also canal fishing. The river has a match stretch. There are reasonable bream swims just upstream of the village and on the same side. A bit further upstream, opposite Inishlosky Island, there are tench and rudd.

PLASSY (sketch map 18)
The last noted coarse fishing venue on the Shannon before it becomes tidal at Limerick is Plassy, noted for large catches of bream. This is tip fishing into very deep water; the best of the swim is fifteen to seventeen feet (4.5–5.1 metres) at normal summer levels. It is as well to use a fairly long trail; when the bream are on, they take on the drop. Fish on the south bank from a point opposite Limerick Pond up to and just past the point where the little River Groody enters the Shannon. Limerick Pond and Clare Pond have quite good rudd fishing, but Clare Pond is difficult to reach without a boat.

3. CAVAN, MONAGHAN & NORTH MEATH

Counties Cavan and Monaghan are in the Republic but they have borders with Northern Ireland. Both counties offer fishing varying from average to excellent for all the Irish species of coarse fish except dace and carp. Cavan is arguably the best county in Ireland for pike angling.

The landscape in most of the fishing areas is dominated by what geographers call 'drumlins'—small, rounded hills. The hills are often wooded and rivers and streams run between them; the streams are continually broadening out into irregularly shaped lakes and ponds. There is a bewildering number of potential angling waters—quite large areas of Co. Cavan actually have more water than land and even getting from one place to another along the small roads and lanes without a map can be difficult. The area is mostly very pretty without developing the grand beauty of say the Clare Lakelands. There are plenty of small guesthouses and farmhouses that take paying guests and camping is also possible. The waterways are mostly too shallow to be navigated by anything but a small boat.

The principal river system in the area is the complex of rivers and lakes that makes up the Erne system. It rises in the Republic and threads a tortuous course through Cavan and Monaghan before turning into Northern Ireland.

Information on fishing the Lower Erne can be found in the chapter on Northern Ireland.

Ten or fifteen years ago, roach were introduced into the Lower Erne in Northern Ireland; before this they were only found in the Blackwater system in the south of the country. Since then roach have spread all the way up to the headwaters of the system in Co. Cavan and have even got out of the system—with the help of pike anglers who illegally transported them for use as live-baits—to invade the Shannon system. This means that the Erne system and many, though not all, of the waters described in this chapter are in an ecologically unstable state. A venue which produces good nets of pound-plus (0.5 kg+) roach one year may, after a good breeding season, only yield thousands of two and three inch (5.0–7.6 cm) fish a few months later. Other species are affected as well; rudd and perch are disappearing, bream populations seem to be fluctuating and the shoal movements have become rather unpredictable. Pike are flourishing on an easy diet of small roach. Of course, it will all settle down eventually and when it does, these rich and varied waters must be capable of producing first-rate angling for a variety of species. But don't neglect Cavan and Monaghan in the meantime; if you do, you'll miss some of the best angling in Ireland. Just make sure that you have up-to-date information if you are intending to fish in waters which have been invaded by roach. Pike angling is, if anything, better than ever. Tench and to a lesser extent, the large bream, are mostly fished for in still waters which have been unaffected by roach. Big roach require up-to-date local knowledge but you can have a lot of fun and polish up your speed-fishing techniques with small roach at many points along the Erne system. These northern counties also offer the winter angler more than many other parts of the country—roach and pike are both good winter species. However, the Erne system is rather subject to winter flooding which can make fishing difficult.

The list of venues below is only a personal selection out of the many reliable waters in the area. It starts in west Cavan and moves eastwards through Monaghan. It ends with a small and rather isolated area of interest to the coarse angler around Drumconrath in Co. Meath. Because of the topographical complexity of the area and the immense amount of water in it, a stranger must provide himself with a good map. To make it easier to locate places, the name of the river or lake in the heading is preceded by the name of a nearby town or village.

BALLINAMORE-ST JOHN'S LAKE (Map 19)

To find this venue, take the road west from Ballinamore which goes to Carrick and Drumshanbo. Stop after you've crossed the bridge at the head of the lake and you will have good access to about half a mile (0.8 km) of clean bank on your left. The principal interest is bream and hybrids; legering is normal.

BALLINAMORE-BALLYDUFF (Map 19)

The straight piece of river that flows out of St John's Lake is part of the Woodford River called the Ballyduff stretch. At the time of writing it is one of the most reliable spots in the area for big winter roach. In fact the Woodford for about two miles (3.2 km) to the east and two miles (3.2 km) to the west of Ballinamore offers excellent roach fishing and is an attractive river for trotting.

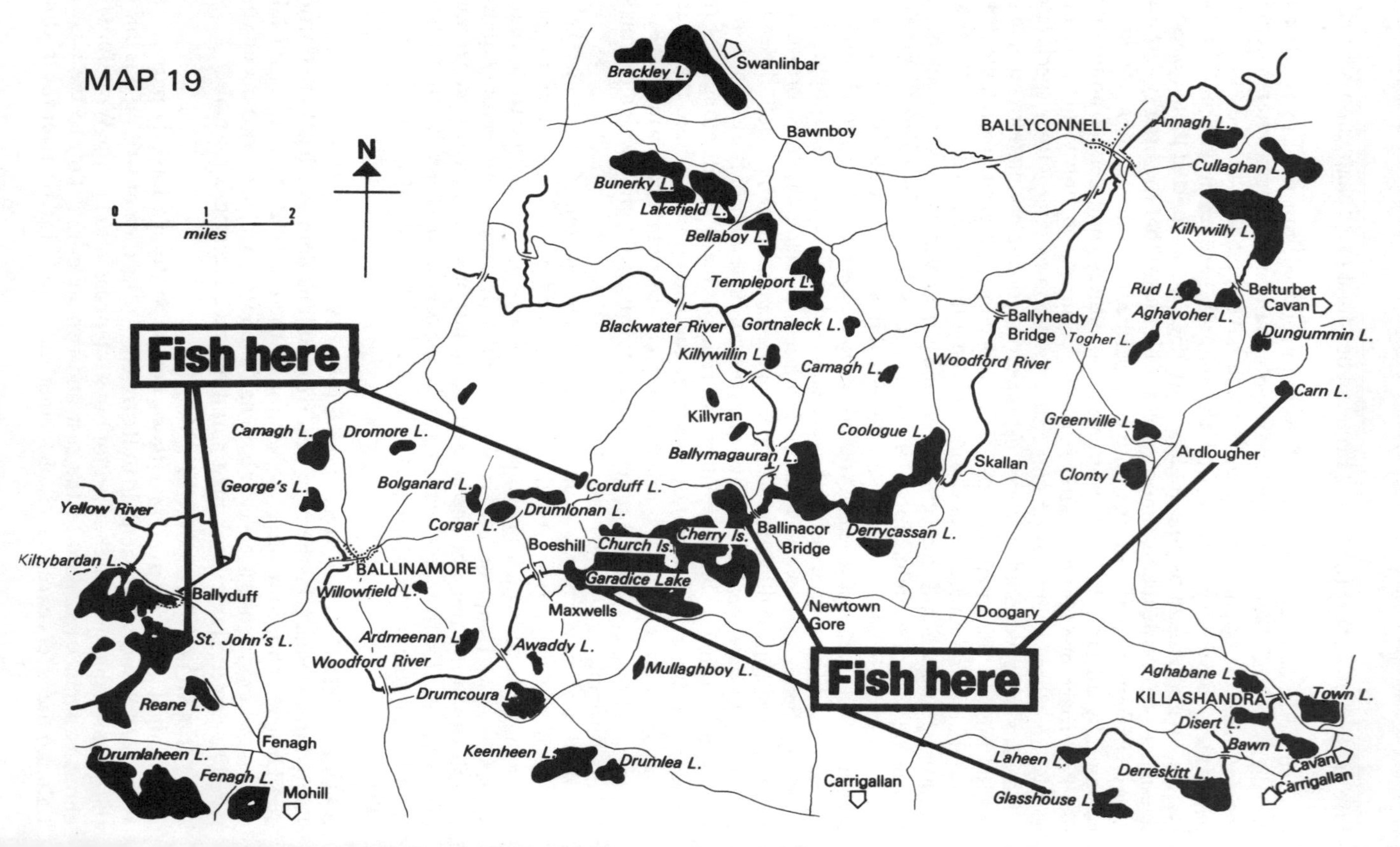

MAP 19
0
1
2
miles
N
Brackley L.
Swanlinbar
Bawnboy
BALLYCONNELL
Annagh L.
Cullaghan L.
Bunerky L.
Lakefield L.
Bellaboy L.
Killywilly L.
Templeport L.
Rud L.
Belturbet
Cavan
Aghavoher L.
Blackwater River
Gortnaleck L.
Ballyheady
Bridge
Togher L.
Dungummin L.
Fish here
Killywillin L.
Camagh L.
Woodford River
Carn L.
Killyran
Camagh L.
Dromore L.
Coologue L.
Greenville L.
Ardlougher
Ballymagauran L.
Skallan
Clonty L.
George's L.
Bolganard L.
Corduff L.
Yellow River
Drumlonan L.
Corgar L.
Cherry Is.
Ballinacor
Bridge
Derrycassan L.
Boeshill
Church Is.
Kiltybardan L.
BALLINAMORE
Garadice Lake
Ballyduff
Willowfield L.
Maxwells
Newtown
Gore
Doogary
St. John's L.
Ardmeenan L.
Awaddy L.
Woodford River
Mullaghboy L.
Fish here
Aghabane L.
Reane L.
Drumcoura
KILLASHANDRA
Town L.
Disert L.
Fenagh
Bawn L.
Drumlaheen L.
Keenheen L.
Drumlea L.
Laheen L.
Fenagh L.
Cavan
Derreskitt L.
Mohill
Carrigallan
Carrigallan
Glasshouse L.

Lower stretches of the river, which produced well in former years, have suffered recently from slurry pollution.

BALLINAMORE-GARADICE LAKE (Map 19)

A few miles east of Ballinamore the Woodford river flows into a large lake called Garadice Lake. It has all the local species except tench but is probably best known for bream. There is access and good fishing at the extreme west end of the lake just south of the river mouth, which is called Maxwell's Shore and at the east end of the lake where it narrows. This can be fished from both sides, the most popular being the south east side called Haughton's Shore.

BALLINAMORE-CORDUFF LAKE (Map 19)

Corduff Lake is a small water to the north of Garadice. It's right beside the Ballinamore/Killashandra road on the left if you're coming from Ballinamore. It has good tench and some worthwhile rudd.

KILLASHANDRA-GLASSHOUSE LAKE (Map 19)

About two miles (3.2 km) to the south west of Killeshandra is a complex of lakes of which the most popular with anglers is Glasshouse Lake. It has all the local species except tench but is best known for its shoals of good bream.

BALLYCONNELL-CARN LOUGH (Map 19)

Carn Lough is a small lake between Ballyconnell and Belturbet. It is reached by taking the second right turn if you're going from Ballyconnell to Belturbet; it has good tench.

CAVAN TOWN-LOUGH OUGHTER: GENERAL (Map 20)

To the north east of Cavan town is an immensely complex system of small to medium sized lakes and short stretches of river. It's part of the Erne system and is sometimes referred to as 'Lough Oughter' (pronounced 'ooter') after one of its larger lakes. It offers fairly difficult fishing for large bream, fairly straightforward fishing for medium sized pike and easy fishing for small roach. It is one area of Ireland where dead-bait fishing for pike seems to be consistently more successful than the use of artificials, although floating plugs can be very effective in the warmer months. The main problem it presents the visiting angler is that there is such a bewildering choice of attractive looking water with good access that he doesn't know where to begin. By using an Ordnance Survey map and the sketch map in this book, anglers should be able to find the venues selected below which offer some of the most consistent fishing.

CAVAN TOWN-ARDAN LAKE (Map 20)

Ardan Lake is just south of the village of Milltown at the north end of the Lough Oughter complex. There is good fishable shore alongside the road; there are bream, roach and pike and it is also a good winter venue, particularly for the last two species.

CAVAN TOWN-BAKERSBRIDGE (Map 20)

Just to the east of Ardan Lake is the small village of Bakersbridge with a bridge across the River Erne. There is good bank access to the river here and swims that provide pleasant fishing in running water for bream and roach with the possibility of trotting for the roach. Most of the roach are small, but there is a reasonable percentage of medium sized fish up to a pound or a little over (about 0.5 kg). Just upstream of the bridge there is a wide spot in the river with an island

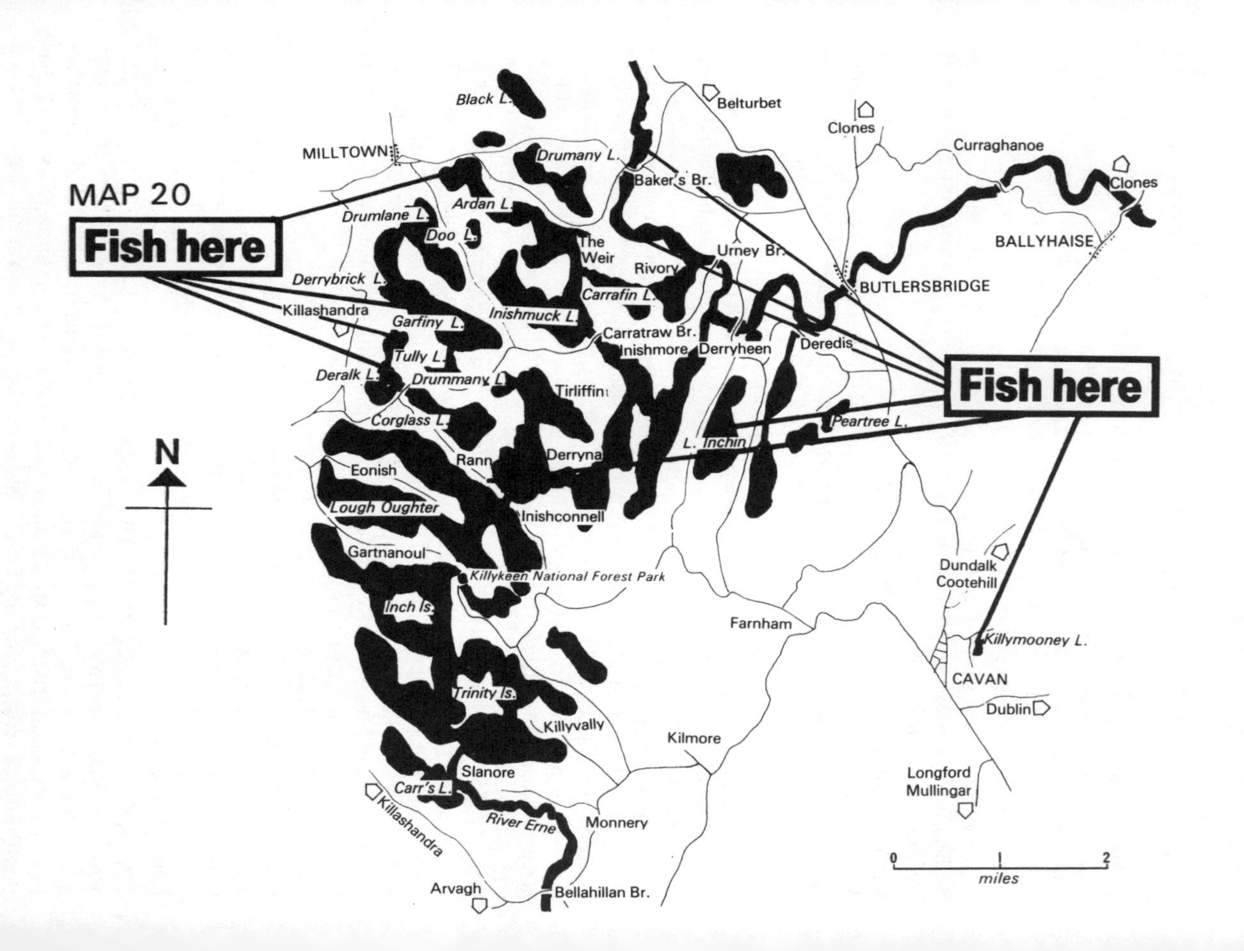

MAP 20
Fish here
Fish here
MILLTOWN
Black L.
Drumany L.
Baker's Br.
Belturbet
Clones
Curraghanoe
Clones
BALLYHAISE
Drumlane L.
Ardan L.
Doo L.
The Weir
Rivory
Urney Br.
BUTLERSBRIDGE
Derrybrick L.
Carrafin L.
Killashandra
Garfiny L.
Inishmuck L.
Carratraw Br.
Inishmore
Derryheen
Deredis
Tully L.
Deralk L.
Drummany L.
Tirliffin
Corglass L.
Peartree L.
L. Inchin
Rann
Derryna
Eonish
Lough Oughter
Inishconnell
Gartnanoul
Killykeen National Forest Park
Dundalk
Cootehill
Inch Is.
Farnham
Killymooney L.
CAVAN
Dublin
Trinity Is.
Killyvally
Kilmore
Slanore
Longford
Mullingar
Carr's L.
Killashandra
River Erne
Monnery
0
1
2
miles
Arvagh
Bellahillan Br.
N

in it. The depth here is up to sixteen feet (4.8 metres) at normal summer levels and the current slack; best access is from the east bank. This is probably the best spot for bream. Downstream of the bridge, which is better approached from the west bank, the river also broadens into a small lake and deepens from about two feet six (0.76 metres) to about eight or nine feet (2.4–2.7 metres). This is a better venue for roach and there are some good pike. Unlike the last venue, this is primarily summer fishing.

CAVAN TOWN-DERRYHEEN/DEREDIS (Map 20)

There is a competition stretch of the River Annalee just before it joins the Erne. It is between the bridges at Derryheen and Deredis. The main species is roach and they are mostly small, although shoals of fish between eight ounces and a pound (0.25–0.5 kg) can be encountered.

There are a few big bream in the spots where the river broadens out. Fish upstream of Derryheen bridge on the southern bank or downstream of Deredis bridge on the northern bank around the junction of the little River Cavan with the Annalee.

CAVAN TOWN-DERALK, TULLY AND GARFINNY LAKES

The neighbouring lakes of Deralk, Tully and Garfinny on the western side of the complex offer some of the best fishing for large bream in the area. A visiting angler who wants a specimen is advised to visit them, choose a couple of swims and start an active programme of pre-baiting. If he fishes the swims morning and evening for a week in good summer weather, he has a very good chance of catching a fish around the eight pound mark (3.6 kg) or even larger. This is, however, not fast fishing. Leger as far out as you can throw groundbait.

CAVAN TOWN-LOUGH INCHIN (Map 20)

Lough Inchin, on the eastern side of the complex and fairly near Cavan town, holds a variety of species and is noted for pike. Like many of the Cavan lakes, it holds a large population of pike between five and fifteen pounds (2.3–6.8 kg) with the occasional heavier fish. The most productive methods of pike fishing in the Cavan area seem to be using dead roach of three or four inches long (7.5–10.0 cm), either free-lined or suspended under a float. However, quite a lot of fish succumb to floating plugs or large copper spoons fished slowly.

Pike fishing in this part of the country is almost exclusively done from the bank. Foreign anglers should be reminded that live-baiting and the fishing of more than two rods at once is forbidden under Irish law. They are requested not to kill more than a bare minimum of pike as the fish populations are very rapidly depleted by angling pressure.

CAVAN TOWN-LOUGH OUGHTER/RANN ACCESS (Map 20)

Another good spot for pike fishing. Pike can be fished all the year round, with the possible exception of about six weeks in the early spring when they are spawning. The comments under the previous entry apply here also.

CAVAN TOWN-LOUGH OUGHTER/KILLYKEEN ACCESS

Killykeen is a National Forest Park. It has been attractively developed for a variety of recreations including walking, swimming, boating, picnicing and of course angling, and there is a restaurant as well as toilets and ample car parking. Angling matches are held there. There is quite good fishing for small to medium pike; the roach are almost all very small and the bream very scarce, although there are signs that they may be coming back to the venue at the time of writing. All normal methods of angling are practised here, including the roach pole. This is a venue that will primarily interest the family man who wants some alternative amusements to offer the wife and kids while he gets on with a bit of fishing.

CAVAN TOWN-KILLYMOONEY LAKE (Map 20)

Killymooney Lake is a small, shallow, muddy, weedy lake right in the town. The maximum depth in the middle is about seven feet (2.1 metres) and you can walk to the lake if you're staying in the town. It has small rudd, small perch and eels but the primary interest is the good head of very nice tench. At one stage the lake was apparently stocked with some enormous bream, up to thirteen pounds (5.9 kg), but no-one has ever caught these bream since. The lake is oval in shape and you can fish halfway along either of the long sides of the oval.

CAVAN TOWN-UNNAMED LAKE

If you drive south out of Cavan Town and take the right fork signposted to Longford and Mullingar, you'll come to a small lake on the right, less than a mile (1.6 km) from the fork. As far as I can find out, it doesn't have a name. It has provided me with good winter fishing for medium sized rudd, bream and hybrids.

GOWNA. GENERAL (Map 21)

The Lough Gowna complex, lying to the south of the waters in Cavan which have already been described, incorporates the headwaters of the complicated Erne system. Because it's at the head of the many miles of convoluted waterways that make up the system, it is the last part to be colonised by roach. At the time of writing it is not suffering from the ecological shock of having to support an enormous head of stunted roach. Also, because it's at the head of the system, it does not suffer quite as badly from winter flooding as the Lough Oughter complex.

These two facts together mean that it offers the angler some of the best fishing on the Upper Erne. However, these generalisations will probably be out of date by 1981.

GOWNA-CLOONE (Map 21)

The Cloone access to Blue Gate Lake is on your right if you take the road south west from the village of Gowna. It is primarily a bream venue and likely to appeal to anglers who like legering into large waters.

GOWNA-DERNAFERST (Map 21)

Further along the same road there is a car park at Dernaferst where the road bridges the short stretch of river which joins the Blue Gate Lake to Lough Gowna proper. Again the primary interest is bream, although all the local species except tench are present. The best swim is probably on the southern or Lough Gowna side of the road to the east of the river entrance. At this venue and the previous one, bream anglers can also expect to encounter large roach.

GOWNA-DRING (Map 21)

The Dring access at the very southern tip of Lough Gowna is probably the best bet for an angler who wants to try for large roach in the open lake. It can be fished from the bank or from a small portable boat. There is a certain amount of luck involved in locating a shoal in such a large expanse of water but this venue probably holds roach weighing more than the Irish record.

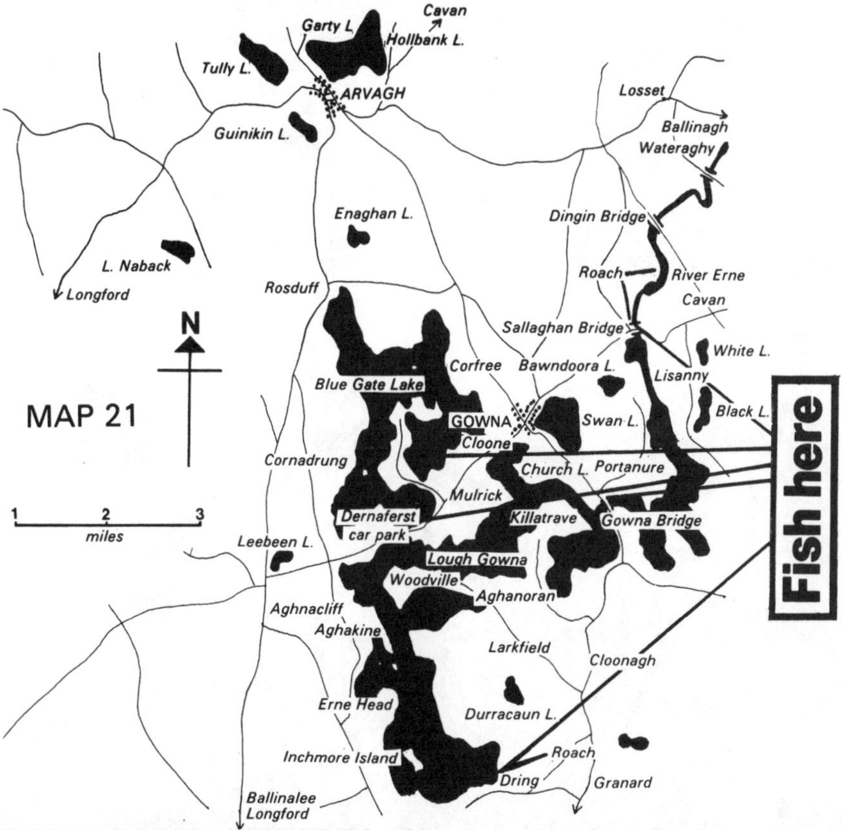

GOWNA-GOWNA BRIDGE (Map 21)

Gowna Bridge is the first bridge you meet on the road south east of Gowna village, the one signposted to Granard. Again, it is over a short stretch of river linking two lakes and offers attractive fishing for medium sized roach with the chance of large ones. It fishes well on the float and the best swims are probably downstream of the bridge.

GOWNA-SALLAGHAN BRIDGE (Map 21)

Sallaghan Bridge is the first bridge you meet if you take the road that heads north east from Gowna village to Cavan town. It provides pleasant fishing, primarily for roach with some bream and roach/bream hybrids. The river downstream to Dingin bridge provides a great choice of swims that can be trotted between weedbeds in summer. The clearer parts can also be fished with light swim-feeder tackle. This is a good stretch for anglers who like to fish a swim for ten minutes and then move on. There is a broad spot in the river about a hundred yards (91 metres) downstream of the bridge which is excellent for the more sedentary angler and can also be fished during winter floods—it's big enough for about three anglers. In winter, anglers should also explore upstream of the bridge where the river is wider and slower.

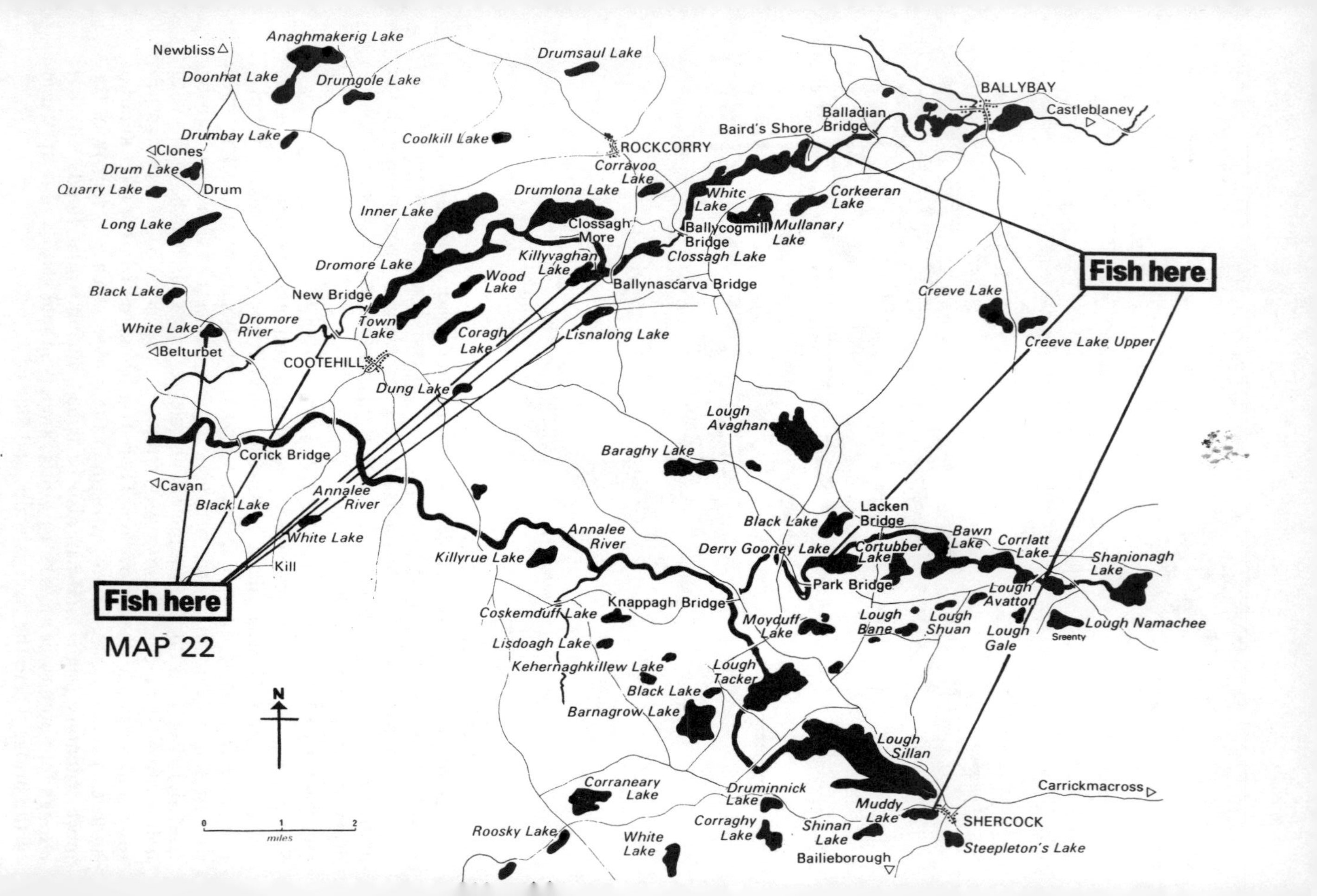
Newbliss
Anaghmakerig Lake
Drumsaul Lake
Doonhat Lake
Drumgole Lake
BALLYBAY
Castleblaney
Balladian Bridge
Baird's Shore
Drumbay Lake
Coolkill Lake
Clones
ROCKCORRY
Drum Lake
Corravoo Lake
Quarry Lake
Drum
Drumlona Lake
White Lake
Corkeeran Lake
Inner Lake
Long Lake
Clossagh More
Ballycogmill Bridge
Mullanary Lake
Killyvaghan Lake
Clossagh Lake
Dromore Lake
Fish here
Wood Lake
Ballynascarva Bridge
Black Lake
New Bridge
Creeve Lake
White Lake
Dromore River
Town Lake
Coragh Lake
Lisnalong Lake
Creeve Lake Upper
Belturbet
COOTEHILL
Dung Lake
Lough Avaghan
Baraghy Lake
Corick Bridge
Cavan
Annalee River
Black Lake
Lacken Bridge
Black Lake
Annalee River
Bawn Lake
Corrlatt Lake
White Lake
Derry Gooney Lake
Cortubber Lake
Shanionagh Lake
Killyrue Lake
Kill
Park Bridge
Lough Avatton
Fish here
Knappagh Bridge
Coskemduff Lake
Moyduff Lake
Lough Bane
Lough Shuan
Lough Gale
Lough Namachee
Sreenty
MAP 22
Lisdoagh Lake
Kehernaghkillew Lake
Lough Tacker
Black Lake
Barnagrow Lake
N
Lough Sillan
Corraneary Lake
Druminnick Lake
Carrickmacross
Muddy Lake
0
1
2
miles
Corraghy Lake
SHERCOCK
Roosky Lake
Shinan Lake
White Lake
Steepleton's Lake
Bailieborough

COOTEHILL GENERAL

Cootehill is in Co. Cavan but most of the fishing around it is in Co. Monaghan, just to the west of the town. Therefore the rest of this chapter can be taken as dealing with Co. Monaghan except for the section at the end under 'Drumconrath' which deals with an area just in north Meath.

COOTEHILL-WHITE LAKE (Map 22)

There are at least three lakes in this area which are called 'White Lake', a source of confusion. This one is a small lake two miles (3.2 km) to the west of Cootehill in Co. Cavan. It has all the local species and is best known for bream. Many of the small lakes in this area are completely surrounded by reeds and some of them are private. White Lake suffers from neither of these disadvantages.

COOTEHILL-NEW BRIDGE (Map 22)

Driving north from Cootehill on the Clones road, take the left fork and in less than a mile (1.6 km) you'll come to the New Bridge over the Dromore River. Fish in Dromore Lake immediately to the east of the bridge from the north shore for good bream and small roach. Both the Dromore River and the Annalee River to the south of it are infested with these small roach.

ROCKCORRY-BALLYNASCARVA BRIDGE (Map 22)

Ballynascarva Bridge about two miles (3.2 km) south of the village of Rockcorry offers roach fishing in the Dromore River both upstream and downstream. There is a better than average chance of contacting decent-sized roach in this stretch and there are some bream in the wider spots. It fishes summer and winter.

ROCKCORRY-KILLYVAGHAN LAKE (Map 22)

Between Ballynascarva bridge and Lisnalong Post Office is a small road which runs into a car park to the west of the shores of Killyvaghan Lake. There is a stony peninsula opposite the car park which gives access to water about six feet deep (1.8 metres). But if you walk up to the left for about half a mile through a belt of trees you come to an open flat bank which gives access to swims of about eleven feet (3.3 metres) and better fishing. This is a good big-fish water containing bream, rudd, roach, perch and roach/bream hybrids. Many bream over eight pounds (3.6 kg) and some over nine (4.1 kg) have been taken. The lake and the nearby stretches of the Dromore River also provide active sport for small to medium pike.

ROCKCORRY-LISNALONG LAKE (Map 22)

This lake lies just to the south of the crossroads at Lisnalong and has some good tench.

ROCKCORRY-WHITE LAKE (Map 22)

White Lake (this is a different White Lake to the one mentioned earlier) is a long, thin lake between Rockcorry and Ballybay to the east. It offers good bream and moderate roach. The best access is at Baird's (formerly Woods) Shore at the east end and is signposted.

SHERCOCK-MUDDY LAKE (Map 22)

Muddy Lake is practically in the village of Shercock at the west end. It has all the local species and is best known for bream. It is aptly named.

SHERCOCK-DERRYGOONEY LAKE (Map 22)

There is a complicated series of small and medium sized lakes to the north of

Shercock. The best of them is probably Derrygooney Lake. It has sound bream fishing and is an excellent pike water on a tributary of the Annalee. It's not easy to find without a map.

CARRICKMACROSS-BROTHERS/LISANISK LAKE

This small lake, which goes by both the names given above, is practically in the town of Carrickmacross. It has some stands and some bank access and competitions are fished on it. The lake has a large head of small bream and small rudd and is fairly easy fishing. A good water for children and beginners.

CARRICKMACROSS-MONALTY LAKE

Monalty is on the Dundalk road out of Carrickmacross and, like all the local lakes, is well signposted. It is a stark contrast to the previous water, being a remarkable big-fish venue. Some anglers regard it as the top specimen water in the country. It produces bream, rudd and rudd/bream hybrids, some tench and some perch. All of these species have been caught over specimen weight and some of them very close to record weight. Strangely enough, small fish are a rarity. Like all big-fish waters, it is fairly slow fishing and produces best to all-night sessions. Legering as far out as you can throw the groundbait is the method, and for the night sessions butt indicators are normally used. Avoid using worms or maggots in the groundbait or you will be pestered by eels.

CARRICKMACROSS-LOUGH NA GLACK

This venue, formerly a prime bream water, is not now recommended due to pollution.

CARRICKMACROSS-CAPRAGH LAKE

Capragh, on the Crossmaglen road out of Carrickmacross, is a similar lake to Monalty but slightly deeper, slightly easier and not producing such a remarkably high proportion of big fish. It is unusual in containing carp, although they are seldom caught. The lakes in this area generally produce best to maggots, although worms can be good. Bread also works but is more difficult to use for night sessions involving long range fishing.

CASTLEBLAYNEY-TOWN LAKE

The lake is beside the Carrickmacross road just outside the town and has big bream.

DRUMCONRATH. GENERAL (Map 23)

There is an area around the village of Drumconrath in the north of Co. Meath where a number of small lakes in a drumlin landscape have been developed for coarse angling. The area is attractive and the development—building stands, car parks and stiles—has been well carried out. Some competition angling goes on and there is an annual festival. On the other hand, the fishing itself seems to be a little unpredictable; some anglers have had very heavy nets of bream and there are undoubtedly big tench in the area. On other occasions, large parties of highly skilled anglers have had very disappointing results. Because the area is isolated from the main coarse fishing areas of the country it does not get much pressure and not a lot is known about some of the smaller lakes.

DRUMCONRATH-CORSTOWN (Map 23)

Corstown Lake, two miles (3.2 km) to the north of the village of Drumconrath, is probably the best known fishery in the area. It consists of a medium sized, very deep lake with a small lake connected to the top of it. Most of the angling is from

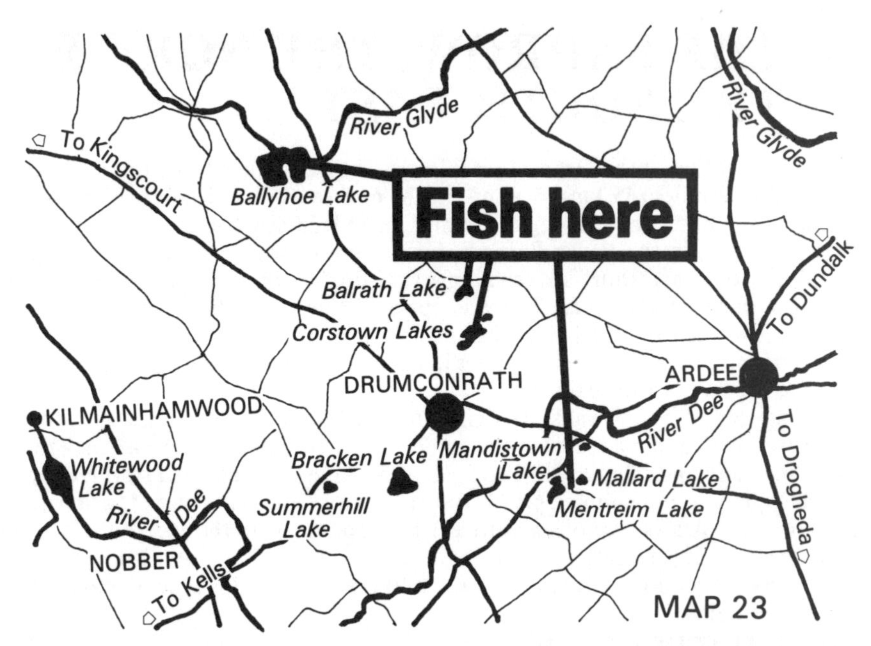

stands, access is good and there is reasonable wind protection. Primary interest is in the bream and because the water is over twenty feet deep (6 metres) it is usual to leger or fish with a sliding float. There are also rudd, tench, perch and pike; the pike provide moderate winter fishing for medium sized fish. Nets of over a hundred pounds (45 kg) have been taken, but the water has a reputation for being moody.

DRUMCONRATH-BALRATH LAKE (Map 23)

To the north of Corstown lies Balrath Lake, a small and attractive piece of water which has bream, rudd, tench, perch and pike. It's partly bank fishing and partly from stands. The southern end of the water is very shallow and weedy. The bream and rudd tend to be small and I've no information about the tench.

DRUMCONRATH-BALLYHOE LAKE (Map 23)

Ballyhoe Lake, on the river Glyde, is five miles (8 km) to the north west of the village and is the largest water in the area. It has bream, pike, perch and rudd and is said to hold tench as well as trout and salmon. There is bank fishing and fishing from stands and boats is available. The pike fishing is average. Night sessions in summer can produce heavy nets of small to medium bream.

DRUMCONRATH-MANDISTOWN, MALLARD AND MENTREIM LAKES (Map 23)

This group of lakes to the south east of the village of Drumconrath is where the big tench are supposed to be. Apparently a scientific survey of the area using nets came up with a number of very big fish including at least one over the Irish record weight. The lakes are not fished much, but there are some stands and some bank access. The lakes would almost certainly repay extensive exploration by specimen hunters, and because they are small this is a feasible proposition.

4. THE BARROW, THE NORE & THE SOUTH-EAST

The Barrow line of the Grand Canal leaves the main line at Lowtown and runs south the 28 miles (45 km) to Athy. In the course of this distance can be found some of the best canal fishing in Ireland, or indeed anywhere else. At Athy the navigation joins the River Barrow. From here down to the tidal limit of St Mullins, there are short stretches of canal dug so that boats can bypass the shallow parts of the river. There is coarse fishing of a high quality in these stretches of the canal and river, but little is known about it. At St Mullins, the Barrow enters a large estuary which it shares with the Nore and the Suir; there are coarse fish in this estuary.

The Inland Waterways Association of Ireland publishes a guide to the Barrow which may be useful to the angler. The Ordnance Survey half inch to the mile sheets 16 and 19 cover the region. In general the area covered by this chapter holds high quality fishing in pleasant surroundings and is the place to make for if you like the idea of exploring with a fishing rod as, with the exception of a few canal venues, it is largely a coarse angler's 'terra incognita'. Some known venues and some indications of areas that seem likely to repay this type of exploration are listed below.

BALLYTEAGUE (Map 24)

Shortly after the Barrow line of the canal leaves the main line at Lowtown, it is joined by the Milltown Feeder, which has recently been made navigable through to the summit level, and passes Ballyteague Castle. There is a lock up into the feeder and two locks close together just below the castle. The area is easily reached from Robertstown, Allenwood or the village of Kilmeague; there is road access on both banks and two road bridges. The canal can also, of course, be crossed on foot at all the locks. The fishing here is principally for rudd, which grow up to two pounds (0.9 kg) and have a considerably better average size than is normal in the canal. Because these fish have a wandering nature, it is best to start proceedings by looking for signs of activity between the junction of the two canals and the 20th lock. Rudd like to feed near the surface, so this activity is often evident, particularly on warm days. Bread flake is a good bait and it should be free-lined or fished under a light self-cocking float. Groundbaiting should not be heavy-handed.

RATHANGAN (Map 25)

The village of Rathangan provides fishing for rudd, hybrids, perch and eels, as well as some quite good bream fishing. The swims are above (north of) the village on the opposite bank and the better swims are the ones quite near the village, opposite and just up from the large galvanised iron silos.

Matches are fished on this stretch. The towpath is driveable. The bream can be fished for with light legering tackle or by laying-on just off the shelf on the far side of the channel. In general, bread tends to be a better bet in summer and maggots or worms in spring or autumn—it is little fished in winter.

UMERAS

Umeras bridge is reached by taking the Monasterevan road south from

Rathangan and taking the second turn right off it which is about three miles (4.8 km) from Rathangan. Again, this is fairly ordinary canal fishing without tench and the bream seem to have a lower average size than at Rathangan. However, the fish are very willing and a good net of smaller fish can usually be had fairly quickly and easily. Interestingly, this is one stretch of canal which consistently seems to produce fish in winter. Moderate pike and small rudd can be caught all

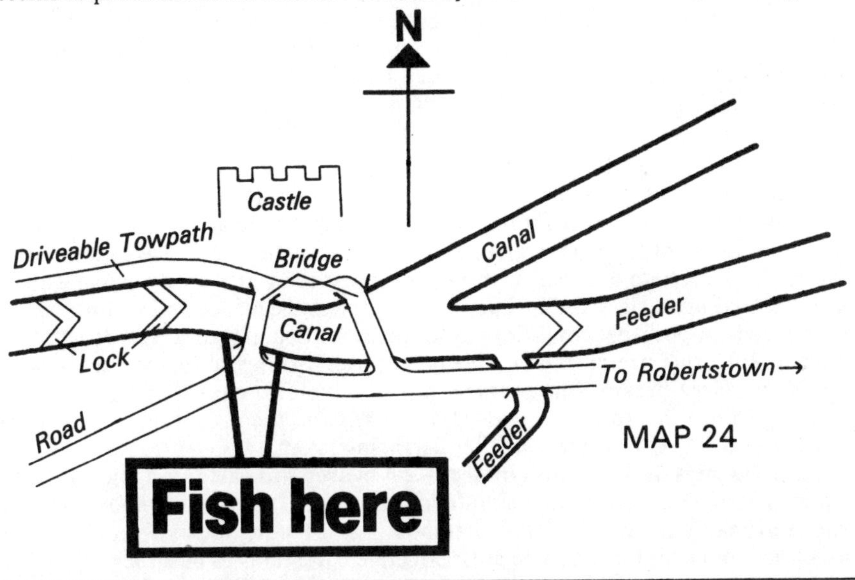

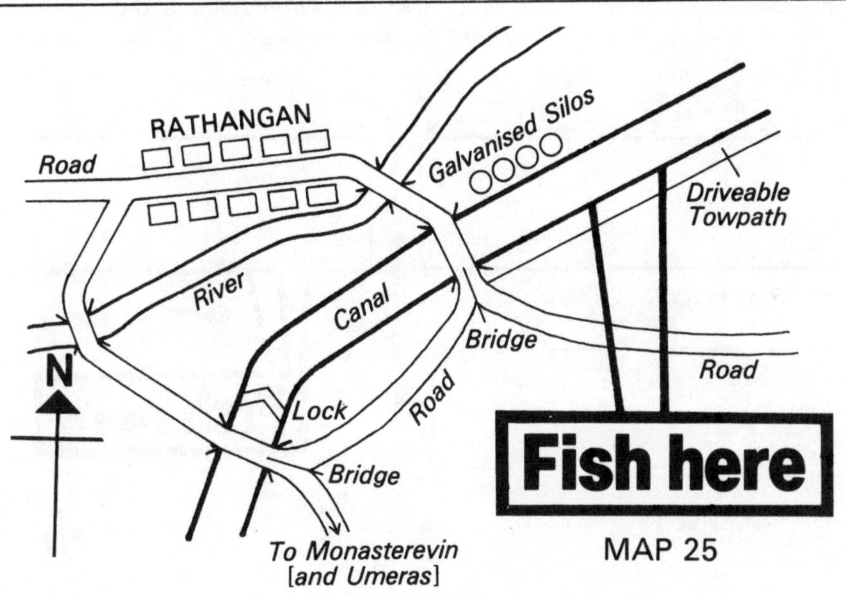

the time and bream on the milder days. Park at the bridge and fish north of it on the east bank; the best swims are within a hundred yards (91 metres) of the bridge.

VICARSTOWN

At Vicarstown, there is a road south which hugs the bank of the canal almost all the way to Athy. There is fishing for rudd, perch, bream and hybrids in the stretch south of the village but it tends to be dominated by small rudd. Because of this, Vicarstown is a popular venue for anglers looking for pike baits. A mile or so (1.6 km) north and south of the village are a couple of small tributaries of the Barrow which have pools where the roving angler can catch small to medium pike and large perch.

BALLYMANUS BRIDGE (Map 26)

Ballymanus Bridge is the first bridge over the canal south of Vicarstown, about a mile and a half (2.4 km) from the village. The swims are along the east bank of the canal north of the bridge and south of the aqueduct. There are reeds along the canal bank here but two or three swims just above the bridge have usually been cleared by anglers and it is possible to park at the bridge and set up a basket in the reeds. In the right conditions in summer, particularly on a warm evening in June or July, this stretch can provide magnificent fishing for mixed bags of large tench and large bream. The averages are very high for canal fishing, the tench running from three to five pounds (1.4–2.3 kg) and the bream from four to six pounds (1.8–2.7 kg) with few smaller fish being taken.

The Canal is deep (up to eight feet—2.4 metres—in parts along here and the water is opaque. Legering in the centre of the channel with a fairly short swingtip rod is probably the most effective method. Float fishing is possible, but a little awkward in the high reeds. The most effective bait seems to be either a bunch of maggots or a cocktail of maggots and redworm. Groundbaiting should take the form of accurate loose-feeding with handfuls of maggots and should be fairly

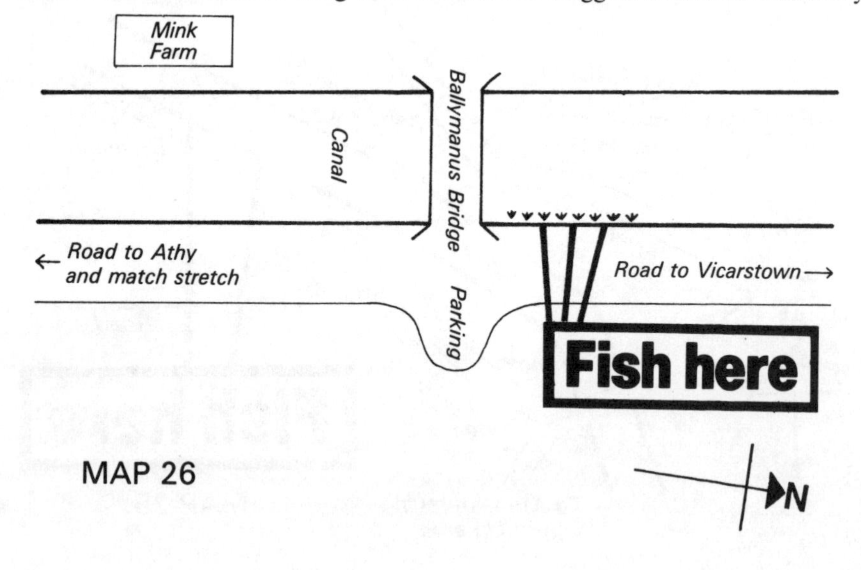

generous because of the large quantities of large fish that are present. Nets weighing over a hundred pounds (45 kg) are quite common.

If the conditions seem right but the swims are not producing, it is worth walking or driving slowly along the towpath for a few hundred yards in each direction, looking for muddying of the water and in particular, for those clumps of very small bubbles fizzing up to the surface which are characteristic of feeding tench. There are some water lilies, both floating and submerged, in the canal in this stretch and they can cause problems if large fish are hooked on a line of less than 5 lbs (2.3 kg) breaking strain.

PEG 108

If you continue driving south along the towpath from Ballymanus bridge, after a few hundred yards you will notice numbers painted in white in the middle of the road every so often. These are the peg numbers for a popular match stretch. Top pegs are around 108 where the canal takes a bend and widens slightly. Although all the normal canal species are present, again the real interest is in the big bags of quality tench and bream which can be taken. This stretch receives quite a lot of pressure and the fish have a degree of sophistication not common in Ireland. They can be put down by undue noise and movement on the bank, which means that matches are quite often won with fairly low weights. They are also used to feeding on goundbait, particularly in the summer months, and can become preoccupied for a while with one or the other of the common baits. A visiting angler can ask about this at the local angling club (see appendix).

Some local anglers groundbait by using plain, ordinary mud! However, this stretch is capable of producing nets as good as those taken at Ballymanus bridge and is probably a better venue for the dedicated float fisherman, as it is a little shallower and the banks are more open. This match stretch also has a high density of moderate to good sized pike; a scientific survey found an average of one double-figure pike for every four hundred yards (365 metres) and one fish in the stretch over twenty pounds (9.0 kg). Between the north end of the match stretch and Ballymanus bridge is a mink farm; the owner also breeds ducks. Rumour has it that an enormous pike feeds on these ducks and there is a reward for its removal. Rudd deadbaits are effective for pike fishing in this part of the canal.

THE RIVER BARROW

It is important that a guide book of this nature should have the courage to admit its shortcomings and it must be said that the information here about coarse angling in the River Barrow is liable to be sketchy and inaccurate. This is because the river, although it undoubtedly has excellent fishing, has been very little explored by anglers. This will probably change over the next few years and the author would welcome any information which will help to make future editions more comprehensive. In the meantime, perhaps it's a blessing that we have a river of great beauty and character which has produced our largest rod-caught coarse fish (the record pike of 42 lbs—19.1 kg), is capable of producing many more record breakers, and which is virtually unknown. The Barrow may have more unrealised potential than any other coarse fishery in Europe. It should tempt pioneers, who should bear in mind that the river is navigable and boats can be hired. The species available, apart from game fish, are large pike, perch of above average size, tench, bream, rudd, hybrids, eels, large gudgeon and shad.

The venues listed below should repay further exploration.

ATHY

Stretches around the town produce good sized perch. The usual method is spinning and this is most conveniently done from a small boat. There are also bream.

CARLOW

Stretches in the town and above and below it have been stocked with tench some years ago, as well as containing rudd, bream, hybrids, pike and perch.

LEIGHLINBRIDGE

Stretches just upstream of the village provide convenient access for fishing for rudd, bream, hybrids, pike and perch. Tench are probably present.

BAGENALSTOWN (MUINE BHEAG)

There is a short stretch of canal bypassing a weir in the town. It contains specimen hybrids as well as good rudd and bream.

GORESBRIDGE

There is a swim downstream of the bridge on the east bank in the pool where the canal leaves the river. The towpath is driveable. There are large hybrids.

GRAIGUENAMANAGH

Noted for pike fishing; also bream, rudd and hybrids.

SAINT MULLINS

Below here the river is tidal. This is the only place in Ireland noted for angling for thwaite shad; they are caught below the sea lock, usually on small spinners, for a few weeks every year around the end of May.

THE NORE

The River Nore joins the estuary of the Barrow below the limit of the tide at Saint Mullins. Even less is known about it as a coarse fishery than is known about the Barrow, but it can be assumed to hold the same range of species. Certainly hybrids of a good size are found in the estuary below the confluence of the two rivers—in fact as far down as New Ross. A convenient base from which to explore the lower reaches of the Nore would be Inistioge. The river has a reasonable run of spring salmon and much fishing is preserved.

MISCELLANEOUS

Before leaving the south east, it is worth mentioning Belle Lake, on the road from Waterford to Dunmore East, which has quite good pike fishing, moderate rudd and which was stocked with tench some years ago. A boat can be hired. It is rumoured that counties Waterford, Kilkenny and east Tipperary have a number of small private lakes on large estates as bequests from their Norman pasts which contain monstrous carp. Any information about these would be most gratefully received! Finally there have recently been reports of large rudd at a couple of points on the River Suir. These have not yet been properly investigated.

5. MUNSTER BLACKWATER & LOUGH IN CORK

The province of Munster is primarily territory for the sea angler and the game fisherman. There are, however, two important exceptions to this rule—the River Blackwater and the Lough in Cork City.

The Blackwater is a river of some size and great beauty. Despite the fact that it flows past spectacular limestone cliffs, it is an acid-water, reflecting its origins in the bogs of Kerry. It has a claim to being Ireland's best salmon river, has mediocre brown trout fishing in the main river but quite good stretches in the tributaries and some reasonably good fishing for white trout in the lower reaches. From this, it can be deduced that the river is fast flowing for most of its course and given to flooding and that much of the fishing is carefully preserved. The situation with regard to coarse anglers on water preserved for game fishing is a little complex and is more often a question of custom and practice, common sense and courtesy than it is of legal niceties. When fishing on the Blackwater it is however, very important to ask permission first and to make it quite clear what species you are going for. The swims on the river detailed in the text of this chapter all offer free fishing without the necessity of asking permission.

The interest of the Blackwater, apart from the beauty and challenge of its fast-flowing swims, is that it is the only river in Ireland which has dace and was the only river with roach, until recently. The dace fishing is superb and is strongly recommended to anyone who appreciates this small but sporting species.

The Blackwater was also, until recently, one of the top two or three roach rivers in the world. As the roach is a twelve-months-of-the-year species, it offered welcome sport in winter when the river wasn't in flood—the principal species of coarse fish in Ireland, with the notable exception of pike, are primarily summer quarry. But the biology of the roach is complex and not yet fully understood by the scientists. Roach are subject to population surges and unpredictable migrations and there is some evidence that this is happening at present on the Blackwater. The fishing is not as consistent as it was—roach are deserting well-known swims and turning up in unexpected places.

This has been exacerbated by the fact that many of the great roach catches of the past were made in Cappoquin at the famous 'Bacon Factory' swim where the discharge from a food processing plant concentrated huge shoals of fish. The factory has changed its method of operation and no longer discharges scraps into the river and the roach have dispersed. However there is no cause for alarm. There are still great shoals of roach in the Blackwater and it remains a river in which two pounders (0.9 kg) are a reasonable ambition and even larger fish are not out of the question. It's just that over the next few years, anglers may have to do a bit of exploring and a bit of thinking for themselves instead of relying on the pioneering efforts of those who fished before them. Apart from roach and dace, the river has eels and some large perch.

CAPPOQUIN (Map 27)

The river is tidal here; it used to be the prime venue for roach. The upstream

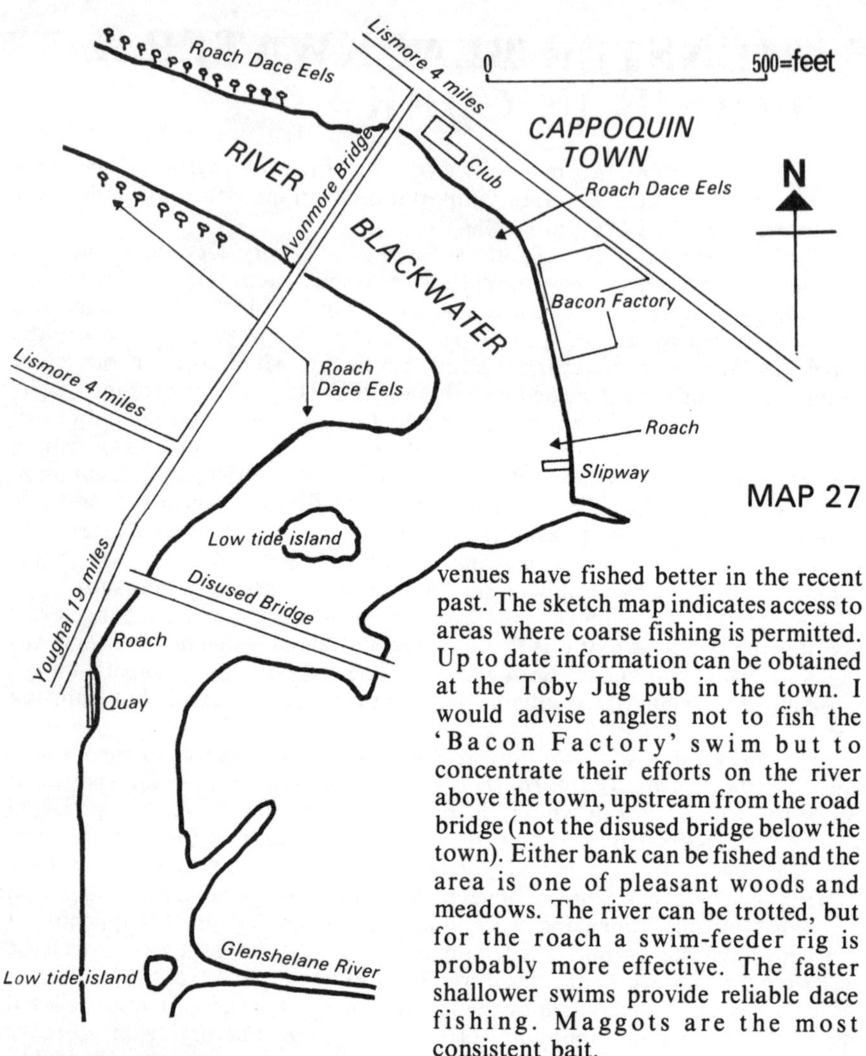

venues have fished better in the recent past. The sketch map indicates access to areas where coarse fishing is permitted. Up to date information can be obtained at the Toby Jug pub in the town. I would advise anglers not to fish the 'Bacon Factory' swim but to concentrate their efforts on the river above the town, upstream from the road bridge (not the disused bridge below the town). Either bank can be fished and the area is one of pleasant woods and meadows. The river can be trotted, but for the roach a swim-feeder rig is probably more effective. The faster shallower swims provide reliable dace fishing. Maggots are the most consistent bait.

FERMOY (Map 28)

Fermoy offers excellent dace fishing and the possibility of very large roach. It is possible to fish in the town itself above the weir from the south bank—this is a popular venue for night fishing as the street lights help to avoid tackle tangles. Just downstream of the town there is access off the main Cappoquin and Waterford road on the north bank down a pathway beside a house—room for only two or three anglers. The main access is on the south bank downstream of the town off the Tallow and Youghal road. There is a car park and a sign post saying 'Fishing' on the left, coming from Fermoy, opposite the hospital.

There is good fishing directly below the car park. It is probably even better a little further downstream if you walk through a small wood and past the viaduct,

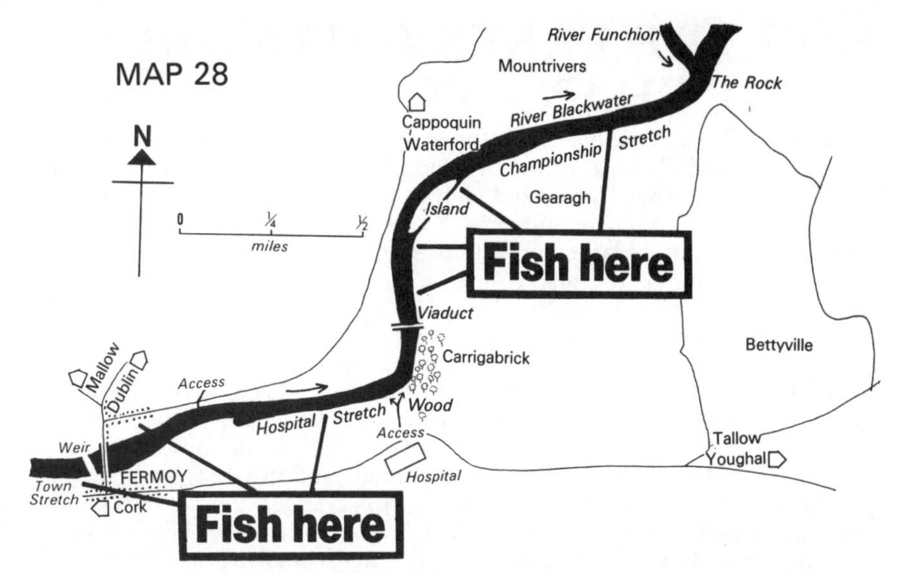

a distance of about a quarter of a mile (0.4 km). Fish from just past the viaduct to just before the long island. About another quarter of a mile (0.4 km) further on, just past the island, is the start of the 'Championship Stretch' where a former World Championship was held. All the normal methods of river fishing for roach and dace can be used but the most consistently successful approach is probably to use a quiver-tip rod and a swim-feeder full of maggots.

MALLOW

Around Mallow the river is generally shallower and faster. This is the cream of the dace fishing and the roach have been improving in recent years. It is best to ask locally for permission to fish for coarse fish.

THE LOUGH, CORK CITY

The Lough is shallow pond in a housing estate in Cork City. It can be reached by bus. The pond contains a fairly dense population of small rudd and bream and matches are occasionally fished there. It has also produced specimen eels. However its chief interest to the angler is that it provides the only consistent public carp fishing in Ireland at present. The Lough has produced fish of over eighteen pounds (8.2 kg) in weight. (The current Irish record fish is 18 lbs 12 ozs—8.54 kg—which is not large by international standards; it came from a private lake.) There are undoubtedly fish over the record weight in the Lough.

The Lough is set in a park which means that during the day there is rather too much activity from children and mendicant ducks for successful carp fishing. During the night or very early on summer mornings are the times to fish. Of double-figure fish reported in 1977, ten took floating crust, five maggots and two bread paste.

6. CLARE LAKES & WEST OF THE SHANNON

By and large, Ireland west of the Shannon drainage has little to offer the coarse angler. Kerry and Donegal have, for all practical purposes, no freshwater fish except game fish. Sligo, Mayo and Galway (except for some of the Shannon drainage in east Galway) are primarily of interest to the game angler and the sea angler. There are quite large populations of pike and perch in these last three counties and some of the pike fishing is worth investigation. However, the development of the large western lakes for trout fishing has resulted in pike stocks being depleted by extensive netting and electro-fishing. Also, any angler interested in pike fishing in Sligo, Mayo or west Galway will have to do a considerable amount of research for himself, as there appears to be little reliable information available about venues. There are some populations of rudd scattered through these three countries and isolated populations of bream.

Lough Corrib in west Galway contains bream and fish up to specimen size have been taken by anglers trolling for trout. However, locating a bream shoal in this huge expense of water without any pointers as to where they might be would be a daunting task. There are some small lakes at Moycullen near Lough Corrib which offer much better prospects for dedicated bream anglers unlucky enough to be spending their holidays in Galway City—they are mentioned in the text. Otherwise, it's a rather unproductive 'terra incognita'; information on new venues would be very welcome for future editions of this book.

The big exception to the generalisation that no coarse angler in his right mind goes west of the Shannon drainage is the Clare Lakelands. (To forestall any criticism, the Clare Lakelands can be described as belonging to the Shannon drainage as they drain principally through the Fergus River which itself empties into the Shannon estuary. However, for the purposes of this book, it seems simpler to treat them separately.) They consist of a maze of large and small lakes and bits of river in a high PH limestone landscape of great natural beauty. There is good access along small roads and local tourism interests have done a good job of signposting the better-known fishing spots, developing guesthouses and making car parks. There are also some first-class resident coarse anglers in the area and some active clubs, notably the one in Tulla. There is far too much water in Clare for a comprehensive guide to be possible within the limited scope of this book. The venues listed below are chosen because they offer contrasting fishing in beautiful surroundings at places that can take a reasonable amount of angling pressure.

DOON LAKE (Map 29)

Doon Lake is a relatively large lake, or to be more exact, two lakes joined by a channel. Its PH is lower than most of the others in the area because it is fed by mountain streams that come off peat. There is a lot of woodland round the shores which has been developed for recreational purposes and picnicing. The road access is excellent and there are a number of car parks. Boats are available locally, but most of the lake can be fished from the shore.

Much of the water within casting distance of the bank is however, rather shallow. One exception to this is the Doorus Shore in the north; this gives the

0 1 2
miles
FEAKLE
Scarriff
Gort
Ayle
Derrynaneal L.
Derrycaghra L.
Biddy Early's L.
Dromore L.
Kilbarron L.
Errinagh L.
Clondanagh L.
Rosslara L.
Derrinterriff L.
Loughinaloon L.
Clandoorney L.
Maryfort L.
Clooncoose L.
Castle L.
Killaloe
Lough
Bridget
Ballynahinch L.
Garrura L.
Tench
Bream
TULLA
Coolbawn L.
Silvergrove L.
Blacksticks
L. Nacronia
Ennis
O'Hara's L.
Kilgory L.
Lecarrow L.
Liskenny L.
Fish here
Hogan's
P.O.
Bream
Doorus Shore
Cullaun L.
Doon L.
Garr L.
Gortnacorragh L.
Craggaunowen L.
Broadford River
O'Donnell's
Shore
Derragher L.
Kilkishen
Clonlea L.
BROADFORD
Rathluby L.
Stone's L.
Kilcornan L.
Limerick
Quinn
Kilkishen L.
Owenagarney River
N
Shandangan L.
Clonbrick L.
Kilmurry
Castle L.
MAP 29
Limerick

bank angler access to a hole which is up to thirty feet (9.1 metres) deep and big enough to accommodate thirty or forty anglers at the one time. This venue produces heavy nets of fairly small bream (a three pounder—1.4 kg—is a good fish). A car park has recently been laid out on the Doorus Shore, about 150 yards (137 metres) from the swims. The lake also contains rudd, hybrids, pike, perch and eels. The eels can be a nuisance at times as the most popular local bait is brandling worms. The other species are not present in the size or quantity to be of interest to the serious angler, except for the pike, which go up to specimen weight. Pike are normally caught on artificial lures. The normal method for bream fishing is long-distance legering and the bites have a reputation for being hard to hit.

KILGOREY LAKE (Map 29)

Kilgorey Lake, to the north of Doon, has a higher PH and probably because of this, a considerably higher average size of bream. The fish run to specimen weight but the fishing is more difficult than Doon. Pre-baiting is strongly recommended and some local knowledge of the recent shoal movements is a big help. The same species are present as in Doon and there are reports of occasional tench. There is good access on surfaced roads and fishing stands have been built around the lake.

SILVERGROVE (Map 29)

Further to the north again is Silvergrove, a serpentine lake that gets its name from the groves of birch and alder that surround it. Like most of the Clare lakes, it is a very attractive venue; it is also primarily a bream water, although more tench turn up in it than in the last two lakes mentioned. There is good road access and much of the bank is fishable—the parts that aren't are mostly provided with stands. It's also a leger water. Up to date information on movements of the shoals can be had by polite enquiry from Jack Kelly of the Silvergrove Guesthouse.

THE CULLAUN CHAIN (Map 29)

The Cullaun chain consists of one large lake to the west of the ones previously mentioned and a number of small loughs and ponds stretching out to the south and south west. It is all high PH water and contains notable pike and rudd as well as good bream. Some of the smaller lakes in the chain also provide tench up to specimen weight. Cullaun lake itself is a notable pike water which responds to deadbaits and artificials. There is also good fishing for rudd, which can run up to specimen weight, off the reed beds in the early morning and late evening. A boat is advisable. Further down the chain to the south west, Stones Lake can be reached by parking on the road which runs south from the cross at Hogan's Post Office and walking east down onto a platform of limestone from which you can either float fish or use long distance legering tactics to reach out into water up to forty feet (12.2 metres) deep. There are specimen tench and bream in this particularly beautiful fishing spot. Further to the east, the little Kilkishen and Kilcornan lakes are not far from the road and offer excellent tench fishing.

MOYCULLEN LAKES (GALWAY AREA) (Map 30)

The coarse angler in Galway City who is unwilling to face the long drive east to the Suck at Ballinasloe or south to the Clare Lakelands is recommended to try the Moycullen lakes, a series of gravel pits near the village of Moycullen on the

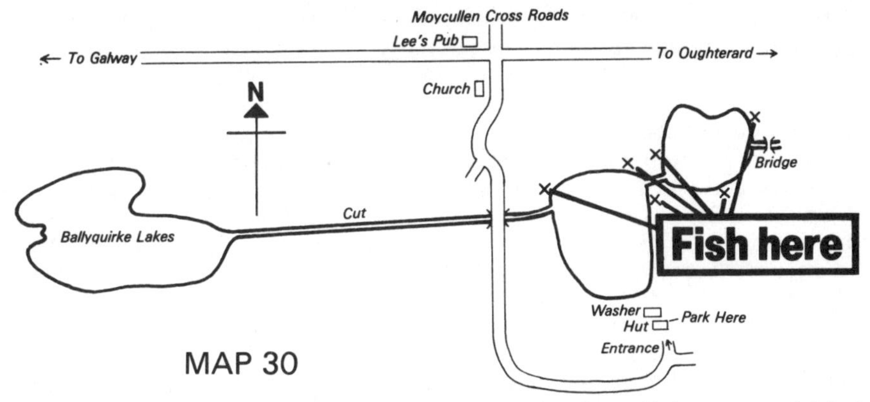

road from Galway to Oughterard. If you're coming from Galway turn right at the Moycullen crossroads, just after passing Lee's pub. Drive into the gravel workings, park beside the hut (on weekdays) and walk past the washer through the gates to the pits. The swims are marked on the sketch map. There are bream up to about five pounds (2.3 kg); the best bait is worms, although bread can also be good. The pits seem to also go under the name of the Ballyquirke Lakes.

7. NORTHERN IRELAND

This chapter is concerned with coarse fishing in Northern Ireland, which, like the Republic, has no close season for coarse fish. But while coarse fishing in the Republic is free, in Northern Ireland you need permits for nearly all waters. The licensing system is complicated and there are exceptions to the general rules which are noted in the text. In general, though, a coarse angler who buys a Department of Agriculture Annual General Coarse Fishing Permit and a Conservancy Board licence (just over £1 each) is then entitled to fish for coarse fish anywhere in Northern Ireland, except on privately owned waters. These permits are available from fishing tackle shops and in some cases from general shops and pubs. The Northern Ireland Department of Agriculture publishes annually a booklet called the 'Angling Guide' which contains details of the waters it is developing (mostly game fishing waters), details of licence requirements and a full list of places where you can buy licences.

The fishing itself does not offer quite the variety, either of water types or species, that one finds in the Republic but there is angling of a very high quality indeed for some species. With the preponderance of good roach and pike waters, there is excellent winter fishing. Co. Fermanagh in the south west of the province offers first class roach and pike angling and good bream and perch. Co. Tyrone has quality roach and some good pike, while Co. Armagh has roach fishing which may not offer quite the size of fish found in the Fairy Water in Tyrone, but compensates by the quantity of fish that can be caught in a session. There is one important venue in the south eastern county of Down, which offers challenging angling for small to medium bream in large quantities, quality pike and a sprinkling of other species. The two northern counties of Derry and Antrim have populations of pike and perch but are not of great interest to the coarse angler. The principal species, then, are roach, bream, pike and perch. There are hybrids between roach and bream and rudd and bream. The rudd themselves are declining under the onslaught of the roach, there are no dace, practically no tench, no carp to my knowledge, some large gudgeon and a lot of eels.

Also there are not many anglers. Coarse fishing is a fairly new sport to Northern Ireland, although it is catching on fast and many of the local anglers are very highly skilled. Also, political troubles in this part of Ireland have tended to discourage the sort of influx of angling tourists that occurs at some venues in the Republic.

Despite this, the authorities have carried out quite a lot of development of coarse angling waters in the form of car parks, signposts, stiles, stages and so on. There is also a cruiser hire industry on Lough Erne and much of the angling water in Fermanagh is navigable. The availability of bait and specialist tackle in Northern Ireland is a bit patchy. Shops which stock selections of bait and groundbait include Rod and Tackle, Holywood Road, Belfast, J. K. Falloon, Lisburn, Lakeland Tackle, Enniskillen; and Tyrone Angling Supplies in Omagh.

There is a developing match circuit in Northern Ireland, taking the form of a few big-money matches held during the English close season and a more modest club circuit. Because of the quality of the roach fishing, the Ulster Winter League draws anglers from all over Ireland during the colder months. It was during one of the big-money matches, the Benson and Hedges Fishing Festival, that Ian Heaps from England, who was World Champion at the time, broke the World Open Five Hour Match Angling Record with 166 lbs 11 ozs (74.9 kg), almost entirely roach, on the Erne in Co. Fermanagh.

Anglers from the Republic and foreigners who visit Northern Ireland are likely to do so because they are interested in the superb roach fishing, probably the best in the world. It is worth noting that most of the roach in N. Ireland live in large lakes like Lough Neagh and Lower and Upper Lough Erne. However, most of the roach angling is done on the rivers that flow into these lakes or connect them. This is because roach are very hard to locate in these enormous stretches of water—Lough Neagh is the largest lake in the British Isles.

There are roach in the rivers all the year round, but there are more in winter than in summer. However, in May, enormous concentrations of roach move up the rivers from the lakes to spawn and this is probably the single best month of the year for catching large quantities. The principal method is long-trotting maggots, although quiver-tipping can be more effective in high water. Pike fishing on the other hand is mainly done in still water and it should be noted that live-baiting, which is banned by law in the Republic, is allowed in Northern Ireland.

The following list of venues starts in Co. Down in the south east of the province and moves westwards to Co. Fermanagh. The Fermanagh venues can be hard to find because of the complexity of the Erne system of waterways and the small roads which twist among them. Visiting anglers are advised not to rely solely on the sketch maps in this book for navigation in this area but also to buy Sheets 4 and 7 of the One Inch Ordnance Survey map of Northern Ireland. The list of venues is not exhaustive, but it is reliable; a number of known venues have

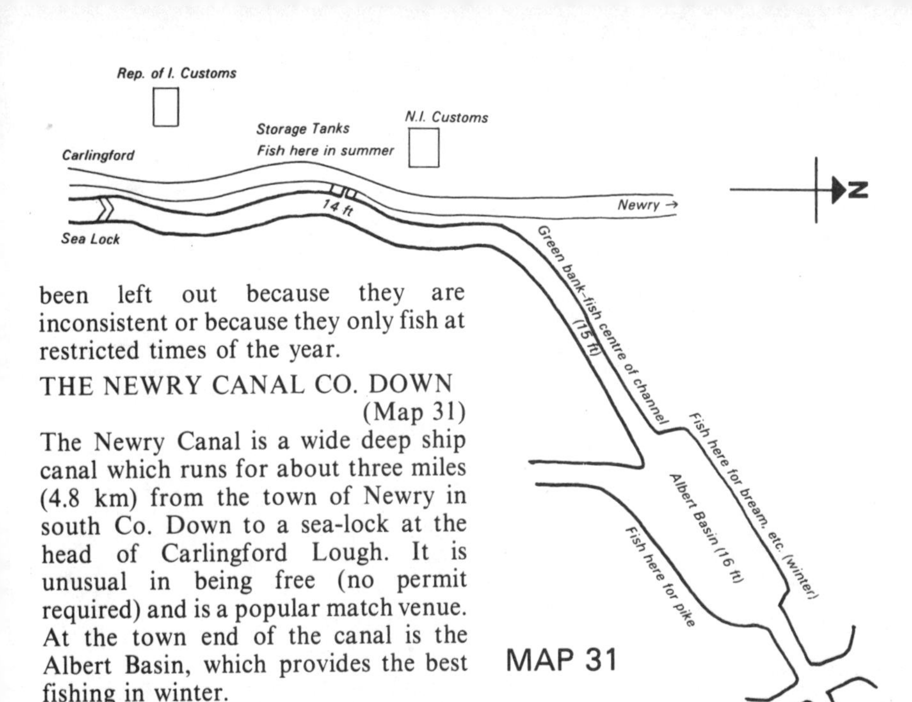

been left out because they are inconsistent or because they only fish at restricted times of the year.

THE NEWRY CANAL CO. DOWN (Map 31)

The Newry Canal is a wide deep ship canal which runs for about three miles (4.8 km) from the town of Newry in south Co. Down to a sea-lock at the head of Carlingford Lough. It is unusual in being free (no permit required) and is a popular match venue. At the town end of the canal is the Albert Basin, which provides the best fishing in winter.

The Basin contains large pike, which are usually fished for from the east bank, and quantities of bream averaging a half to three-quarters of a pound (0.25–0.375 kg) but running up to about three pounds (1.4 kg); these are usually fished from the west bank. There are also some rudd, perch and hybrids; a few roach and tench have appeared recently. The bream are very finnicky biters. To be successful, it is necessary to plumb the depth exactly (it is usually about sixteen feet—4.87 metres—and a couple of feet—0.6 metres—less in the canal) and fish exactly on the bottom, neither over-depth nor under, with a shotting arrangement calculated to show the smallest bite.

The usual arrangement is a rod with a sliding float, although it can be fished on the pole. Maggot and worm are the baits and it responds to steady feeding—a bait dropper is useful. The stretch on the west bank immediately below the basin is known as the Green Bank and the middle of the channel here also fishes in winter. In summer it is best to take the Newry/Carlingford road and fish the stretch between the two Customs posts—about half-way along this stretch there are a couple of large storage tanks and this is a good landmark. The difficulty with this stretch is that there is deep water in the middle and shallow at the side with a pronounced ledge between. It is easy to lose a fish hooked in deep water by knocking it off on this ledge, but it is also possible to gather fish in the shallower water by using groundbait sensibly.

THE RIVER BANN AT PORTADOWN, CO. ARMAGH (Map 32)

The Upper Bann is a short but fairly wide river which flows into Lough Neagh. The best angling on it is in the town of Portadown itself; there is superlative

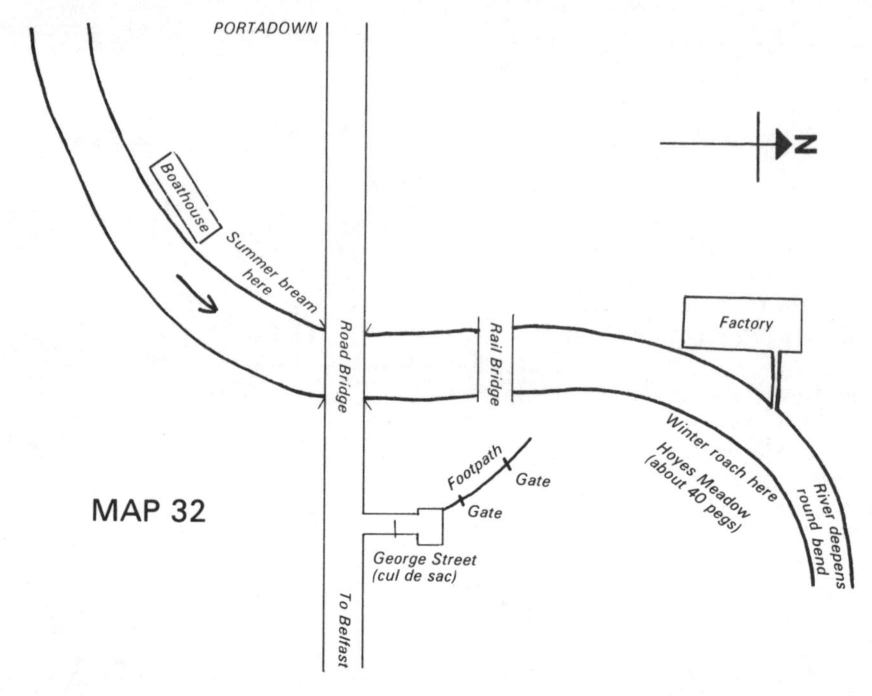

winter roach fishing and reasonable summer bream. The roach are mainly in the one to one and a half pound range (0.5–0.75 kg) with a sprinkling of smaller fish. An indication of the quality of the winter fishing is that when matches are fished here, it is usually necessary to catch 100 to 130 pounds (45–58.5 kg) to win, which is a lot of roach. The match anglers use six pound (2.7 kg) line and bunches of maggots on a 10 or 12 hook; pleasure anglers who don't have to horse their fish in so fast may like to fish a little more delicately. The method is trotting in about eight feet (2.44 metres) and the flow is normally quite heavy. Poles are sometimes used. Quiver-tipping is also possible. The roach fish from September to April and the best swims are in Hoyes Meadow downstream from the railway bridge. In summer there is quite good bream fishing on the Boathouse stretch upstream from the road bridge.

THE RIVER BLACKWATER AT MOY, CO. TYRONE

The River Blackwater also flows into Lough Neagh and also offers winter roaching, although not to quite the same standard as the Bann. Just upstream from the bridge where the Dungannon to Armagh road crosses the river in Moy itself, there is a factory belonging to Moy Meats. There is an outfall pipe from this factory and fish tend to congregate round it; unfortunately, rather revolting objects come out of the pipe from time to time. There are also bream to specimen weight here.

THE FAIRY WATER, CO. TYRONE (Map 33)

The Fairy Water, a tributary of the River Strule, is the place where roach were first introduced into the Erne system some time after the end of World War II.

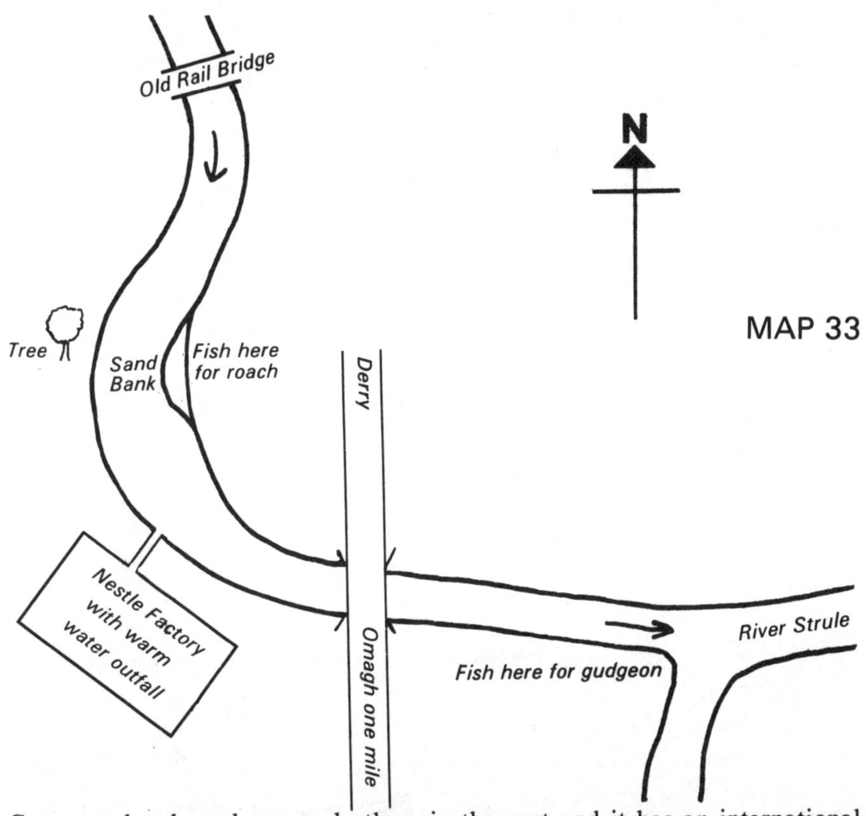

Great catches have been made there in the past and it has an international reputation. Today, it has become a bit overshadowed by venues in Co. Fermanagh and Co. Armagh which produce larger quantities of roach. But the Fairy Water is still of interest because it has very large roach—certainly three pounders and possibly four pounders (1.4–1.8 kg). The best place to fish is a broad bend beside the Nestle factory about a mile outside the town of Omagh on the Derry road. It fishes well in high water, in fact the rise or the fall of a flood seem to produce the best results. December, January and March are the best months.

The method is to float fish maggots in the middle or towards the far bank on about a 3AAA Avon. The depth is six to seven feet (1.82–2.13 metres) and the best part of the swim, the sandbar marked on the map, has room for four or five anglers. It is a free water. There is also roach fishing and excellent pike fishing on the Fairy Water at a place called the Priest's Bridge, about six miles (9.6 km) from Omagh on the old Drumquin road. Downstream from the Nestle factory, the river joins the Strule and the junction of the two waters is noted for large gudgeon.

THE RIVER COLEBROOKE, CO. FERMANAGH (Map 34)

This moderately sized river is a tributary of the Erne. It varies a lot in depth and

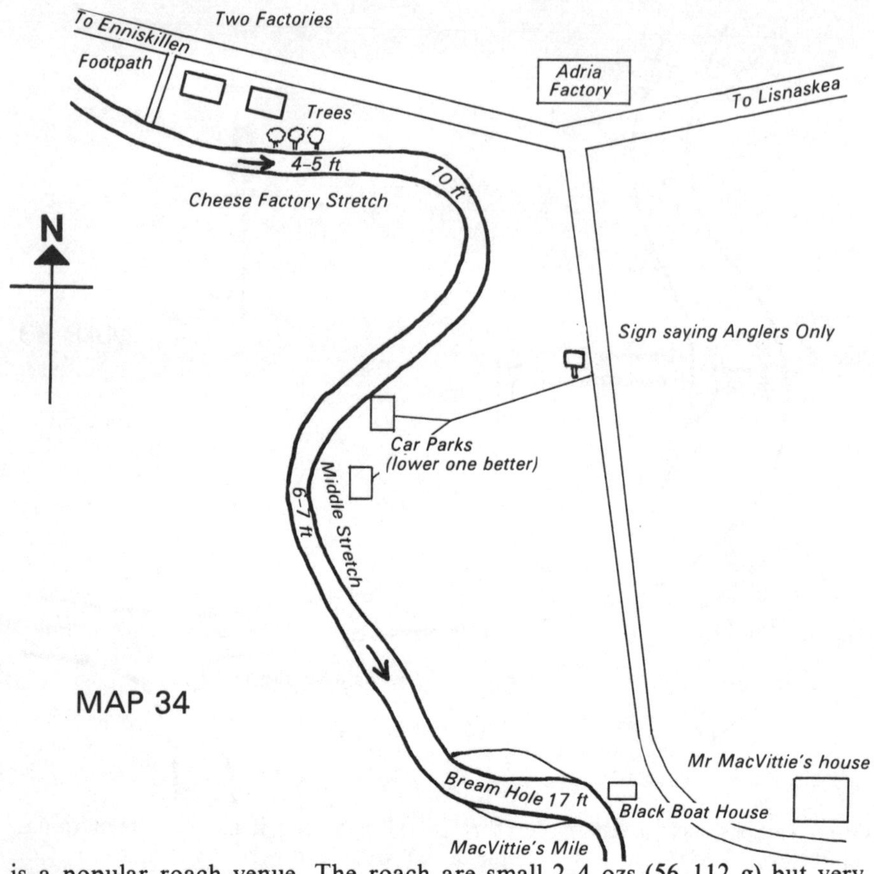

is a popular roach venue. The roach are small 2–4 ozs (56–112 g) but very plentiful.

The Cheese Factory stretch fishes particularly well in winter, even in high water. The swims average four to five feet (1.2–1.5 metres) and up to ten feet (3.04 metres) around the bend—it is better to seek out this deeper water in frosty weather. The method is trotted maggots. The Middle Stretch, reached from either of the two car parks marked on the sketch map, has good roach/bream hybrids as well as roach and the odd bream. MacVittie's Mile is private but can be fished by asking the permission of Mr MacVittie who lives in the house marked on the sketch map. The 'Bream Hole' marked on the map in this stretch is up to 17½ feet deep (5.33 metres) and contains nice bream in the three to four pound range (1.4–1.8 kg). The method here is quiver-tipping the far bank. There are also some nice perch and the odd rudd in the Colebrooke. In May a much better quality of roach move in from Lough Erne for spawning. Access to all the swims on the Colebrooke is from the Lisnaskea/Enniskillen road.

THE RIVER ERNE—THE 'SCHOOLS' AND 'CORRIGANS' (Map 35)

Four or five miles (6.4–8 km) further along the Lisnaskea to Enniskillen road is a

Former world champion, Ian Heaps, who broke the World Open Five Hour Match Angling Record on the Erne at Enniskillen

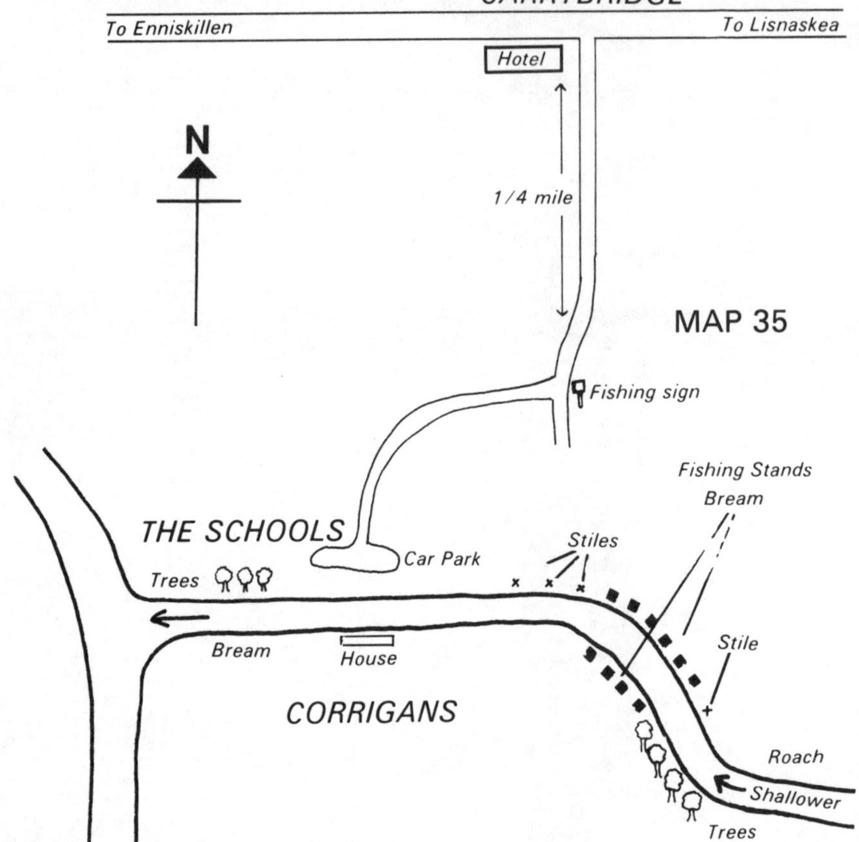

place called Carry Bridge. If you turn left here and follow the signposts which say 'Fishing' until the road ends in a car park, you'll come to the 'Schools', a famous stretch on the River Erne itself. The opposite bank is called 'Corrigans' and is also well-known, but it is rather complicated to approach and doesn't fish quite as well. This stretch fishes summer and winter, although high water can be a problem in winter. The winter fishing is pretty well restricted to roach, which are average by Northern Irish standards. There are also good bream either side of the clump of trees downstream from the car park, although they tend to be well out in up to twelve feet (3.65 metres) of water. Three fields upstream are a number of fishing stands and there's good bream fishing here also. Further upstream again the river shallows and roach predominate.

THE RIVER ARNEY, CO. FERMANAGH

The Arney is a tributary of the Erne which enters from the west, not far from 'Corrigans'. It is a pleasant smallish water with a maximum depth of about eight feet (2.44 metres). It is best trotted except in high water when a quiver-tip is effective. It fishes consistently for quality roach in May but is patchy the rest of

FII 4

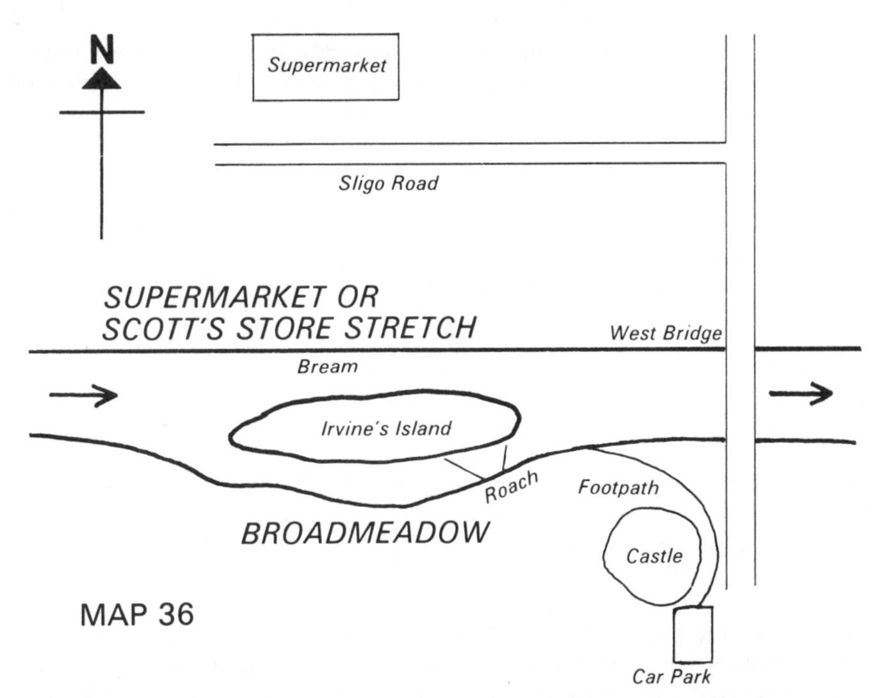

the year. The best swims are near its junction with the Erne and access is by taking the A 509 south from Bellanaleck in the direction of Belburbet and taking the second turn left (the first of these left turns, incidentally, leads to 'Corrigans').

THE RIVER SILLEES, CO. FERMANAGH

This is another smallish west bank tributary of the Erne which offers similar fishing to the Arney and even more massive concentrations of roach in the spawning season. It flows in between the Arney and Enniskillen and there is access off the A 509.

THE ERNE IN ENNISKILLEN, CO. FERMANAGH (Map 36)

There is excellent fishing on the River Erne in the town of Enniskillen itself. The top roach swims are in the Broadmeadow stretch. To find this stretch, look for the castle; there is a car park beside it and a path down from it to the river. Fish anywhere from the castle up to the far end of Irvine's Island. In May huge quantities of roach move up the river to spawn from Lower Lough Erne and they tend to be concentrated in the fairly narrow channel beside the island; many of the famous large roach catches from Co. Fermanagh have been caught then. The far bank opposite the island is known as the 'Supermarket' or 'Scott's Store' stretch and fishes better for bream.

THE BALLINAMALLARD RIVER, CO. FERMANAGH

The river flows into the top end of Lower Lough Erne from the north. To find it, take the Ballinamallard/Omagh road north from Enniskillen until you come to a left turn signposted to St Angelo airfield, turn off and take a second left signposted to the Flying Club. Drive down this and out onto the runway (keeping a look out for aircraft—the runway is in use!). Drive to the end of the runway and park beside the river. It fishes excellently for roach during the first three weeks of May and is starting to fish consistently for roach and bream throughout the year as soldiers stationed in a local garrison are feeding the swims.

BOA ISLAND, LOWER LOUGH ERNE, CO. FERMANAGH

Boa is a large island off the northern shore of Lower Lough Erne and it is connected to the mainland by a bridge at each end and has a road down the middle. The best bank fishing is around the east end near the village of Kesh. There are stages on both sides of the bridge; the northern side is better. Fish out in the middle. There are large perch, small bream and roach. Lower Lough Erne also provides excellent pike fishing for small to medium sized fish. It is probably best fished from a boat but if you do want to fish from the bank, Boa Island offers good access.

RIVER ERNE AT ROSSCAR, CO. FERMANAGH

The River Erne after it leaves the Lower Lough and heads for the sea offers reasonable fishing, particularly for bream. There is good access beside the road bridge just to the north of the village of Rosscor. The bream are about three rodlengths out in six to ten feet (1.8–3 metres) of water.

THE LOWER BANN, COLERAINE, CO. DERRY

This is not the same River Bann that flows into Lough Neagh via Portadown. It is a longer river that flows from the vicinity of the north shore of Lough Neagh into the Atlantic below Coleraine. There are reports of bream up to specimen weight having been taken on stretches near the town of Ballymoney and further downstream near Coleraine, but it does not seem to be seriously fished.

USEFUL ADDRESSES FOR COARSE ANGLERS

Northern Ireland Tourist Board,
River House,
High Street,
Belfast BT1 2DS.
Tel: (0232) 31221
Bord Failte, Irish Tourist Board,
Baggot Street Bridge,
Dublin 2.
Tel: (01) 765871
The Board also operates a number of offices abroad and Tourist Information centres around the country. They provide an efficient service for such things as accommodation and boat hire but the quality of the angling information supplied is variable.

Inland Fisheries Trust Inc.
Balnagowan,
Mobhi Boreen,
Dublin 9.
Tel: (01) 379206

The Trust can provide accurate and up to date information on the better-known venues and information on specimen claims and returns. It is currently being reorganised into the Central Fisheries Board. Full details should be published in the national and local papers in the Republic.
Northern Ireland Department of Agriculture,
Fisheries Division,
Hut 5,
Castle Grounds,
Stormont,
Belfast BT4 3TA.

Fisheries Conservancy Board for Northern Ireland,
21 Church Street,
Portadown,
Co. Armagh.

National Coarse Fishing Federation of Ireland,
Hon Secretary: Joe Murphy,
Mountshannon Road,
Scarriff,
Co. Clare.
PRO: Victor Refausse,
20 Gortmore Gardens,
Omagh,
Co.Tyrone.
Tel: Omagh 45363

The Federation, amongst other things, publishes an annual calendar of match events, is available for 40p from the PRO.

REGIONAL CONTACTS

The following list is of centres that have angling clubs affiliated to the National Federation (a body that operates in both the Republic and Northern Ireland). The people named are very generous about giving up-to-date information on their local waters, but in most cases are not paid for this. A courteous approach and a stamped addressed envelope would help.

ATHLONE (Midland Angling Club)
Barry Brill, 31 Battery Heights, Athlone, Co. Westmeath.

ATHLONE ANGLER'S ASSOCIATION
Aidan Gallagher, Ardkeenan, Drum, Athlone, Co. Westmeath.

ATHY
Mrs Jo Ann Snell, 25 Avondale Drive, Athy, Co. Kildare.

BALLINAKILL
Denis Bergin, The Square, Ballinakill, Co. Laois.

BELFAST (The Pikers)
Larry Nixon, 7 Sharmon Park, Stranmillis, Belfast 9.

BELFAST A.C.
Robert Buick, 7 Knockvale Grove, Belfast 5.

BALLYFORAN
Michael Donohue or Frank Grogan, Ballyforan, Co. Roscommon.

BALLYGAR
Patsy Scanlon, Ballygar, Co. Galway.

BALLINAMORE
P. J. Martin, Ballinamore, Co. Leitrim.

BALLYMOTE
Michael Wilcox, Ballymote, Co. Sligo.

BALLINASLOE
Patrick Lawless, 4 Hillcrest Park, Ballinasloe, Co. Galway.

CASTLEPOLLARD
Vincent Baker, Castlepollard, Co. Westmeath.

CAVAN
Mrs B. O'Hanlon, St Martin's, Creegham, Cavan.

COOTEHILL
B. J. Greenan, The Beeches, Cootehill.

CAPPOQUIN
William Deavy, Richmond House, Cappoquin, Co. Waterford.

CARRICKMACROSS
Tom Ward, Coolfore, Carrickmacross, Co. Monaghan.

CRAIGAVON (Exquisite)
Terry Clifton, 112 Maylin Estate, Craigavon, Co. Armagh.

DRUMCONRATH
Jim Meade, Drumconrath, Co. Meath.

DUBLIN
Nicolas Bolger, 36 Farney Park, Dublin 14.

ENFIELD
Bill Carey or Declan O'Donoghue, Enfield, Co. Meath.

ENNISKILLEN (Erne Anglers)
Ken Stewart, 114 Windmill Heights, Enniskillen, Co. Fermanagh.

FERMOY
Jack O'Sullivan, 4 Patrick Street, Fermoy, Co. Cork.

LANESBORO
Tony Dalton, 24 The Green, Lanesboro, Co. Longford.

LOCH GOWNA
Jimmy Sloan, Loch Gowna, Co. Cavan.

LOUGH ALLEN A.C.
B. McGourty, Carrick Road, Drumshanbo, Co. Leitrim.

LISNASKEA
Bob Maher, Sir Richard Arkwright A.C., Derryharney, Enniskillen.

MALLOW
David Willis, 7 Dromore Drive, Mallow, Co. Cork.

MONAGHAN
Thomas McEntee, 46 Dublin Street, Monaghan.
MOHILL
Willie Burns, Mohill, Co. Leitrim.
NEWMARKET-ON-FERGUS
R. G. V. Boelens, Carrowmeer, Newmarket-on-Fergus, Co. Clare.
NEWTOWNABBEY
Joseph Catherall, 22 Glevacoole Avenue, Glengormley, Newtownabbey, Co. Antrim.
NEWRY C.F.A.C.
Oliver McGauley, 18 College Gardens, Newry, Co. Down.
NEWRY & DISTRICT
R. McAllister, 77 Main Street, Newry, Co. Down.
OMAGH
Victor Refausse, 20 Gortmore Gardens, Omagh, Co. Tyrone.
PLASSEY
John Morrison, 42 Rossa Avenue, Limerick.
PORTADOWN
Bill Clarke, 265 Ballyoran Park, Omagh, Co. Tyrone.
PROSPEROUS
Oliver Reilly, Prosperous, Co. Kildare.
ROOSKEY
Mrs Bride Duffy, Hon. Sec., Rooskey & District Anglers, Rooskey, Co. Roscommon.
SHANNON TOWN
Miss Mary Byrne, Shannon Town Centre, Co. Clare.
SCARRIFF, MT SHANNON & WHITEGATE A.C.
P. Cahill, Mountshannon, Co. Clare.
CHIPBOARD A.C. SCARRIFF
Joe Murphy, Mountshannon Road, Scarriff, Co. Clare.
SHANNONBRIDGE
Dermot Kileen, Shannonbridge, Co. Offaly.
TULLA
Brian Culloo, N.T., Tulla, Co. Clare.

Sea Angling Areas

SEA ANGLING
Kevin Linnane

INTRODUCTION

Sea angling in Ireland is still a comparatively young sport. It is only in the last twenty years or so that it has become prominent, with the growth of the Irish Federation of Sea Anglers and increased publicity in the Irish, British and Continental press. There are now almost two hundred sea angling clubs scattered all round the coast and they hold various competitions and festivals each year. As many as 220 competitions are fished annually under the auspices of the IFSA. From 1980 onwards all these competitions will be fished on a conservation basis. The emphasis may change from area to area but generally as many fish as possible will be returned alive to the water during competitions.

The guide cannot hope to describe all the fishing hotspots in Ireland. This would take volumes and it would need to be revised almost monthly, because so much of our coast is still virgin territory. New marks and hotspots are being discovered weekly while some old marks fade out due to ever changing trends. What is contained here can only be an indication of the fishing to be had in various areas. In some centres where a considerable amount of angling has already been done, more detailed information will be given where possible.

Any angler worth his salt will know his own locality intimately and this guide cannot be of great value to him at home, but if he travels to a new area, it will at least give him a fair idea of the sea angling to expect. Even so, every angler in a strange locality should enquire from the local tackle shop or angling club about local conditions. No amount of writing can be as informative as a friendly chat with a fellow angler.

GEOGRAPHICAL

Ireland is approximately 300 miles long by 150 miles wide. (483 km × 241 km). It lies at the extreme western edge of Europe. Its western and southern coasts are washed by the warm North Atlantic drift, which is an extension of the Gulf Stream. This has great influence on our weather and in summer the offshore water temperature can be as high as 17° C. The coastline is extremely varied with beaches, cliffs, headlands, estuaries and almost landlocked bays interchanging rapidly all along its 3,000 miles (4,828 km). The fish population varies from warm water species, such as bass and blue shark, to coalfish and cod, which are primarily cold water fish. The prevailing winds are between south and southwest.

SPECIMEN FISH COMMITTEE

The Irish Specimen Fish Committee is a voluntary body representative of all angling and fishery interests in Ireland. Its purpose is to authenticate and record

WHEN TO FISH

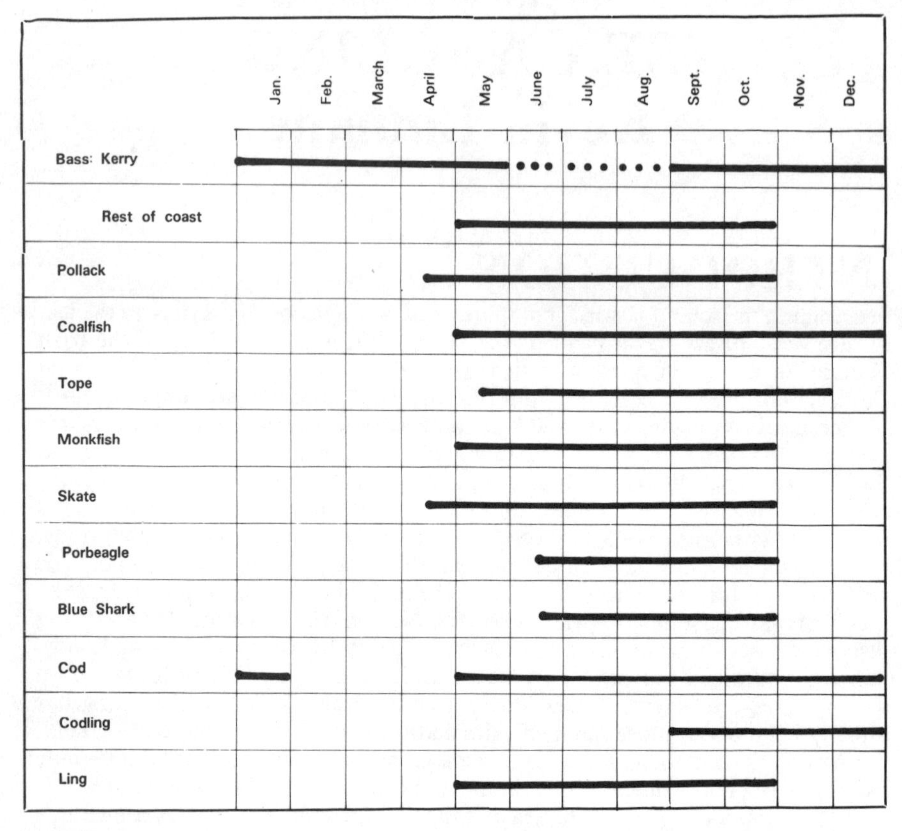

the capture by fair angling of record and specimen fish in Irish waters.

The term "Specimen" means a fish of exceptional size for its species and whose capture merits recording. The committee has drawn up a schedule of minimum qualifying weights and is available at most angling centres or can be obtained direct from the Hon. Secretary, Irish Specimen Fish Committee, Mobhi Boreen, Mobhi Road, Glasnevin, Dublin 9. Tel: (01) 379206.

All anglers are requested to co-operate fully with the committee by recording the capture of specimen and record fish. In doing so they are making a valuable contribution to the knowledge of the presence and distribution of the various species. They will also be providing fishery biologists with essential scientific information which would not otherwise be available to them. The captors of ratified specimen and record fish are presented with awards annually at presentation ceremonies in Ireland, Britain and at various centres on the Continent.

THE MORE COMMON FISH

BASS (Dicentrarchus labrax). Specimen weight 10 lbs (4.5 kg). The bass is a favourite quarry of many sea anglers. It usually weighs between 2 and 6 lbs

(0.9–2.7 kg) except where there are 'schoolies' (small fish of 1½ lbs—0.75 kg—or

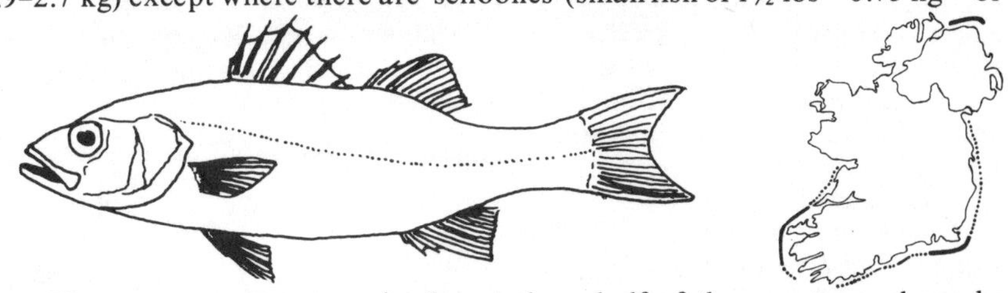

less). They are most common in the southern half of the country and can be fished on beaches, areas of low rough and in estuaries. They can be taken on lugworm, ragworm, crab, mackerel and by a variety of spinners and rubber eels. Although the best season is usually June to October they can be taken all the year round in the south western part of the country, particularly in counties Cork and Kerry.

BLUE SHARK (Prionace glauca). Specimen weight 100 lbs (45 kg). Most blue shark caught around Ireland are between 20 and 80 lbs (9.1–36 kg) but fish in excess of 100 lbs (45 kg) are common. They are summer visitors to the south and west coasts, arriving in mid-June and departing in October. A number of deep sea angling centres cater especially for blue shark anglers and boats and tackle can be hired at a reasonable charge. When fishing for blue shark it is essential to

use 'rubby dubby', and charter boat skippers are well accustomed to this technique.

PORBEAGLE SHARK (Lamna nasus). Specimen weight of 150 lbs (68 kg). The normal run of porbeagle shark is between 40 and 100 lbs (18–45 kg), but the record is 365 lbs (164.3 kg). A very powerful fish and an excellent predator. They appear to have a liking for reefs and are generally encountered within a half mile

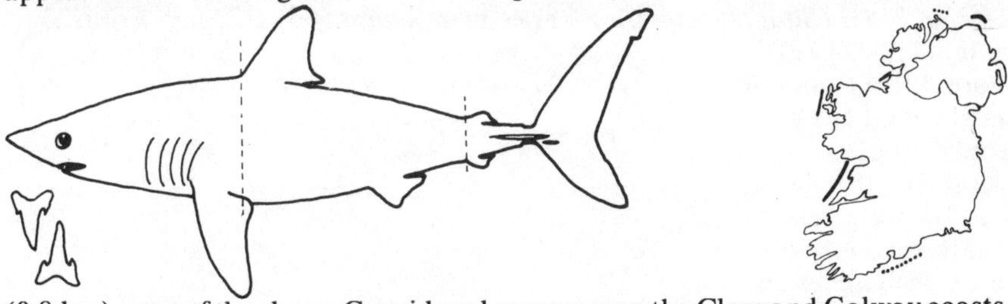

(0.8 km) or so of the shore. Considered common on the Clare and Galway coasts, but they have been taken all round the coast at some time or other.

MAKO SHARK (Isurus oxyrinchus). Specimen weight 200 lbs (90 kg). An aristocrat among fish, renowned for its ferocity on the end of a line. They are true oceanic sharks and are occasionally encountered along the south coast in summer, although unfortunately very few are landed. They are reputed to have a preference for reefs, but are mostly encountered while fishing for blue shark.

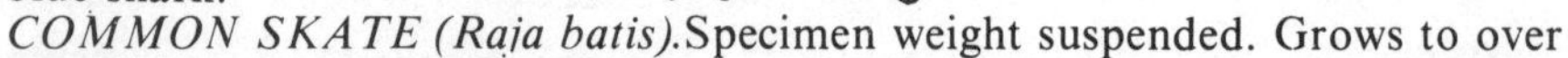

COMMON SKATE (Raja batis). Specimen weight suspended. Grows to over 200 lbs (90 kg) and regularly caught on the south and west coasts. Most common on mixed ground in deep water but they are also taken frequently in inshore waters. Generally taken by bottom fishing at anchor with fish baits. The season is generally April to September but they can be caught all the year round. These great fish are not so common now as they were in former years; anglers are requested to return them alive to the water.

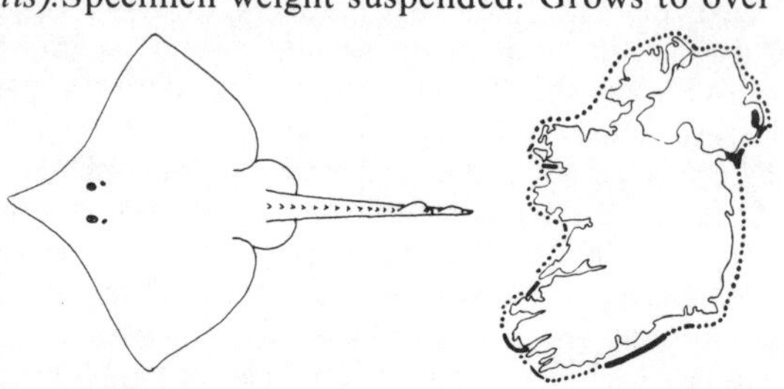

WHITE SKATE (Raja alba). Specimen weight 120 lbs (54 kg). Fairly common all along the west coast in deep water. Fished at anchor with fish baits and can be found on mixed or clean ground although it has a preference for muddy sand or gravel.

RAYS—various species. Thornback—specimen weight 20 lbs (9.07 kg). Homelyn—specimen weight 5 lbs (2.3 kg). Undulate—specimen weight 14 lbs (6.4 kg). Painted—specimen weight 10 lbs (4.5 kg). Sting—specimen weight 30 lbs (13.6 kg).

The various species of ray are abundant in certain areas, but are mostly caught on sandy or muddy bottoms on fish baits. Some can be taken from the shore and the most common is the Thornback, which can be caught almost everywhere. Great care should be taken identifying rays, as a "small thornback" could easily turn out to be a record of one of the smaller species. If in doubt, ask the local club secretary for advice.

MONKFISH (Squatina squatina). Specimen weight 50 lbs (23 kg). From 25 to 50 lbs (11.3–23 kg) or more. Most common on the west coast on sandy or muddy bottoms in fairly shallow water, particularly near estuaries or in sheltered bays. They can be quite

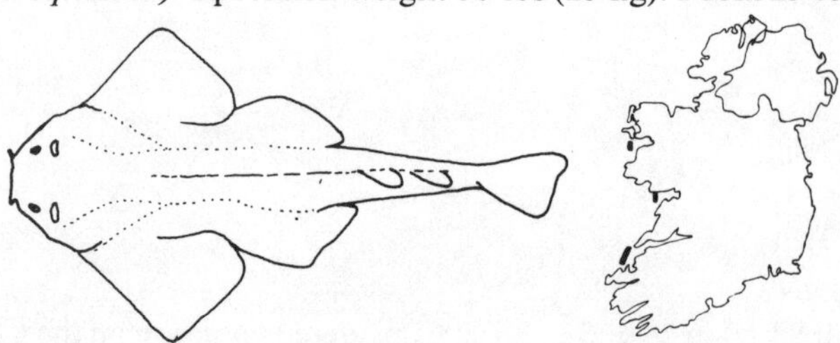

common locally but are not to be confused with the "Angler" fish which is marketed as "Monk".

TOPE (Galeorhinus galeus). Specimen weight 40 lbs (18 kg). Normally weights

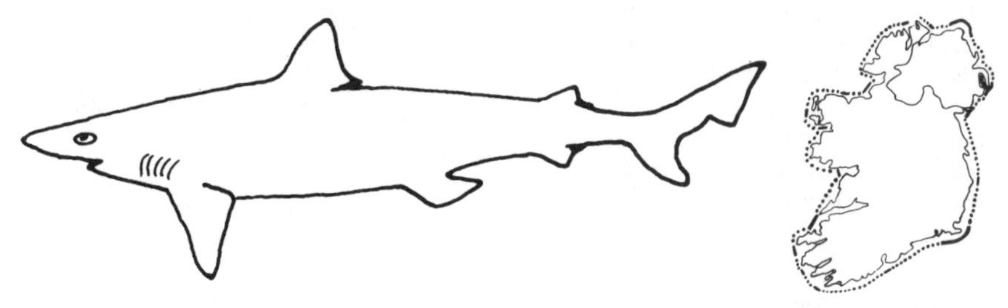

between 17 and 25 lbs (7.7–11.3 kg). It is found all round our coasts, mostly on a sandy bottom but it can be very abundant locally. In places, it can be fished from the shore but generally is taken from a boat with a large mackerel bait. A very strong sporting fish, especially in shallow water.

HALIBUT (Hippoglossus hippoglossus). Specimen weight 50 lbs (23 kg). A leviathan among flatfish, the halibut can grow to 600 lbs (270 kg). Occasionally taken on the west coast, generally in deep mixed ground by people fishing for skate or tope. It has a liking for big baits such as 3 lbs (1.4 kg) pollack fished close to the bottom.

FLOUNDER (Platichthys flesus). Specimen weight 2½ lbs (1.15 kg). A very common flatfish found all round the coast and known as "fluke" in parts of the south and west coasts. It can be taken on beaches, in creeks and estuaries, frequently going well into fresh water. It likes a muddy or sandy bottom and is very partial to a lug or ragworm trolled slowly behind a "flashy" spoon. Average weight ¾ to 1½ lbs (0.37–0.75 kg). Season from May to November, except in isolated estuaries when they can fish best in January.

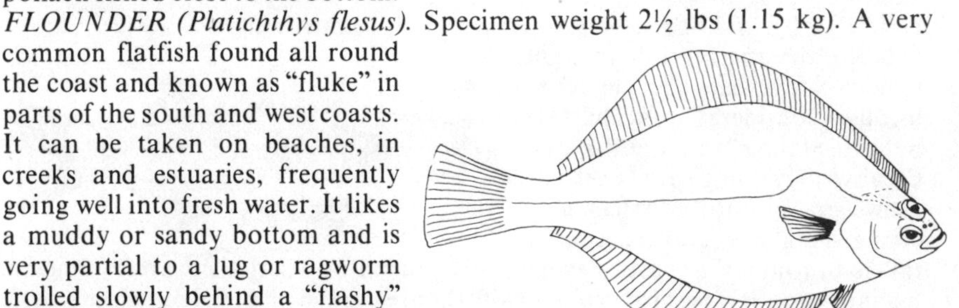

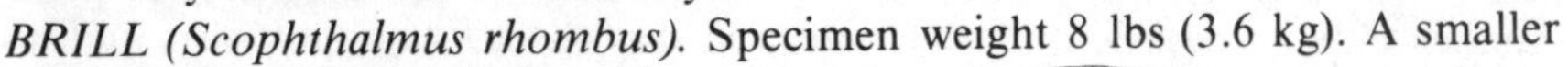

BRILL (Scophthalmus rhombus). Specimen weight 8 lbs (3.6 kg). A smaller species than the turbot, with which it is frequently confused. The brill has not got tubercles on its back. It can grow to 15 lbs (6.8 kg) but is usually between 2 and 5 lbs (0.9–2.3 kg) likes the same terrain as the turbot and is fished in a similar fashion.

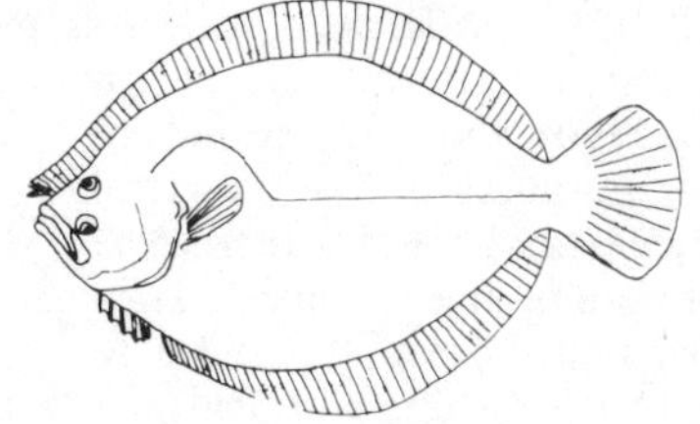

PLAICE (Platessa platessa). Specimen weight 4 lbs (1.8 kg). It can grow to 6 or 7 lbs (2.3–3.2 kg), but commonly taken between 1½ and 3 lbs (0.75–1.4 kg). Usually found on sandy banks where there are plenty of small shell fish, such as queen scallops, mussels and cockles. Normally taken in fairly shallow water or from the shore. Bait-ragworm, lug, mussel etc. from May until October.

TURBOT (Scophthalmus maximus). Specimen weight 18 lbs (8.2 kg). The turbot is a highly prized flatfish which can grow up to 50 lbs (23 kg) or so, but it is normally between 7 and 15 lbs (3.2–6.8 kg). It is found on all coasts but tends to be rather localised. Smaller sizes like sandy areas and can be taken from the beaches, but the larger fish go deeper and have a preference for gravelly banks. Usually caught between May and October at anchor or drifting with slips of mackerel or sandeel on the bottom.

GREY MULLET (Crenimugil Labrosus). Specimen weight 5 lbs (2.27 kg). A fish for the specialist with light tackle. A few years ago they were locally considered uncatchable because of their "soft mouths" and because they "only eat plankton". However this attitude has now changed and grey mullet are being taken all round the coasts, particularly in harbours where there are commercial fishing boats. It is best to "ground bait" the area first with bread or fish cuts to get them feeding and then float fish with very sensitive tackle using as bait whatever they are feeding on. They have been known to take a small black wet fly in places. Once "hooked" on mullet fishing, it is quite possible for any angler to become a mullet addict. They are extremely wary and very powerful fighters when hooked.

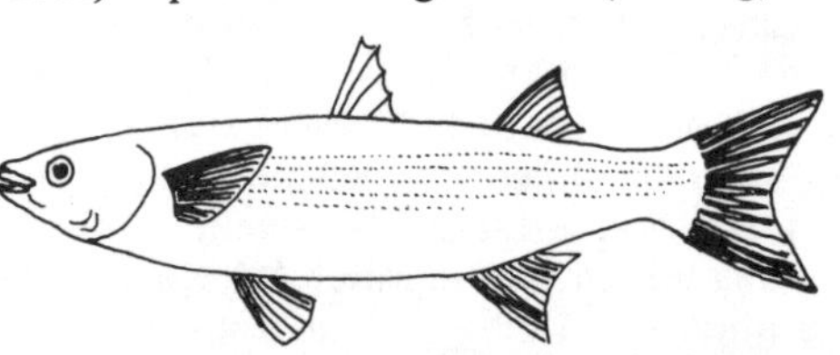

POLLACK (Pollachius pollachius). Specimen weight 12 lbs (5.4 kg). Very abundant where there is rough ground, but they are found in greater numbers on the west and south coasts where they tend to be larger than on the east coast. They can be fished from the shore in many places, fishing with feathers or lures or from boats trolling or jigging. They will also readily take fish baits. Dawn and dusk are the best times between May and November. In some places it is possible to catch pollack averaging between 8 and 10 lbs (3.6–4.5 kg). They love peaks, pinnacles, reefs and wrecks. In the south they are often called "whiting pollack".

COALFISH (Pollachius virens). Specimen weight 15 lbs (6.8 kg). Coalfish tend to travel in large shoals and are most frequently encountered when feathering for mackerel. These are normally small fish of 1 to 2 lbs (0.5–0.9 kg) and can be great fun on light tackle. Shoals of larger fish can be found on the west and north coasts during summer and these fish can be 14 or 15 lbs (6.4–6.8 kg) in weight. Unlike the pollack, which is normally taken close to the bottom, the large coalfish is usually encountered in mid water. They take feathers, large fish baits or pirks.

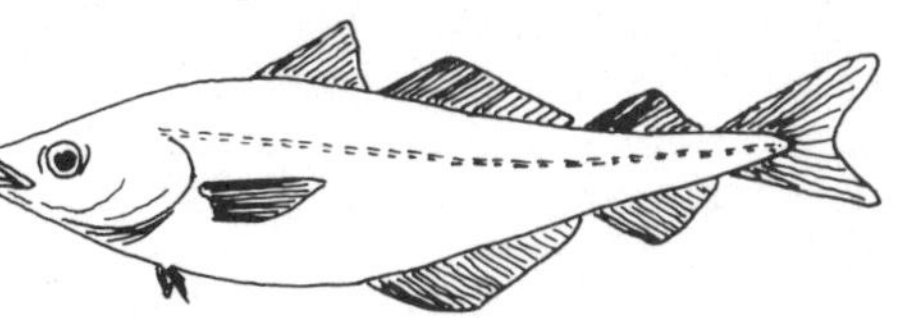

COD (Gadus morhua). Specimen weight 25 lbs (11.3 kg). During summer and autumn, most coasts have codling fishing—fish less than 6 lbs (2.7 kg). They are found in roughish ground at the mouth of large estuaries and can be taken on crab, lugworms or mussel. Some bigger fish up to 16 or 17 lbs (7.3–7.7 kg) are taken on reefs during summer using fish baits, baited feathers, rubber eels or pirks and on clean ground on fish baits or lugworm. In winter there is reasonably good codling fishing on the east coast; in some places they can be taken from the shore.

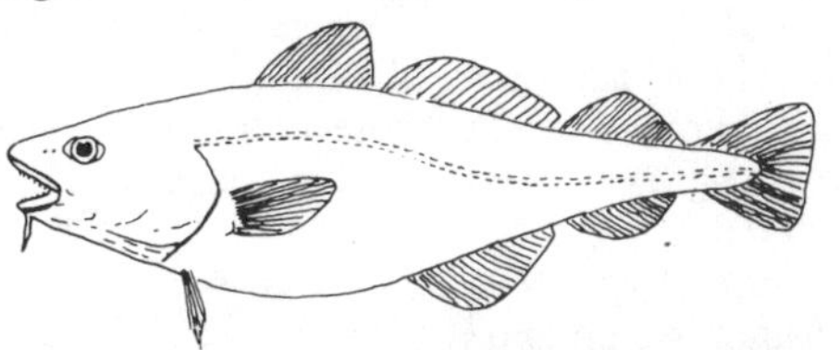

LING (Molva molva). Specimen weight 25 lbs (11.3 kg). Grow up to 50 lbs (23 kg) but are normally taken between 12 and 20 lbs (5.4–9.1 kg). They live on the bottom in rough ground such as reefs and wrecks. They like deep water and are taken mostly on the south and west coasts. Best fished at anchor with large fish baits but they will also take a baited pirk or baited feathers.

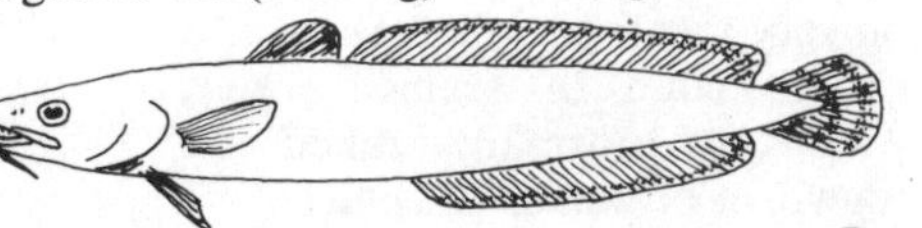

WHITING. (Merlangius merlangus). Specimen weight 3 lbs (1.4 kg). Can grow to 6 lbs (2.7 kg) but are usually between one and two pounds (0.5–0.9 kg). They are demersal fish who like mud and sand and can be taken on small fish baits or worms. They usually stay deep in summer and come inshore in winter, especially on the east coast.

POUTING (Trisopterus luscus). Specimen weight 3 lbs (1.4 kg). Can grow to over 4 lbs (1.8 kg) but are generally about 2 lbs (0.9 kg). Most plentiful during summer on the south and west coasts on rough ground in deep water. They are normally taken on small fish baits.

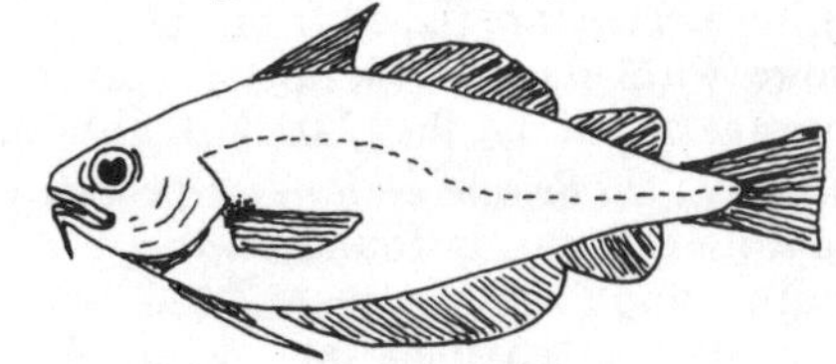

HADDOCK (Melanogrammus aeglifinus). Specimen weight 7 lbs (3.2 kg). A demersal fish with a liking for sand or gravel banks. They are very abundant in some localities and are fished with fish baits at anchor or on the drift. They can also be taken on lugworm. The haddock population seems to rise and fall very rapidly with many fish being caught some summers and very few in others.

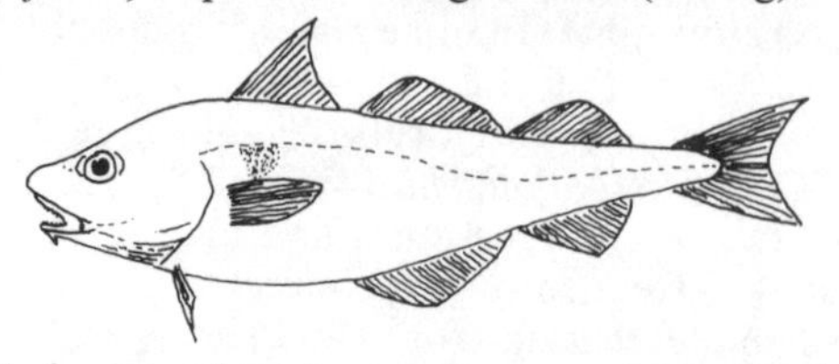

HAKE (Merluccius merluccius). Specimen weight 10 lbs (4.5 kg). A deep water fish normally encountered in mid water on the west and north coasts. They were plentiful but are now scarce. Hake can be taken on baited feathers, fish baits or pirks.

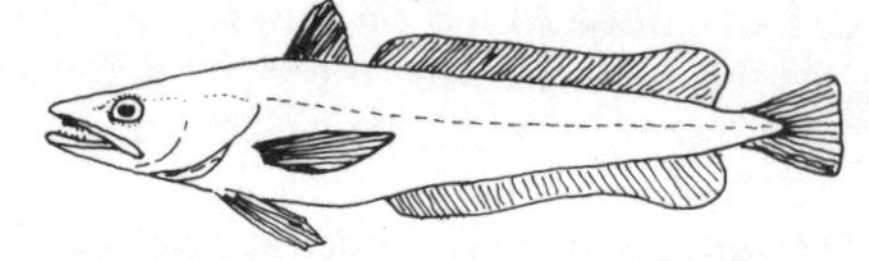

MACKEREL (Scomber scombrus). Specimen weight 2½ lbs (1.15 kg). Mackerel are probably the most abundant fish in these waters during summer. They are available almost everywhere close inshore from May until October usually weigh about 1 lb (0.5 kg). They can give excellent fun on light tackle from the shore, spinning with lures or feathers, but from boats are usually fished with feathers for bait purposes.

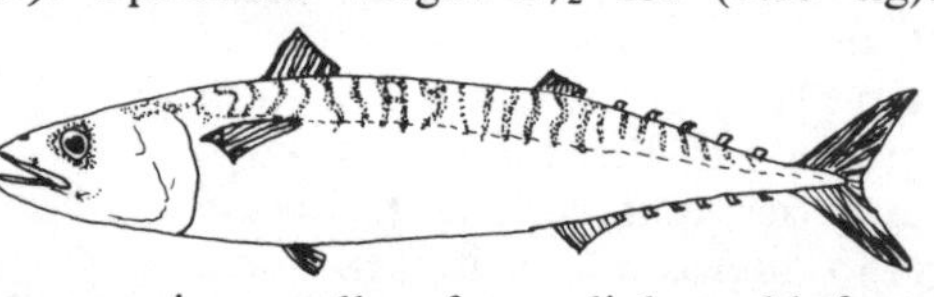

RED SEA BREAM (Pagellus boraraveo). Specimen weight 4½ lbs (2.05 kg). A beautiful summer visitor to the west and south coasts. They can be very localised in shoals over a rough patch in deepish water. They are normally taken on lugworm or small fish baits.

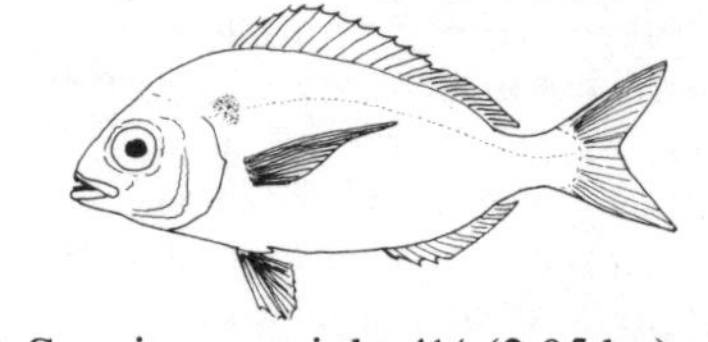

BALLAN WRASSE (Labrus bergylta). Specimen weight 4½ (2.05 kg). A much ignored fish which, given a chance, can give enormous pleasure to the beginner and the competent angler alike. They are available almost everywhere on the south and west coasts wherever there are rocks in 4 or 5 fathoms (7.3–9.1 metres) or closer inshore. They are fished from the shore with lugworm, limpets, crab, even garden worms. In places they can average about 4½ lbs (2.05 kg), although in general they are smaller.

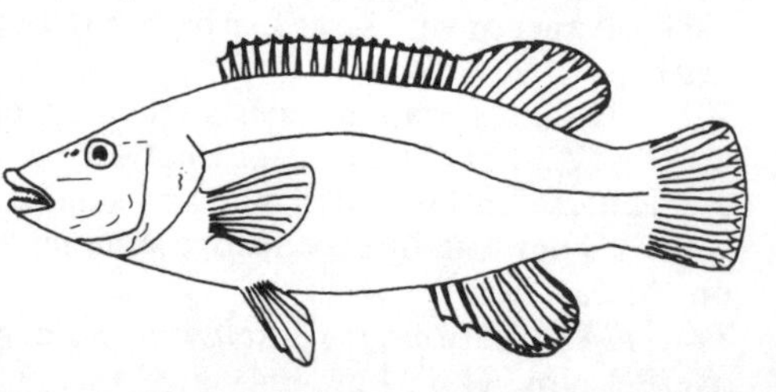

GARFISH (Belone bellone). Specimen weight 2½ lbs (1.15 kg). A wonderful fighting fish mostly found on the south and west coasts and generally in association with

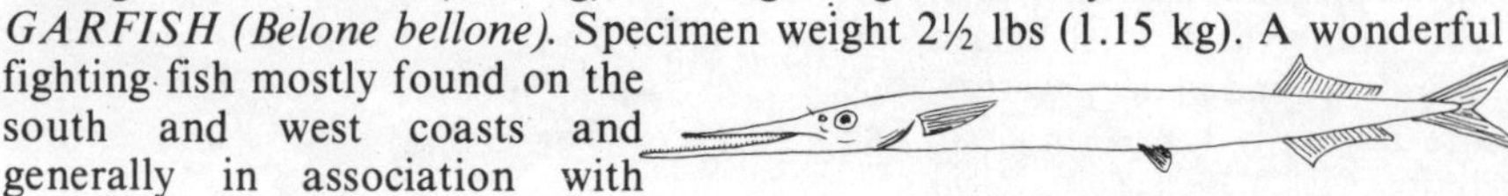

mackerel shoals. Can be taken spinning from the shore or float fishing with a tiny piece of mackerel in the "rubby dubby" trail while waiting for shark to come along.

CONGER (Conger conger). Specimen weight 40 lbs (18 kg). The conger is a bottom dweller living either on or very close to rocks in all depths all round the coast. Fish of between 12 and 25 lbs (5.4–11.3 kg) can be taken from most piers and jetties and from the rocks in certain places.

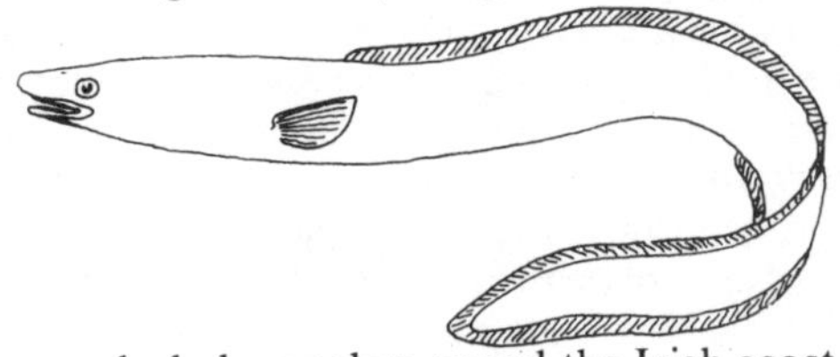

These are some of the fish taken regularly by anglers round the Irish coast. For a more complete list, see the Specimen Fish Schedule in the Appendix.

TACKLE

The choice of tackle for sea angling in Ireland depends on the fish sought, the preferred fishing method of the angler and local fishing conditions, all of which can vary enormously. To simplify descriptions it can be divided into shore tackle and boat tackle.

The equipment for shore angling can be further divided into beach fishing and rock or pier fishing. For beach fishing, distance casting is fairly important, particularly for bass, flounder, ray and codling. A long fibre-glass beach casting rod of 10 to 12 feet (3.04–3.6 metres) with a matching fixed spool or multiplier reel, capable of holding 200 yards (182 metres) of 12 to 18 lbs (5.4–8.2 kg) breaking strain monofilament is required. This tackle can also double up for rock and pier fishing for wrasse, ray, small conger and for "feathering" for mackerel and pollack, where 3 to 6 ozs (84–168 g) weights are required, either for distance casting or holding the bottom.

If spinning with lures or artificial eels is preferred, then a double handed spinning rod of 8 to 10 feet (2.4–3.04 metres) and a smaller reel containing 100 yards (91 metres) of 8 to 12 lbs (3.6–5.4 kg) monofilament will suffice. For bottom fishing from the rocks for conger, tope or ray, a strong beach caster with 18 to 25 (8.2–11.3 kg) monofilament is necessary. This stronger equipment is also useful if fishing over rough ground where getting snagged is inevitable.

The equipment required for boat fishing is a bit more complicated but it can be roughly described as light, medium and heavy gear. Much depends on the marine conditions, but in general the light gear is a 6 or 7 foot (1.83–2.14 metres) spinning rod and a reel containing 12 to 20 lbs (5.4–9.1 kg) monofilament. This tackle is very suitable for fishing in less than 10 fathoms (18 metres) in slack waters for dab, plaice, whiting, pouting, small pollack, coalfish and turbot or for drifting in deeper water for pollock.

The medium gear is a light boat rod of about 20 lbs (9.1 kg) test curve and a multiplying reel up to a 4/0 with 20 to 30 lbs (9.1–14 kg) line. This is a great all-round set of equipment and can be used for deep water pollock, ling, conger, ray, tope and cod; if used properly it can take skate and shark. However if shark, skate or big conger are the quarry then use the heavy gear. This is a strong rod of about 30 lbs (14 kg) test curve and a 6/0 reel filled with 40 lbs (18 kg) line or over.

Local conditions, however, nearly always dictate the choice of equipment and it is very wrong to go to sea with set ideas about the tackle you will use without knowing the speed of the current, the nature of the bottom, the drift of the boat, the depth of the water and many other related factors.

METHODS OF FISHING

For all types of beach fishing, the object is to get a natural bait as far out as possible and lying smack on the bottom. This applies to bass, cod, ray, small turbot and whiting. It is always advisable for safety reasons to use a shock leader and for everything other than ray, a one or two hook monofilament paternoster is sufficient. For ray, a single hook leger is best. If fishing a heavy surf, a grip lead is always desirable and a pair of waders is also generally necessary.

For wrasse fishing from rocks, a single paternoster attached to an adjustable float is best; the adjustable float allows the angler to keep the bait just off the bottom where the fish are located. If "feathering" from the rocks, it is best to use a set of three feathers with the lead attached to the end, but if you are using an imitation eel, it is better to have the eel about 3 or 4 feet (0.9–1.2 metres) below the lead. For any of the bottom dwellers, such as conger and ray, a running leger is superior.

Flatfish are reputed to be full of curiosity and a baited spoon can be very effective. A large "flashy" spoon tripping along the bottom attracts their attention and they take the bait which is 6″ to 8″ (15–20 cm) behind it.

For boat fishing, once again everything depends on local conditions and whether the boat is drifting or at anchor. If drifting over the rough ground, it is best to have the lead at the extreme end of a two or three hook paternoster, but if at anchor, it is always good to have a large natural bait on the bottom. The general idea is to have the baits on or as close to the bottom as possible. Natural baits such as mackerel or lugworm will take most of the bottom dwellers, but on occasions, "pirking" with a heavy pirk and two artificial eels can be very effective for pollack, coalfish and cod.

A very reliable and productive bottom rig for boat anglers is a set of three baited feathers. This consists of three heavy duty feathers with a small piece of mackerel on the hooks and the weight at the end. Almost every species of fish has at some time or other been taken on this rig.

If fishing at anchor for skate, tope, conger or ling, a running leger with 9″ to 12″ (22.5–30 cm) of wire is essential, as some of these fish can make short work of monofilament when they get their teeth to it. Shark, of course, demand special traces and these are usually about 12 to 15 feet long (3.6–4.5 metres) are made of steel wire. This is necessary because shark tend to roll on the trace when hooked.

NATURAL BAITS

The most commonly used natural baits in Ireland are the mackerel, lugworm, ragworm, sand-eel and peeler crab. This is not to say that they are necessarily the best, but they certainly catch most fish. Outside of Dublin it is usually up to the angler himself to catch or collect his own supply. In Dublin, however, there are a number of tackle shops which sell lugworm and ragworm. It is only on the very odd occasion that fishing suffers from lack of bait and this usually applies to boat fishing when mackerel are hard to come by. The normal procedure when a boat goes to sea is for the first hour or so to be spent fishing for mackerel; this is invariably successful.

If lugworm are required, they can be dug on flat beaches and estuaries almost everywhere in both muddy and firm sand. Shore crabs can be collected in most places where there are low, weedy rocks uncovered by the receding tide. Ragworm are mostly confined to the muddy areas of the east coast, but mussels are very abundant in all estuaries and tidal inlets. Razorfish and clams are fairly localised and can be dug at low water, but sand-eels are even more localised and can be purchased in a few centres either frozen or preserved.

TIDES

Every 25 hours approximately, the entire coastline has two high waters and two low waters. Generally speaking, the tides on the south and west coast are "opposite" to Dublin, i.e., when it is high water in Dublin, it is low water in the south and west. This means that high water on the south and west is about six hours ahead of Dublin.

The east coast is more complicated. For example, high water at Wicklow is about three quarters of an hour, Courtown 3½ hours and Wexford 4½ hours earlier than Dublin. High water in Dublin occurs half an hour before high water in Dover. High water spring tides on the south and west coasts are about 6 p.m. G.M.T. and the rise and fall varies between 3 feet (0.9 metres) in Wexford Harbour and 16 feet (4.9 metres) in the Shannon estuary.

CHARTER BOATS

On the south and west coasts, there are a number of centres operating angling charter services. Boat seats or entire boats can be booked for a day's deep sea fishing and many of these offer a limited amount of tackle for hire. Before planning a trip it is best to get in touch with one of the local tourist information offices, or the local operator, club or tackle shop to find out about cost, time of departure and so on. At the time of writing there are angling services being offered at the following centres: Dungarvan, Youghal, Ballycotton, Cork Harbour, Kinsale, Courtmacsherry, Castletownshend, Baltimore, Schull, Kenmare, Derrynane, Ballinskellies, Valentia, Caherciveen, Dingle, Fenit, Quilty, Liscannor, Ballyvaughan, Galway, Clifden, Leenane, Westport, Achill, Belmullet, Killala, Enniscrone and Mullaghmore.

1. WEXFORD AND WATERFORD

A guide must start somewhere and I propose to start at Wexford in the sunny south east of Ireland. From here I will move along the south coast, up the west of Ireland, across the north and down the east coast back to Wexford. There is no particular significance in starting at Wexford, other than it is a very pleasant place in which to start our sea angling tour of Ireland. The town's history goes back to the time of Ptolemy and the name comes from the Viking "Waesfjord", meaning the "harbour of mud flats". This is a good description, even if rather unkind since the town is really quite charming.

WEXFORD AND ROSSLARE

Wexford Harbour faces east and is basically the estuary of the River Slaney which enters the harbour at Wexford town. Two sandy headlands, Raven Point and Rosslare Point mark the entrance to the harbour, a large portion of which dries out at low water. The channel flows out close to Raven Point on the

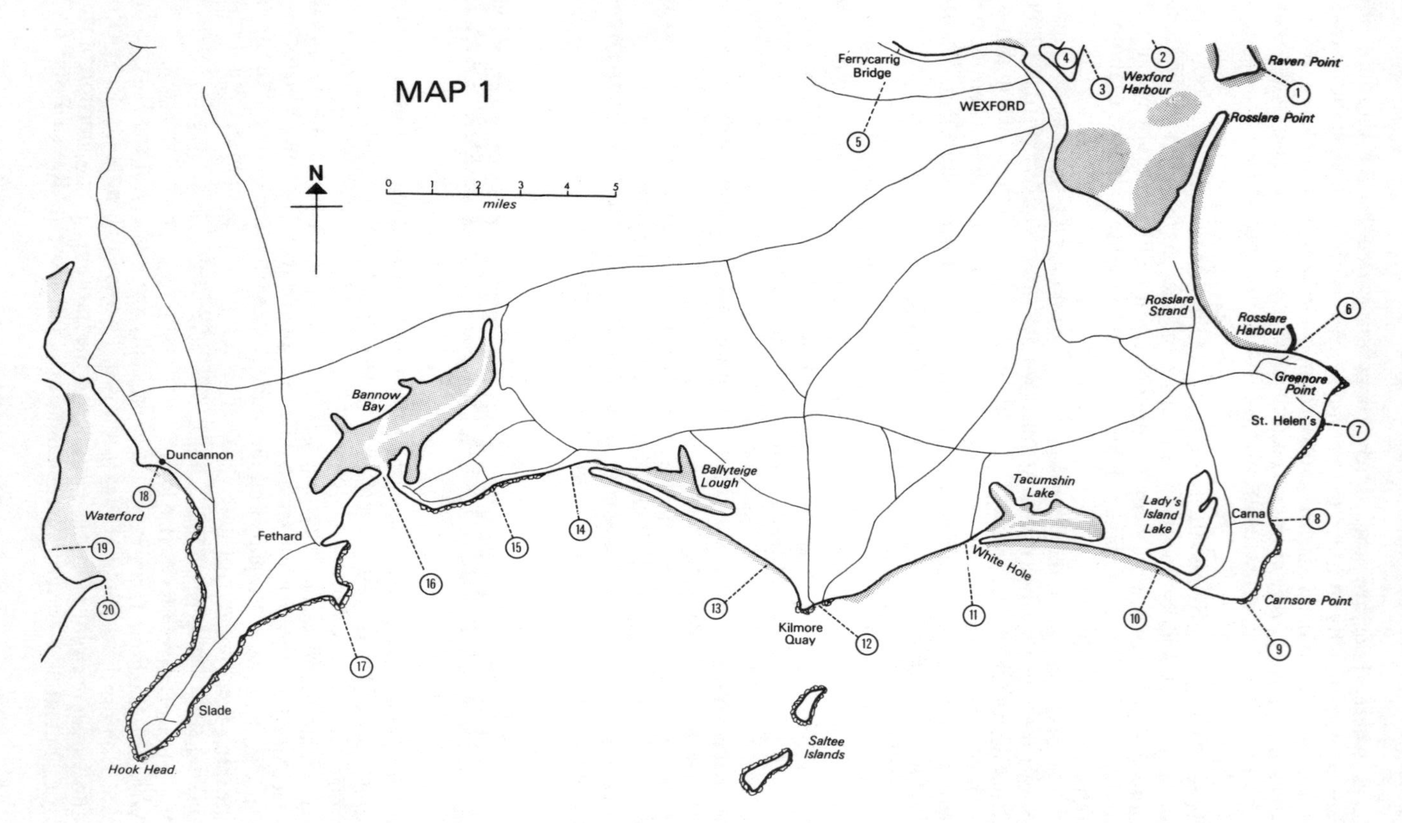
MAP 1
N
0
1
2
3
4
5
miles
Ferrycarrig Bridge
WEXFORD
Wexford Harbour
Raven Point
Rosslare Point
Rosslare Strand
Rosslare Harbour
Greenore Point
St. Helen's
Carna
Lady's Island Lake
Carnsore Point
Tacumshin Lake
White Hole
Ballyteige Lough
Kilmore Quay
Saltee Islands
Bannow Bay
Fethard
Duncannon
Waterford
Slade
Hook Head
1
2
3
4
5
6
7
8
9
10
11
12
13
14
15
16
17
18
19
20

northern shore. Bass and flatfish can be taken surf fishing at the Point [Map 1 (1)]. Care should be taken in this area if fishing during the flood tide, as an angler is liable to be cut off by the tide while fishing on the eastern sand banks. A long walk is necessary to get out to the Raven Point, but it can be worth the effort.

Bass and flounder are taken all along Ardcavan Strand [Map 1 (2)] at the back of the bird sanctuary on which, incidentally, more than half the entire world population of Greenland white-fronted geese winters. Flounder can be very plentiful on the strand just north of Ferrybank [Map 1 (3)], from three hours before high water to two hours after. At the breakwater in Wexford town, bass, flounder and ray are plentiful at times, as are freshwater eels. Still on the north side, on Cats Strand [Map 1 (4)] at the back of the shipyard, flounder, bass and the occasional sea trout are taken at either side of low water. It is unfortunately a rather swampy and unpleasant area and anglers are liable to be cut off by the incoming tide. About three miles (4.8 km) upriver from Wexford, at Ferrycarrig Bridge [Map 1 (5)], small bass and flounder (locally called 'fluke') are plentiful at times, but many of the bass are undersize and must be returned alive to the water. Lugworm, ragworm and mussel are very plentiful in the harbour.

About 12 miles (19.2 km) south east of Wexford is Rosslare Harbour, the terminus of car ferries from Cherbourg, Le Havre and Fishguard. Bass, flounder and dogfish are taken in the cut beneath the inner section of the pier [Map 1 (6)], particularly on the flood tide, and some conger have been taken from the pier head itself. North of the pier a long beach runs right up to Rosslare Point; there are bass and flatfish on this beach, particularly at the northern end, fishing into the mouth of Wexford Harbour. East of the pier on the Back Strand, there are some bass when there is any surf running.

At Greenore Point, the coast turns south in a series of beaches and rocky points. At the Point itself, there is some good fishing for big bass between the rocks. But be warned—the current can be very strong in this area. At Ballyhire, bass, flounder and the odd dogfish are taken and just south of the tiny pier of St Helens [Map 1 (7)], bass can be taken spinning and bottom fishing from the rocks and in the clear patches. The two beaches of Ballytrent and Carne hold bass and flatfish, but a good southerly wind is generally required for the best results. Flounder can be plentiful off Carne Pier [Map 1 (8)].

At Carnsore Point [Map 1 (9)], which marks the south eastern tip of the country, there is a rocky outcrop. Wrasse, bass, codling, small pollack, flounder and lesser spotted dogfish are caught here spinning and bottom fishing. Past the point, the shore turns west and a ten mile long (16 km) beach runs almost to Kilmore Quay. About two miles (3.2 km) from Carnsore Point, behind this long beach, is Lady's Island Lake, the outflow from which can sometimes be blocked after a storm. This area, locally called the "Coome" [Map 1 (10)], has good surf fishing for bass, tope, flounder and codling. From the rather steep beach, sea trout can also be taken at times.

A few miles further west is a similar lake called Tacumshin. The outflow is locally called the "White Hole" [Map 1 (11)] and it is piped out through the beach. There is good surf fishing on the seaward side for bass, sea trout and tope in the summer.

The Wexford area has a reasonable amount of boat fishing. In Wexford

Harbour flounder and ray make up the bulk of the catches, but just outside the harbour mouth bass sometimes shoal during the summer. It is a dangerous area for anyone who does not know the locality. Bass also shoal on the Splaugh Rock south of Greenore Point, particularly in September. They can be fished from small boats out of Rosslare Harbour, St Helens and Carne. Catches of twenty and thirty bass in a session are common. Once again, this is a dangerous place for the inexperienced as the tides run very fast across the Splaugh. The Tusker Rock lighthouse (built in 1815) is six miles (9.6 km) south east of Rosslare and on the rock shoal around it, fishing for cod, pollack, tope, conger and other species can be excellent at times. Beware of the tides—they are very swift and confused.

KILMORE QUAY

Kilmore Quay [Map 1 (12)] is a beautiful little village of thatched cottages, boats and quiet atmosphere. It is primarily a commercial fishing port, but there is good angling in the area. From a boat, if one can be acquired, anglers can fish around the lonely Saltee Islands (a bird watcher's paradise) for pollack, tope, ray, flatfish and occasionally bass. Spur dogfish are so numerous at times that they can be a positive nuisance. On a ridge of rock called St Patrick's Bridge which runs out to sea just east of the harbour there is spinning for bass.

To the west is the rocky headland of Forlorne Point on which there is good bass fishing, although the bottom is quite rough. Lugworm are plentiful in the harbour. West of Forlorne, a long sweep of shelving beach is backed by sand dunes. This stretch is called the Burrow shore [Map 1 (13)], and bass, flatfish, dogfish and occasionally tope can all be taken along its length in a south west wind. A long, narrow lagoon called Ballyteige Lough runs behind the western half of this beach and enters the sea at Cullenstown [Map 1 (14)]. Tides are swift in the channel and there can be good fishing for bass and big flounder. At the entrance on the Cullenstown side, there is good surf fishing for bass, but there is always a danger of being cut off by the flowing tide, so be careful.

Two miles (3.2 km) west of Cullenstown at Blackhall [Map 1 (15)], there is a small beach between the ridges of rock. Bass and flatfish are plentiful at times but it is best to view the fishing area at low water and note the areas of rock. Bannow Bay is a flat sandy inlet, most of which dries out except for some deep channels. It flows out west of Bannow Island in a deep swift channel [Map 1 (16)] in which there are good bass, flounder and the odd tope. Inside the bay, in the many channels, some very big flounder are taken on lugworm which can be dug in the lagoon.

An east facing beach runs from the mouth of Bannow Bay to the tiny harbour of Fethard. Bass and flatfish are taken from it, particularly at the eastern end near the channel.

South west of Fethard the coast is rocky all the way out to Hook Head and for a long way back into Waterford Harbour. At Baginbun Head [Map 1 (17)], 1½ miles (2.4 km) south of Fethard, there is some rock fishing for pollack, wrasse and mackerel. Similar fishing can be had at Slade, at Hook Head under the lighthouse and near Churchtown inside Waterford Harbour.

WATERFORD HARBOUR

Duncannon [Map 1 (18)] is a small fishing port about eight miles (12.8 km) north of Hook Head. It has a small harbour from the back of which some good conger have been caught. South of the town on the strand, which has lugworm, there can be good fishing for bass and flatfish on the flood tide, particularly near the streams. On the western side of the harbour is a long shallow beach running from Passage East straight south to the rocky promontory of Credan Head. At Woodstown Strand [Map 1 (19)], especially towards the southern end and in a few other places, there can be good bottom fishing for bass. At Credan Head [Map 1 (20)], where the tide forms a strong eddy close inshore, some very good catches of bass have been made in the past.

There is quite good boat fishing out of Dunmore East, which is on the west of the harbour entrance. The port itself is one of the leading commercial fishing ports in the country, thus ensuring a constant supply of fresh fish bait. There is good mixed fishing in Waterford Harbour, in the race off Hook Head and on the outside deep water marks for tope, pollack, rays, whiting, pouting, conger, dogfish and flatfish. Blue shark are probably available in the summer but are not fished for.

TRAMORE

The popular seaside resort of Tramore is on the north western corner of Tramore Bay. It is on the landward side of a long spit of sand dunes running east which cuts off the inner portion of the bay called the Back Strand. To the south of the spit, is a beautiful two mile long (3.2 km) surf beach [Map 2 (1)] on which there are bass and flounder, very plentiful at times.

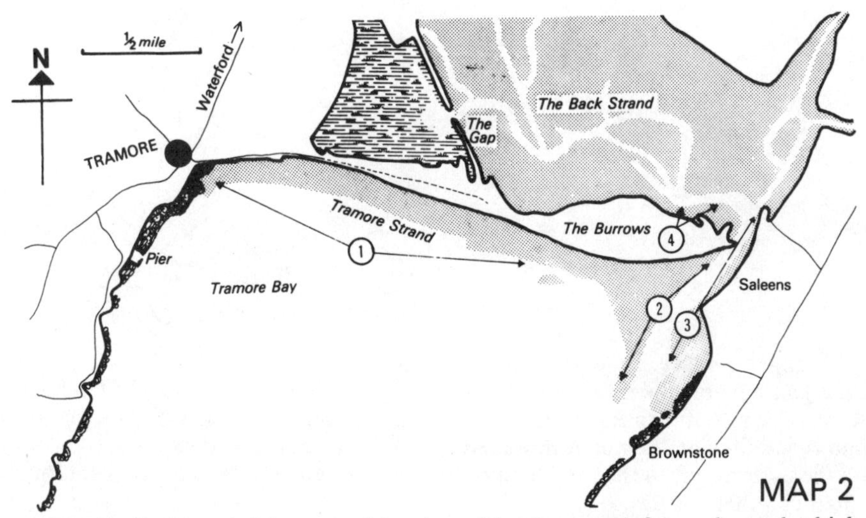

The Back Strand dries out almost completely except for a channel which runs out between the end of the sand spit (called "The Burrows") and the eastern shore of the bay. Bass run this channel and can be caught from either side [Map 2 (2 or 3)], but it is best to fish at low water when the tide is slackest. Just inside the tip of the Burrows the channel turns back in towards the shore; bass and flounder can be taken in the pools [Map 2 (4)]. There is rock fishing for pollock, mackerel and wrasse on either side of the bay at Brownstown Head on the east and Newtown Head on the west. Lugworm are plentiful on the Back Strand.

DUNGARVAN

The coast from Tramore to Ballyvoyle Head, just east of Dungarvan, is for the most part cliffs and rocky headlands, except for two small beaches at Annestown and Bunmahon. Streams flow onto each of these beaches; bass and flatfish are sometimes taken in the surf, but in general this stretch of coast is still virgin territory. Off Annestown there is very pleasant small boat fishing for numerous ray and pollack in summer.

West of Ballyvoyle, a south-east facing crescent-shaped beach called Clonea [Map 3 (1)] runs down to Ballynacourty Point, the north eastern limit of Dungarvan Bay. There are quite a lot of rocky patches on this beach and although bass were plentiful on it some years ago, they are not quite so plentiful now. Flatfish, however, are still caught, mostly on the flood tide.

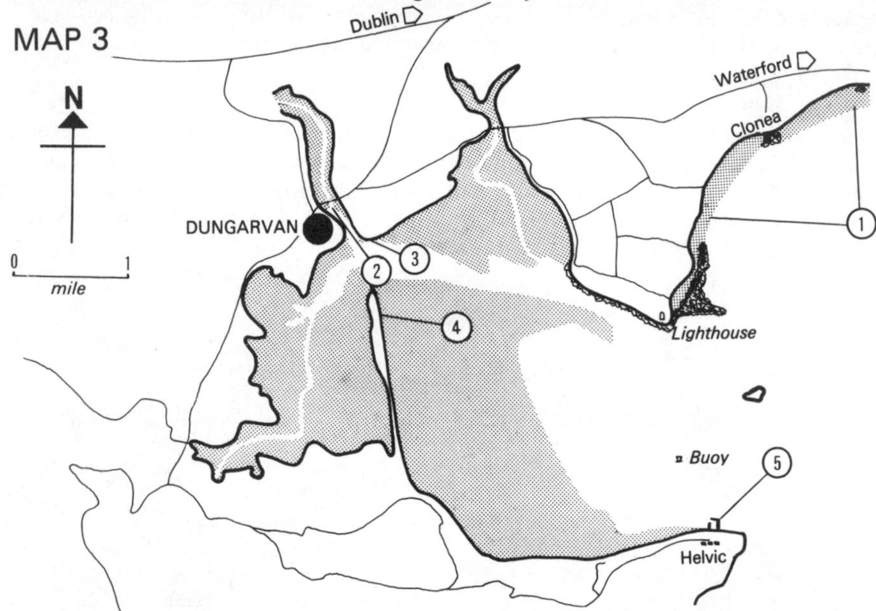

Dungarvan Bay, about two miles wide (3.2 km), faces due east. The Cunnigar sand spit cuts off the inner portion of the bay, which together with the Culligan River, drains out through a narrow entrance between Cunnigar Point on the spit and Abbeyside on the north shore. At low water there are vast expanses of sand on the eastern side of the spit and most of the inner portion dries out, except for a small channel.

In Dungarvan town, in the vicinity of the old railway bridge [Map 3 (2)], excellent flounder fishing can be had, particularly in winter. Bass are regularly taken in the channel at Abbeyside [Map 3 (3)]. In autumn, bass feed avidly on sandeels inside the Cunnigar and good catches are made from small boats on driftlined and float fished sandeels, particularly on spring tides. Sandeels can be collected on the Cunnigar spit and there are lugworm near the swimming pool in the town. When there is a surf on the eastern side of the Cunnigar [Map 3 (4)], bass and flounder can be caught at high water.

Helvic Head marks the south eastern limit of the bay; just inside it is picturesque Helvic Harbour. From the northern pier [Map 3 (5)], mullet are taken on fish bait and small conger (10 to 12 lbs—4.5–5.4 kg) are numerous. There is good ray fishing from this pier also but long casts are necessary. There is a little rock fishing east of the pier for pollack and mackerel during the summer.

Dungarvan, however, is much better known for its deep sea angling than its shore fishing. All through the summer months, boats take out visiting anglers to fish particularly for blue shark, which are quite plentiful in the area between early July and early October. Good mixed fishing can also be had, particularly around Mine Head, for pollack, coalfish, ling, ray, conger and gurnard and there are a number of reasonably productive wrecks in the area. In the bay itself, small boat fishing for bass, flatfish, ray and dogfish can be very enjoyable. Excellent boats and tackle for hire are available in Dungarvan.

ARDMORE

Beyond Mine Head the shore swings west again and continues to be quite rocky and rather inaccessible as far as Ballyquin Strand near Ardmore. Ardmore Bay faces east and in the inner margin is made up of two beaches—Ballyquin Strand [Map 4 (1)] to the north and Ardmore [Map 4 (2)] to the south, separated by a rocky outcrop called the Black Rock. Ardmore Head on the southern end shelters the bay from southerly and westerly winds. The village of Ardmore and its tiny pier are just inside the Head. The two beaches hold bass and flatfish; they fish best in a south wind. It is possible to spin and bottom fish from the Black Rock [Map 4 (3)] for bass, flatfish and the occasional sea trout. Lugworm are plentiful on both ends of Ardmore Strand.

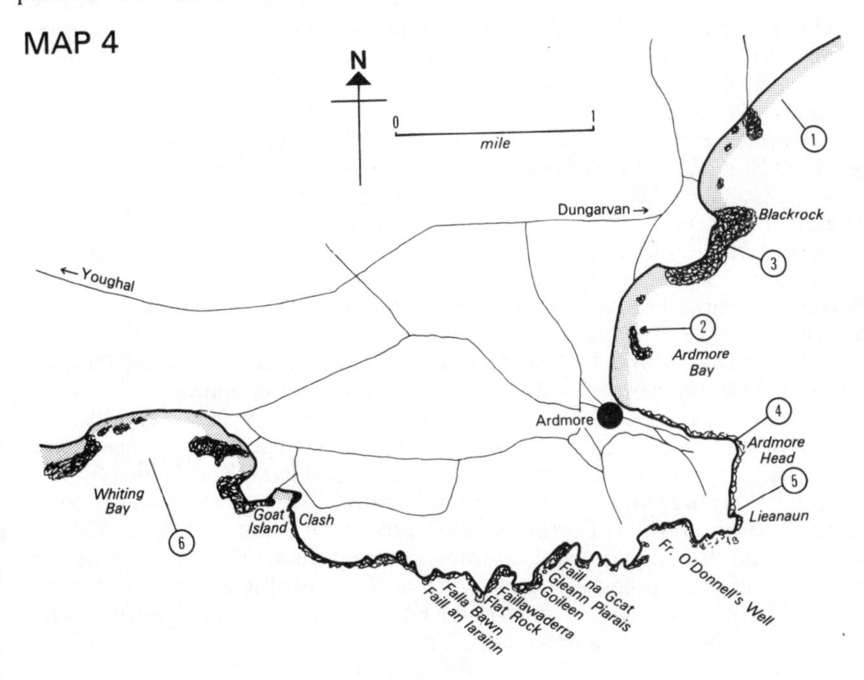

A cliff walk runs from the pier east to Ardmore Head [Map 4 (4)]; pollack, mackerel, wrasse and garfish can be caught from the rocks here. About a half mile (0.8 km) to the south there is another rock mark at Ram Head [Map 4 (5)] for mackerel, pollack and some wrasse.

From Ram Head east to Whiting Bay is about two miles (3.2 km) of rocky shoreline, most of which is fishable. It is all pollack, mackerel and wrasse territory. Faill na gCat, Goileen, Faillawaderra and Flat Rock are but a few of the recognised angling marks.

Whiting Bay [Map 4 (6)] is south-facing and offers excellent surf fishing for bass, flounder, dogfish and at times, ray, particularly painted ray in the autumn. It was from this beach that the current Irish bass record of 17 lbs 1¼ ozs (7.735 kg) was taken in April, 1977.

2. YOUGHAL TO KENMARE

Youghal Bay faces south east and is about eight miles (12.8 km) across from Ram Head to Knockadoon Head. The head of the bay is the major estuary of the Munster Blackwater. The seaside resort of Youghal is on the western side of this estuary, which is tidal for 14 miles (22.4 km) to Cappoquin. The fishing in Youghal is excellent and deep sea, inshore and shore angling are available.

Boats and equipment can be hired in the town for deep sea angling. Blue shark, cod, pollack, ling, whiting, ray, conger and common skate are regularly taken. Catches are usually impressive, with quality fish of a good average size. Small boat fishing in the estuary itself and just outside is very enjoyable. Bass, codling, flounder, coalfish, pollack and the occasional big cod are taken. Spinning, trolling and driftlining from small boats for bass can be very good from Ferry Point (on the eastern side of the estuary) down past Monatrea House and out to Easter Point, but the tides can be very fast and dangerous, particularly at Ferry Point. Sea trout are regularly taken here as well.

There is a lot of shore angling in the area, starting in Caliso Bay [Map 5 (1)] to the east of the estuary mouth. This little beach and Mangans Cove [Map 5 (2)] (about one mile—1.6 km to the west) are steeply shelving with coarse sand and hold bass and flounder. Bass and some pollack are caught spinning from the rocks between the beaches and at Easter Point [Map 5 (3)], which marks the eastern entrance to the estuary.

At Monatrea [Map 5 (4)], south of Ferry Point, there is spinning and light bottom fishing for bass from and between the low rocky ridges.

On the western side of the estuary at Youghal itself, there is a considerable amount of shore fishing for bass, flounder and small conger from the many piers and jetties in the town and from the back of the Green Park. Surf fishing for bass on Youghal Strand [Map 5 (5)] to the south of the town can be particularly good near the railway station. Further south again, in the Pillmore Estuary [Map 5 (6)], bass and flounder are taken at low water near the road. Bait is plentiful on either side of the Youghal estuary. Lugworm can be dug at low water in the harbours in the town and just north of the Ferry Point. Crab are plentiful around Monatrea in the low rough ground.

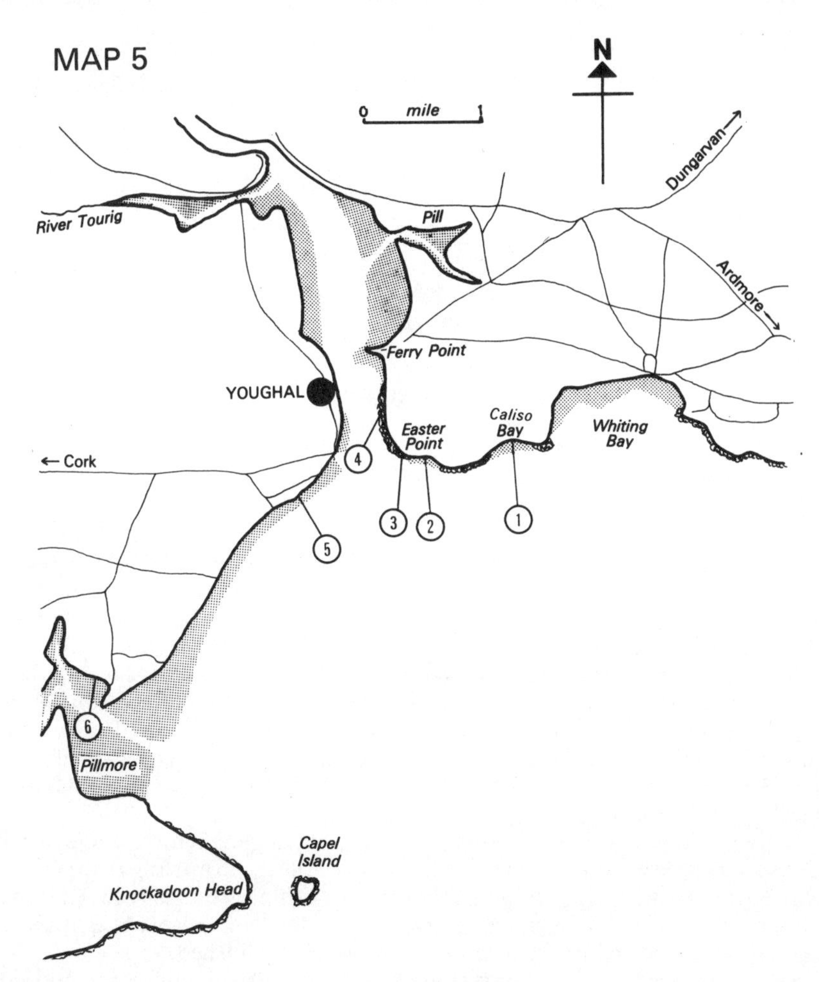

BALLYCOTTON

Ballycotton Bay is the next bay to the west of Youghal. The inner portion faces east and it is about six miles (9.6 km) from Knockadoon Head in the east to Ballycotton Island in the west. Immediately west of Knockadoon [Map 6 (1)], there are a few rock marks for pollack, mackerel and wrasse, but about two miles (3.2 km) to the west, at Ballymakeagh [Map 6 (2)], codling and coalfish are caught in late autumn and winter. The inner portion of the bay is fringed with east and south-east facing beaches, separated by outcrops of low rock.

On the northern beach at Garryvoe [Map 6 (3)] there is good fishing for bass and various flatfish. There is equally good fishing on Ballymona Strand [Map 6 (4)] where, particularly near the streams, bass and flatfish can be plentiful. Occasionally codling are taken here. Lugworm are plentiful on Ballymona, but be careful if you drive on the beach, as cars have been known to sink into the sand.

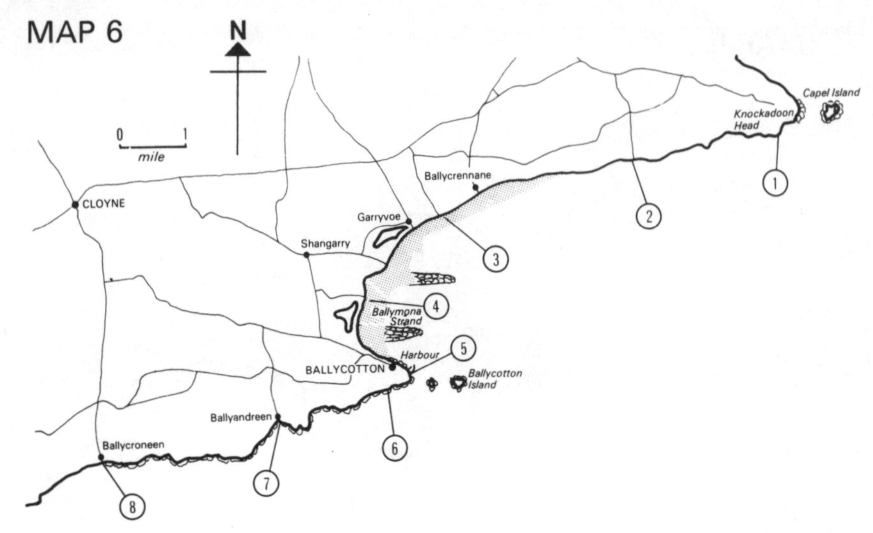

From the end of the East Pier of Ballycotton Harbour [Map 6(5)] some big conger have been taken and mullet can be very numerous. They are normally taken on small pieces of fish or fish gut. A short road runs up the back of the village to the headland and there is a very pleasant cliff walk to the west. Some good ballan wrasse and pollack are taken from the rocks below the walk [Map 6 (6)]. In Ballyandreen Bay, about two miles (3.2 km) west of Ballycotton [Map 6 (7)], there is a small beach where bass are sometimes taken. Pollack and mackerel are also taken from the rocks in this area. Ballycroneen is about three miles (4.8 km) west again [Map 6 (8)], and offers surf fishing for bass and flatfish as well as the occasional tope and dogfish.

Ballycotton was one of the most noted deep sea angling centres in Europe. In fact many people would claim that this was where deep sea angling as we know it today began. In the early part of this century, the fishing grounds between Power Head and Youghal Bay were very heavily fished by members of the British Sea Anglers' Club and many European records were established.

Specimen sized pollack, coalfish, cod, ling, conger, bream, common skate and blue shark were very plentiful twenty five years ago and although still available, very little fishing is carried out from this famous harbour, mainly because boats can be difficult to hire at times.

CORK HARBOUR

The outer portion of Cork Harbour is marked by Power Head to the east and Roberts Head to the west, a gap of seven miles (11.2 km). The entrance to the harbour proper is only about a mile wide (1.6 km) and the depth in the main channel is as much as 16 fathoms (29.2 metres) inside the entrance. Once inside the twin fortifications at the mouth, the estuary of the River Lee expands into a large, deep landlocked natural harbour with islands, sand banks and channels. The tides can be very swift, particularly near the entrance. The surrounding area is now highly industrialised and shipping can be very heavy in the harbour, so be careful in small boats.

*Author Kevin Linnane,
shark fishing
off Kinsale, Co. Cork*

There are a number of places where boats and tackle can be hired for angling, among them Cobh, Glenbrook and Crosshaven. Indeed, many of the boats and skippers are really first class and offer an excellent service. The fishing within the harbour is mostly for demersal fish such as skate, ray, dogfish, turbot, codling, conger and small pollack.

Outside Roches Point, normal good quality deep sea fishing is available for blue shark, cod, pollack, ling, conger and bream. One of the best-known outside marks is the "Daunt Rock". There are a number of wrecks in the area and these are now producing good fishing.

Between Power Head and Roches Point are two small beaches where bass and flatfish are regularly caught. These are Inch Strand and Trabolgan Strand. Around Roches Point there is a considerable amount of rock fishing for pollack, mackerel, wrasse and some bass and tope, especially around the "Foyle" and the "Gut". Inside the harbour there is bottom fishing in White Bay for bass, flatfish and some small ray. Spinning off the slip at Gold Point in East Ferry can produce bass. Some conger, ray and small pollack are taken from the piers and jetties at Cobh and conger and small pollack are taken from Monkstown Pier on the eastern side of the harbour. Crab are plentiful all around the shores of the harbour and harbour ragworm and lugworm can be collected in most of the muddy inlets and creeks.

KINSALE

Kinsale town is beautifully situated at the head of a deep and very safe natural harbour. The Bandon River estuary is roughly "S" shaped and runs out to sea between the very impressive fortifications of Charles' Fort on the east and James' Fort on the west. The town in very old and full of history. In latter years it has become quite famous as a deep sea angling centre with numerous well-run charter boats and equipment available for hire.

The town is probably the top blue shark angling port in Europe and catches are very consistent between mid-June and October. It also has first class general bottom fishing for pollack, ling, cod and conger, particularly on the Ling Rocks, seven miles (11.2 km) due east of the Old Head and in the race off the Old Head itself, where common skate are also taken, altough not as frequently as in previous years. The wreck of the 'Lusitania' lies in 50 fathoms (91 metres) twelve miles (19.3 km) south west of the Old Head lighthouse and although not fished very often, it can produce magnificent catches of quality ling, cod, conger, bream and coalfish.

Kinsale's specialities are the blue shark fishing in season and the light tackle pollack fishing on the Ling Rocks at any time of the year. The Kinsale boatmen are excellent skippers and are most professional in their dealings with experienced and novice anglers alike. The town was established as an angling centre in the mid-fifties and this development has continued up to the present. There is also reasonable inshore fishing in Kinsale Harbour and small boats can be hired in the town.

Shore angling is not very good in the area, but there are a number of places in and near the town worth trying. In particular, some large bass have been taken from the old bridge across the estuary, about two miles (3.2 km) upstream. Codling and flatfish are also available from the new bridge.

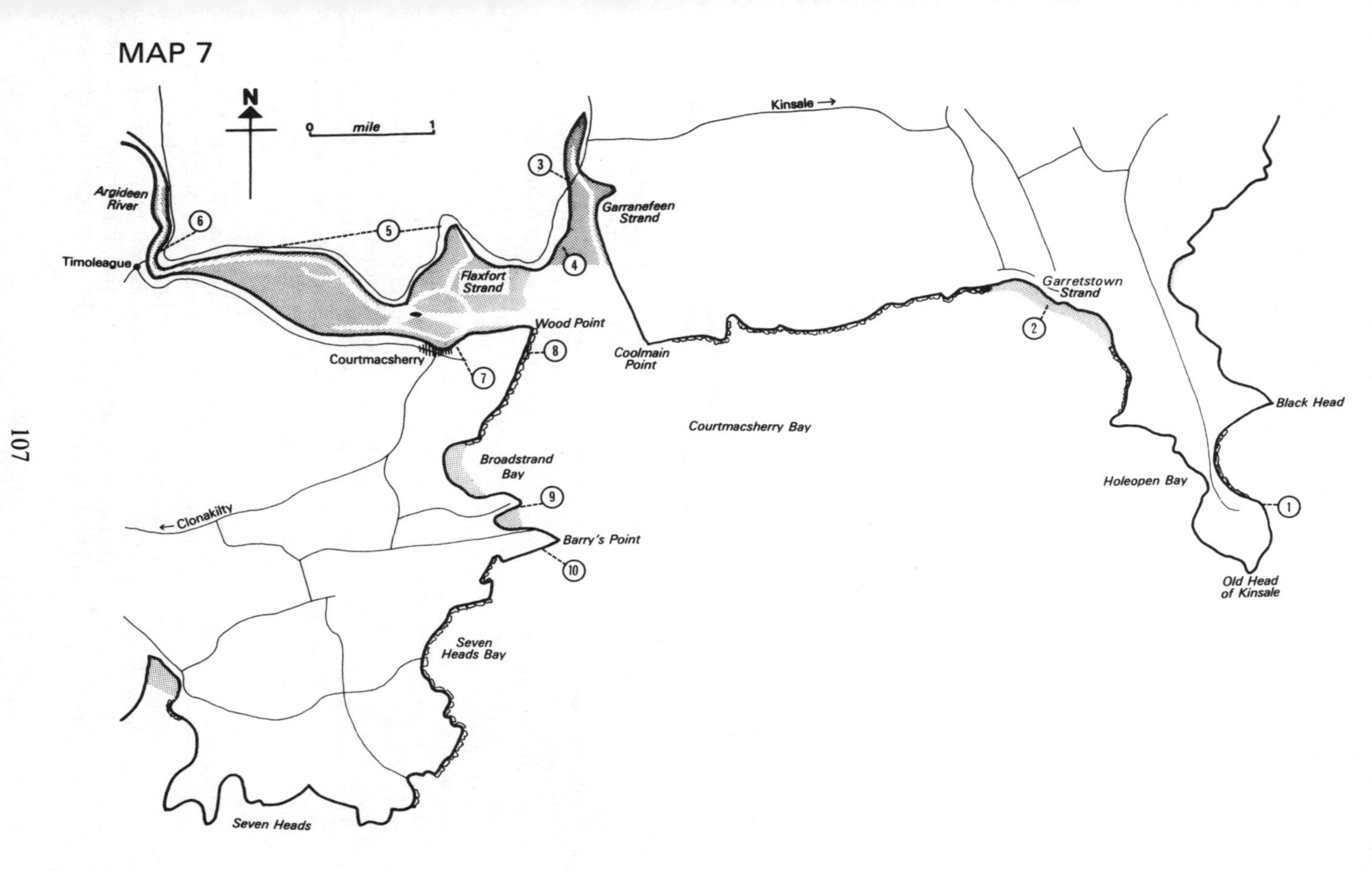
MAP 7
N
0
mile
1
Kinsale →
3
Argideen River
6
5
Garranefeen Strand
Timoleague
Flaxfort Strand
4
Garretstown Strand
Wood Point
8
2
Courtmacsherry
Coolmain Point
7
Black Head
Courtmacsherry Bay
Broadstrand Bay
Holeopen Bay
9
1
← Clonakilty
Barry's Point
10
Old Head of Kinsale
Seven Heads Bay
Seven Heads

Bass and flounder are taken at Jagoe's Point about one mile upstream and mullet are caught from the Quays in the town itself. Immediately inside the Old Head lighthouse [Map 7 (1)], a rock mark offers pollack, wrasse and mackerel, but there is quite a steep climb down. Off the beach at Garretstown [Map 7 (2)], to the west of the Old Head, bass and flounder are taken. It fishes best in a south or south west wind at the western end where a small stream flows in. Lugworm can be dug at Sandycove where there is also a little flounder fishing.

COURTMACSHERRY

The estuary of the Arigdeen River is four miles (6.4 km) long and Courtmacsherry is about two thirds of the way out on the southern side. Kilbrittan creek empties into the eastern end of this estuary and they both flow into Courtmacsherry Bay between Wood Point on the west and Coolmain Point on the east. Courtmacsherry is now well established as a deep sea angling centre with well-run boats and good tackle available for hire. The fishing is much the same as Kinsale, with blue shark the main quarry, but it also offers good general fishing for pollack, conger, ling, cod, wrasse, skate and ray.

Shore angling is fairly popular in the area, particularly in Kilbrittan creek and along the main estuary, which mostly dries out. Kilbrittan creek is crossed by a road bridge [Map 7 (3)] just south of which, especially at low water, bass and flounder can be caught. Above the bridge, mullet are numerous, but I have never seen any caught.

The creek is for the most part flat, firm sand and good lugworm and mussel are plentiful at the bridge. The creek enters the sea at the eastern end of a fine beach near Harbour View; bass and flounder can be taken from it in a good southerly wind [Map 7 (4)].

The Argideen estuary starts at Timoleague and the channel for the most part runs along the northern shore. At low water there are extensive mud flats on the southern side, but near Courtmacsherry this changes to firm sand. At Timoleague [Map 7 (6)], immediately north and south of the Argideen bridge, bass, mullet and flounder can be very plentiful at times. It fishes best from low water to half flood. All along the north shore [Map 7 (5)], bass and flatfish can be taken spinning and bottom fishing through the late ebb and early flood. On the southern side, conger are taken from the pier at Courtmacsherry and bass and flatfish from the beach a little to the east [Map 7 (7)].

In Courtmacsherry Bay itself there are a number of rock fishing marks where pollack, wrasse, mackerel and dogfish are taken. These are at Wood Point [Map 7 (8)], Quarry Point [Map 7 (9)] and Barry's Point [Map 7 (10)]. At Broadstrand Bay, some surf fishing for bass can be had, but a good easterly or south-easterly wind is necessary to build up the surf.

CLONAKILTY

Inchydoney Island is a peninsula jutting out between Clonakilty Harbour on the north and Muckruss Strand on the south. A channel runs along the north and eastern shore of Clonakilty Harbour and enters the sea at Ring Head.

Beginning inside Ring Head [Map 8 (1)], at low water there is fishing for bass and flounder all along this channel and as the tide fills, moving up past Curraghane at half flood [Map 8 (4)]. The best places are near Ring Harbour

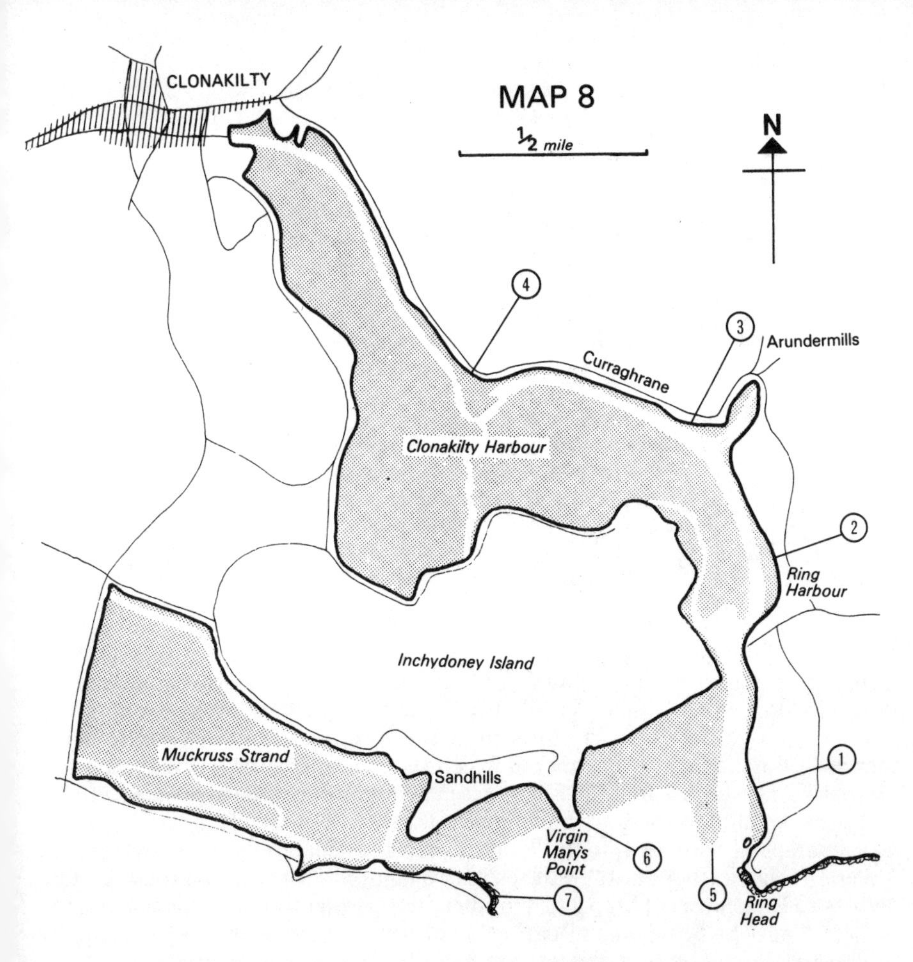

[Map 8 (2)], and from the little pier at Arundermills [Map 8 (3)], where there are also some conger.

On the southern side of Inchydoney Island, a long surf beach faces south, broken in the middle by a rocky outcrop called 'Virgin Mary's Point'. A half mile (0.8 km) walk to the east brings you to the mouth of the channel and fishing the sandbars [Map 8 (5)] at low water can be good for bass, particularly with sandeel. There is surf fishing for bass and flatfish all along the beach and bass and flatfish can be taken spinning and bottom fishing from the rocks at Virgin Mary's Point [Map 8 (6)].

A channel runs along the southern side of Muckruss Strand and some bass and flatfish are taken in it, but the best results are to be had fishing on to the sand off the low rocks around Muckruss Head [Map 8 (7)], Lugworm are plentiful in both Clonakilty Harbour and Muckruss Strand. Bass stocks on the Clonakilty beaches are not as good as in former years and anglers are encouraged to return most of their fish alive.

ROSSCARBERY

There are four fine surf beaches in Rosscarbery Bay all of which produce bass and flatfish, although not as consistently as in former years. Galley Head marks the eastern end of the bay and just inside it to the west is the south west facing Long Strand [Map 9 (1)].

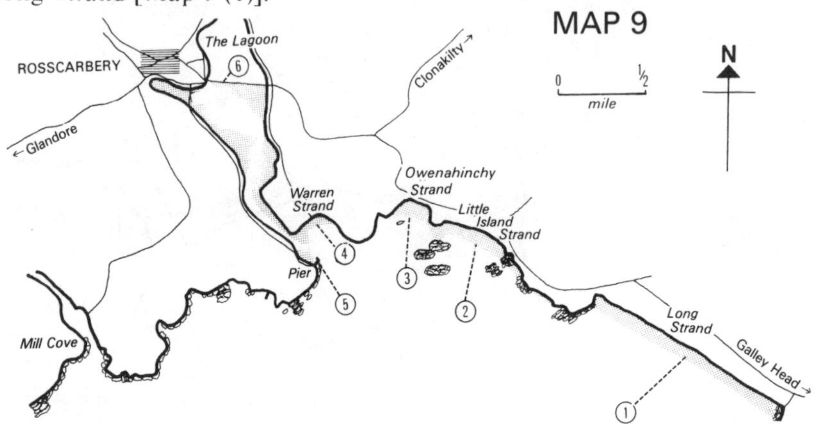

This is the best fished at either end around low water. Little Island Strand [Map 9 (2)], is also best fished at low water, as is Owenahinchy Strand [Map 9 (3)], where a small stream flows in. The last of these beaches is the Warren Strand [Map 9 (4)], which is probably the most consistent.

The Rosscarbery estuary flows in at the western end of this south facing beach through a narrow channel in which the tide can be very strong. Bass and flatfish can be taken spinning and bottom fishing from either side of the mouth at low water, and further up the channel as the tide fills. Outside the estuary there is a small pier [Map 9 (5)] to the south from which small pollack and wrasse are taken. At the northern head of the estuary a lagoon is formed by a road running across to Rosscarbery [Map 9 (6)]; mullet are very plentiful on either side of the bridge. They can be taken on floating bread crust but ground baiting is normally necessary. Lugworm and sandeel are plentiful in the estuary itself.

THE SOUTH WEST CORNER

The shore fishing on the southwest corner of the country between Glandore and Bantry is as yet unknown, except for a few places on the southern side. Just west of Glandore a bridge to Union Hall crosses a large inlet which runs up to Leap [Map 10 (1)]. From the bridge, bass, flounder and numerous dogfish are caught. Immediately east of Union Hall there is a spot where flounder, mackerel and the occasional mullet are taken around low water.

In Blind Harbour [Map 10 (2)], to the east of Castlehaven, fishing from the rocks at the western end of the bay can be good for pollock, wrasse, flatfish, dogfish and ray. On the northern side of Toe Head [Map 10 (3)], a short climb down from the road to a rock mark offers some wrasse and mackerel.

The most interesting fishing in this entire area is in Lough Hyne [Map 10 (4)], a salt water lake about five miles (8 km) east of Baltimore. The lake is very deep (up to 30 fathoms—54.8 metres—in places) particularly on the western side.

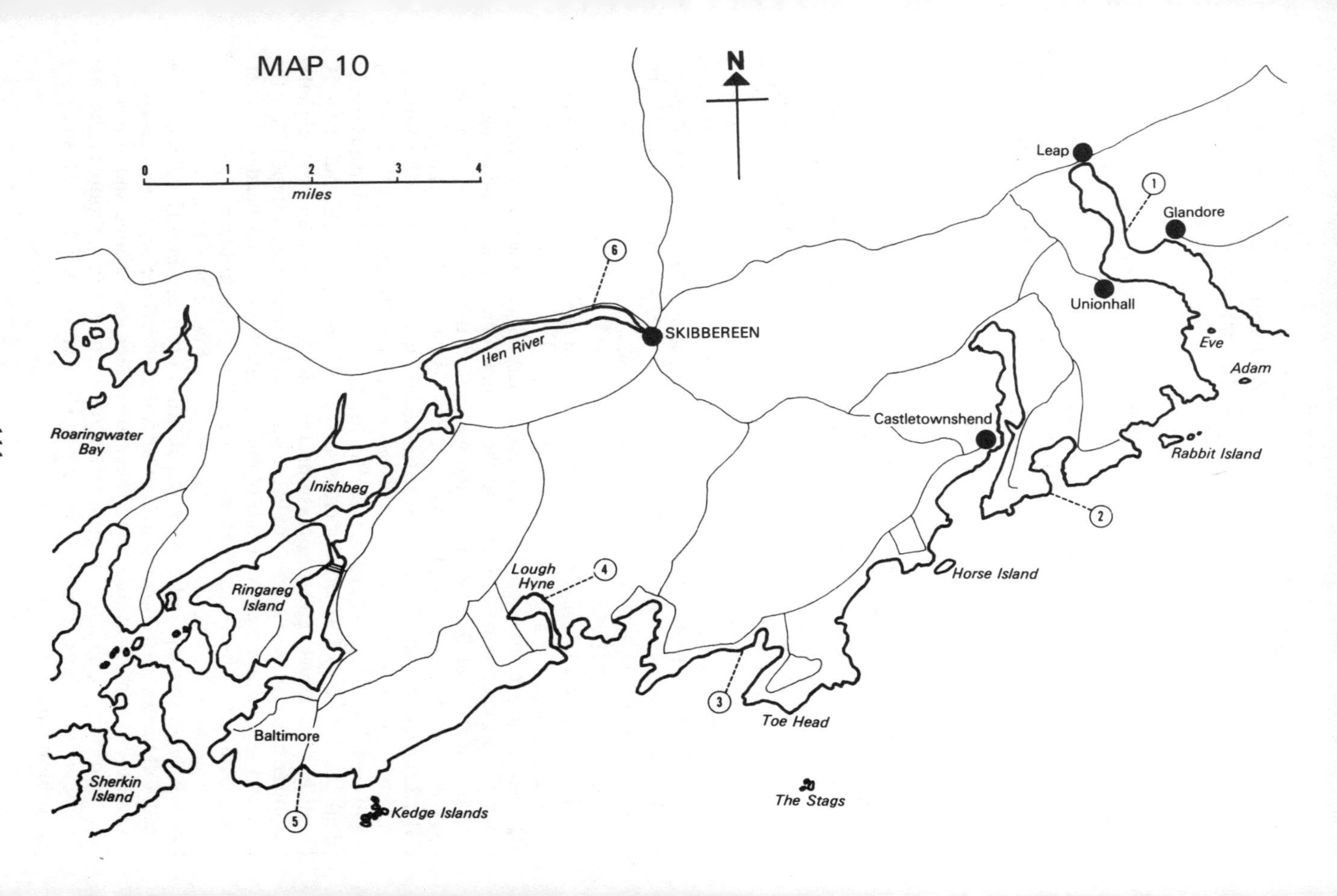

MAP 10
0
1
2
3
4
miles
N
Leap
1
Glandore
Unionhall
Eve
Adam
Rabbit Island
2
Castletownshend
Horse Island
SKIBBEREEN
6
Ilen River
Roaringwater Bay
Inishbeg
Ringareg Island
Lough Hyne
4
3
Toe Head
The Stags
Baltimore
5
Kedge Islands
Sherkin Island

There is unusual "deep sea shore angling" beneath oak trees and ivy for good conger, wrasse, pollack and very large mackerel. Occasional ling are taken here and mullet have been caught on flies from the eastern shore just inside the mouth. There are a few small piers at the northern end of the lake, and dogfish, whiting and mackerel are taken from them. This lake can fish very well in mild weather in the depths of winter.

South east of Baltimore, there is a small cove with a rather dilapidated pier [Map 10 (5)]. By clambering around the headland to the west of the pier, you can reach a good rock fishing mark for pollack, wrasse, conger, dogfish and of course mackerel in season. About a mile (1.6 km) west of Skibbereen a road bridge crosses the Ilen River, which is tidal to Skibbereen. Two hundred yards (182 metres) above this bridge [Map 10 (6)], there is a pool where mullet can be caught on floating bread crust at low water.

Top class deep sea angling is to be had off the south-western corner of the country. There are three harbours from which it is possible to fish—Castletownshend, Baltimore and Schull; only recently have charter boats become available at Baltimore and Castletownshend and Schull. At Baltimore also, small boats can be hired for fishing the fairly safe inshore waters behind the numerous islands for ray, tope, dogfish and flatfish.

Blue shark are numerous in season and such marks as the Stags, the Kedges, Cascanane Sound, Cape Clear, the Fastnet Light and Mizen Head have excellent fishing. Pollack, ling, conger, bream, cod, ray, turbot and gurnards are all in plentiful supply. There is also the occasional skate. There are a number of wrecks within reach of these ports; although they hold quality pollack, ling and conger, they are only rarely fished. A little boat fishing is available from Bantry for tope, ray, dogfish, conger and small pollack.

THE BEARA PENINSULA

Up until recently, there was very little known about the sea angling off this thirty five mile long (56. 3 km) rugged finger of land jutting out into the Atlantic between Kenmare River on the north and Bantry Bay on the south. An angling club was formed a few years ago and the fishing is beginning to be recognised.

The shore from Bantry to Castletownbere on the south coast is all virgin territory, except for the last few miles in Bear Haven itself. This is a stretch of water between the mainland and Bear Island, about a mile wide (1.6 km) and six miles long (9.6 km) with holes in the western end to 10 fathoms (18.2 metres). There are a lot of ray, conger and dogfish in the area, which is best fished from a small boat . East of Castletownbere a road runs down to an old military jetty. Dogfish, small conger and the occasional thornback can be taken from this jetty, but of far more interest are the mullet. Fish offal is sometimes dumped from the jetty and when this happens, shoals of mullet collect just off the head of the pier. Good numbers of fair sized mullet can be caught on fish bait.

The general deep sea angling out of Castletownbere can be quite good. Pollack, coalfish, ling and conger are plentiful off Black Ball Head and Crow Head. Off the western end of Dursey Island, there are three huge rocks called the Bull, the Cow and the Calf. These rocks are rather inaccessible and as a result are infrequently fished, but the general fishing around them is reputed to be first class. Quality pollack, ling, cod, coalfish and bream are taken and blue shark are plentiful in summer.

A cable car connects Dursey Island to the mainland and there is a little boat pier below the cable on the mainland side. Pollack, mackerel and wrasse can be caught here and off the rocks immediately to the north.

A tremendous current thunders through Dursey Sound, both on ebb and flood, so punt fishermen beware! Car top dinghies and the like should be kept well clear of this area.

Below Allihies in Ballydonegan Bay, on the northern side of the headland, there is a nice surf beach. Some bass have been taken from it as well as flounder, small turbot, bull huss, lesser spotted dogfish and the occasional ray. From Allihies east to Ardgroom is again largely untried. However, there are numerous good looking rock fishing areas. Some pollack and wrasse are caught around Ardgroom caves on the western side of the headland running out to Dogs Point.

Between Lauragh and Callorus, moving into Co. Kerry, the main road crosses a few sea inlets and occasinally bass and tiny pollack are taken spinning from the bridges [Map 11 (1)]. Fishing at high water can produce nice conger from Buna Pier [Map 11 (2)]. The occasional bass and flounder are taken off the tiny beach in Ardea [Map 11 (3)]. Pollack, wrasse and an odd tope are caught from the rocks at Reenafreach Point [Map 11 (4)], about seven miles (11.2 km) west of Kenmare. At Killagh [Map 11 (5)], two miles (3.2 km) from Kenmare, there is a little bottom fishing for dogfish and ray.

3. KERRY

The Ring of Kerry is best known for its rugged scenic beauty. Using Killarney as a base, the usual tourist trip is a drive north west to Killorglin, out along the north coast to Cahirciveen, south to Derrynane, east to Kenmare and north again to Killarney. It is without doubt a truly magnificent drive with its mountain passes, cliffs, islands and beaches. Any tourist would consider it time well spent just admiring the beautiful scenery on this peninsula. If, however, he were a sea angler, he could easily get lost for a week on the Ring sampling first class fishing every day in these fantastic surroundings.

This area is best known for the quality of its deep sea fishing, although the rock and beach fishing are of an equally high standard. Boats take anglers out from a number of small harbours such as Sneem and Westcove on the south coast and Derrynane, Ballinskelligs, Valentia Island and Caherciveen on the west. There are plenty of blue shark in the area, but it would normally be necessary to go out beyond Lamb's Head to catch these. The journey would be considered beyond the reach of boats based in the Sneem area.

The general bottom fishing off the west coast is on a par with the best in the British Isles. There is a patch of rough ground about five miles (8 km) west of Bray Head which comes up to 18 fathoms (32.9 metres) from a base of 50 (91.4 metres).

The tides can be very strong on this ground, but common skate well in excess of 100 lbs (45 Kg), big ling, conger, cod, bull huss and a variety of smaller species are regularly taken on it from an anchored boat. The same types of fish are caught around the Skellig Rocks; a particularly good place for skate is just to the south of the Lemon Rock. Other well known marks lie off Puffin Island and the

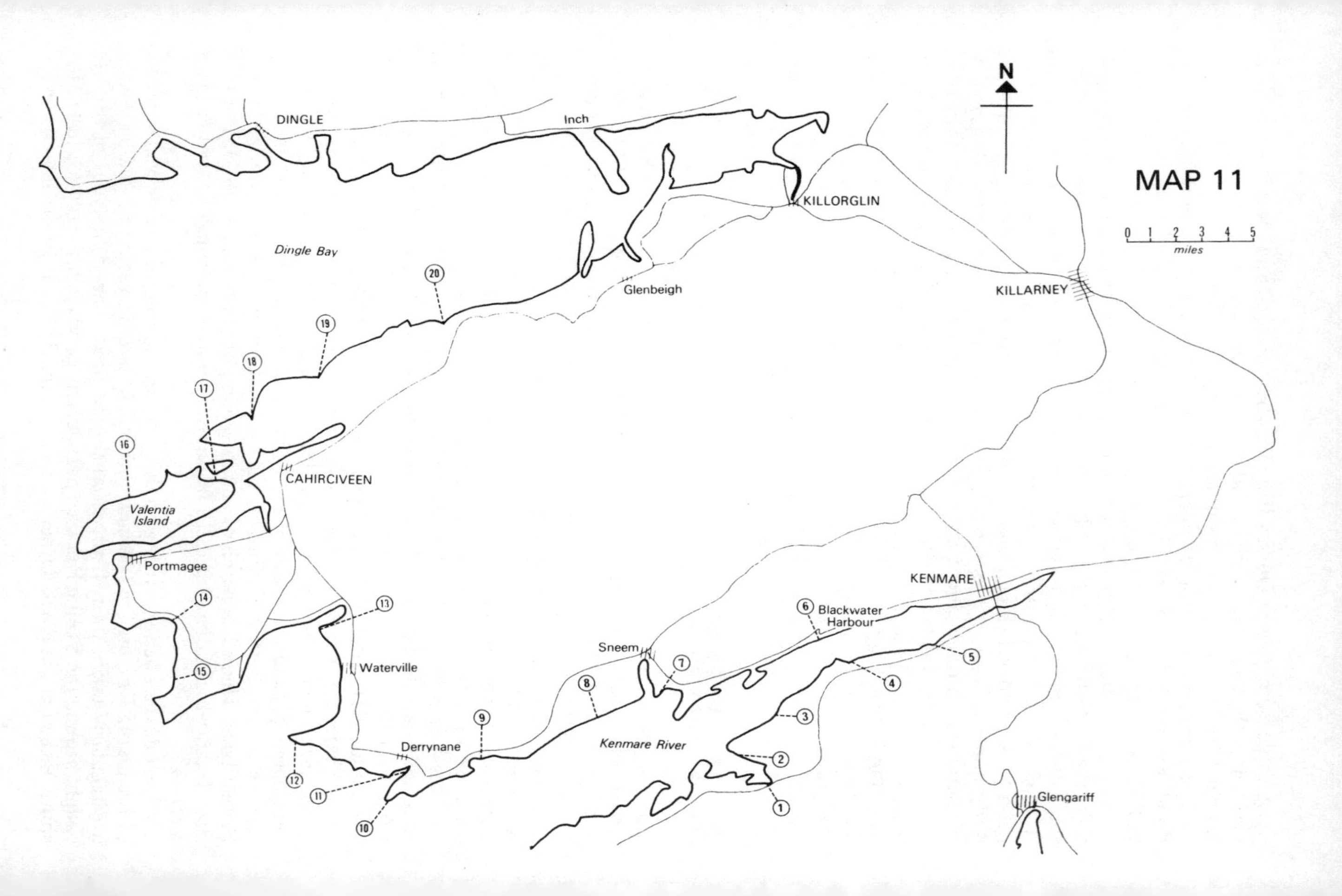
MAP 11
0 1 2 3 4 5
miles
N
DINGLE
Inch
KILLORGLIN
Dingle Bay
Glenbeigh
KILLARNEY
CAHIRCIVEEN
Valentia Island
Portmagee
Waterville
Derrynane
Sneem
Kenmare River
KENMARE
Blackwater Harbour
Glengariff
1
2
3
4
5
6
7
8
9
10
11
12
13
14
15
16
17
18
19
20

north coast of Valentia Island, where there are numerous 'hot spots' such as the Coastguard patch which rises up to 10 fathoms (18.2 metres) from 30 fathoms (54.6 metres).

Giving a list of fish taken regularly off the Ring of Kerry would be like going to an encyclopaedia and listing all the fish available in the British Isles. It was while tagging blue shark off the Skelligs in an effort to trace their migration that I established a personal record in July, 1973. With a crew of two using rod and line, we tagged blue shark at the rate of eleven an hour!

The shore angling is best on the west and north coast, but on the south coast, about eight miles (12.8 km) west of Kenmare, the road crosses the River Blackwater at a rather dangerous bend. Just beyond the bridge there is a road to the north which turns back under the main road and leads down to Blackwater Pier [Map 11 (6)] where there are ray, conger, small pollack and sea trout from the pier itself and a little to the west.

A few miles to the east of Sneem, a road goes south to the Oysterbed Pier [Map 11 (7)]. Conger, ray, ballan wrasse and at times, mullet can be taken on bread and small pieces of fish. At Gleesk [Map 11 (8)], there are small pollack, dogfish, ray and conger. Just inside Lamb's Head, there are a number of rock marks for small pollack, mackerel and wrasse, particularly close to an hotel on the south of the main road [Map 11 (9)].

At Caherdaniel, a road runs down along the headland to a small and beautifully peaceful pier just inside Lamb's Head. A fifteen minute walk directly west brings you to the tip of the headland [Map 11 (10)]. There is deep water in a channel running between the mainland and a small island about 150 yards (137 metres) offshore. Fishing here can produce wrasse, pollack, mackerel, small conger and occasional ray. I have never taken a tope here, but I imagine that they are a serious possibility in early summer. Around the little pier and further east towards the estuary, there are a number of obvious rock marks where pollack and mackerel can be taken spinning during the summer.

The inner portion of Derrynane Bay is a sandy backwater which almost completely dries out. The entrance is at the southern end of a fine clean strand. This surf beach [Map 11 (11)] is particularly beautiful and can be very good for bass and flounder, notably on the southern side fishing out between some large rocky outcrops. It can be a very good beach in autumn. Lugworm are collected in the tiny harbour of Derrynane, close to the museum dedicated to the Irish pacifist patriot, Daniel O'Connell, who lived in the area.

From this area also, boats take tourists on day trips to the Skellig Rock, where there are many stone dwellings of the beehive type erected by the early Christians.

From Derrynane, the road goes north through the breathtaking pass of Coomakista and down into Waterville on the shore of Ballinskelligs Bay. At the southern extremity of this bay is Hog's Head, where there is good rock fishing, particularly on the southern side of the headland [Map 11 (12)], for pollack, mackerel and wrasse. About two miles (3.2 km) north of Waterville, the Inny River flows into the sea through the middle of a long, curved beach which runs from Ballinskellings to Waterville. There is good bass fishing all along this beach [Map 11 (13)], but it is best for about a mile (1.6 km) either side of the river. Plaice and flounder can also be taken at high water below the carpark in

Waterville. Lugworm can be collected on the northern side of the estuary inside the beach.

Bolus Head is on the north western tip of the bay and from here the coast runs north into St Finian's Bay [Map 11 (14)], where there is a tiny beach, good for bass and flatfish and fishing best in autumn. About two miles (3.2 km) south of the beach, there is an excellent rock fishing mark [Map 11 (15)]. A cul-de-sac runs south towards Bolus Head and on the brow of the hill there is a temporary car park. Straight west from this is a rocky point; fishing on the north western side can produce excellent catches of pollack to 8 lbs (3.6 kg) and good wrasse. The bottom is very rough here and quite unsuitable for bottom fishing.

From here north to Portmagee is mostly unsuitable for fishing because of cliffs, but on the north coast of Valentia Island (accessible by road bridge at Portmagee) there is a well known rock mark called Coloo [Map 11 (16)]. Fishing here for pollack, mackerel and wrasse during the summer months is really excellent.

On the eastern side of the island is the village of Knightstown and just to the north west of it, directly below the shipping beacon, is a mark for ray, conger and mullet [Map 11 (17)]. Good fishing for ray can be had from small boats in Valentia Harbour and some small ray can be taken from the mainland around Lough Kay, inside Dolus Head.

From Dolus Head the coast runs east to Glenbeigh and is largely inaccessible except at Cooncrome Harbour [Map 11 (18)], where there is rock fishing on the western side for pollack and mackerel, and at Coonanna Harbour [Map 11 (19)], where flatfish and the occasional ray are taken from the pier. At Kells [Map 11 (20)], pollack, mackerel and wrasse can be caught from the rocks at Kings Head. Just west of Glenbeigh [Map 12 (1)], a long narrow spit of sand dunes called 'Rossbeigh' runs straight north for three miles (4.8 km); the western side of this spit is a magnificent bass beach. Flatfish and occasional ray and tope are also

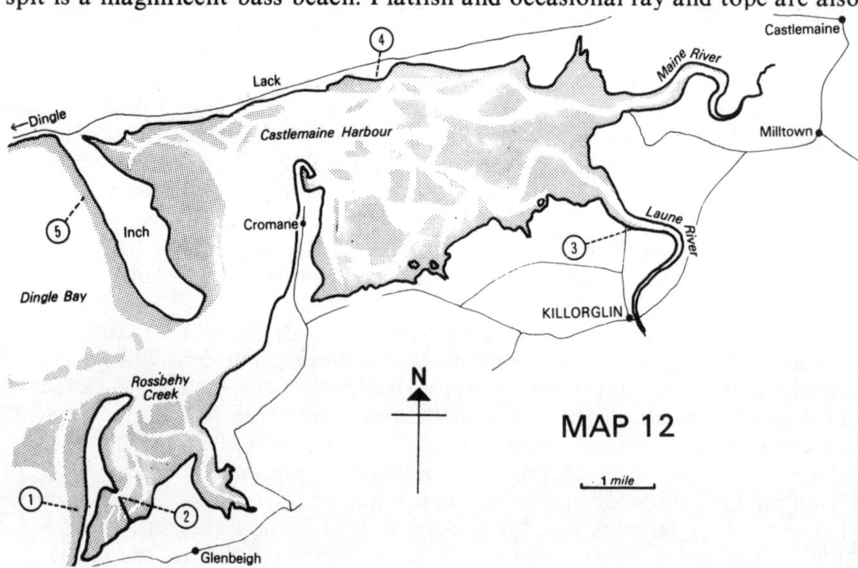

taken. Inside the sand dunes is an old causeway with a breech [Map 12 (2)] where bass can be taken spinning in the channel at low water. Lugworm are plentiful in the area. During early summer there is excellent tope fishing to be had here from small boats hired at Cromane, four miles east (6.4 km) of Glenbeigh.

The best mark is about 150 yards (137 metres) off the tower on the end of Rossbeigh beach; the best time is early flood tide, but be warned—the tides can be very strong.

The little pier of Ballycasane [Map 12 (3)] is just two miles north (3.2 km) of Killorglin on the Laune estuary. The river is about three hundred yards (274 metres) wide at this point, but at low water, a mud bank dries out in the middle. Once the flood tide covers this bank there can be good bass and flounder fishing from the pier itself or from the bank directly opposite. Some bass and sea trout are also taken spinning here. There is an interesting monument on the pier dedicated to the men who, on their way to meet Sir Roger Casement when he landed further north in 1916, took a wrong turn in Killorglin, drove off the end of the pier and were drowned.

THE DINGLE PENINSULA

The Dingle Peninsula is the most northerly of the five 'fingers' of land jutting out into the Atlantic from the south west corner. The peninsula is about 35 miles (56.3 km) long and varies in width from eight to fifteen miles (12.8–24.1 km). The scenery is superb and so too is the fishing, particularly the bass angling from the magnificent beaches which has deteriorated somewhat of late and the rock fishing for wrasse, pollack and conger. A notable feature of this area is that bass can be caught all through the year; the peak comes in late autumn and early spring. The only time it tends to go off a little is in July and August, when the rock fishing is at its best. Fish can be taken in virtually all weather conditions because there are beaches facing in almost every direction.

On the southern side, the inner section of Dingle Bay is a wide and meandering estuary, the confluence of the Laune, the Maine, the Behy and the Caragh rivers. The first fishing point is in this estuary, approximately midway between Castlemaine and Inch. A short dirt road leads down to the water at a point where the channel from the River Maine cuts close inshore [Map 12 (4)]. The fishing is best for two hours either side of high water, when bass and flounder can be taken on lugworm and clam. There are also occasional sea trout taken spinning. It is essential to fish well into the channel here.

Inch Strand [Map 12 (5)] is a long, clean storm beach stretching about three and a half miles (5.6 km) south by south east. Access is easy from the main road and there is a car park just below an hotel at the northern end. It is possible to drive onto the beach, but be warned, cars sink in the soft sand, particularly near the southern end. The bass fishing here can be tremendous, especially just below the car park and for about a mile south (1.6 km). It fishes best when there is a nice surf rolling in, but when conditions are calm it is well worth fishing by night. Some flatfish and the occasional codling are also taken as is the odd tope in autumn. Lugworm can be dug at the back of the sandhills. On the rocks immediately west of the beach, there is some spinning for bass in calm conditions. I personally have had catches of twenty bass in a day on Inch Strand.

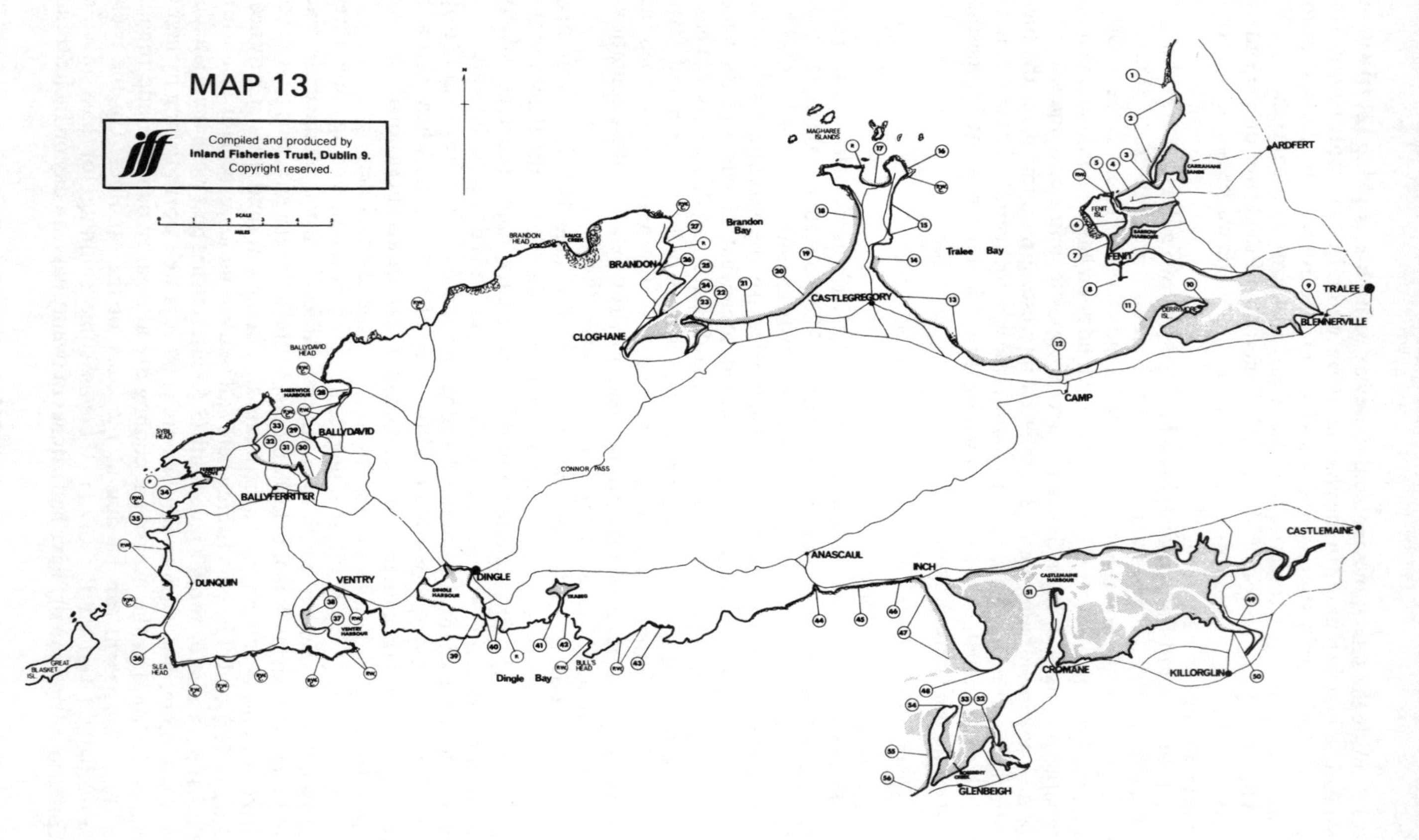
MAP 13
Compiled and produced by
Inland Fisheries Trust, Dublin 9.
Copyright reserved.
SCALE
MILES
ARDFERT
FENIT
FENIT ISL.
TRALEE
BLENNERVILLE
DERRYMORE ISL.
MAGHAREE ISLANDS
Brandon Bay
Tralee Bay
BRANDON HEAD
BRANDON
CASTLEGREGORY
CLOGHANE
CAMP
BALLYDAVID HEAD
SMERWICK HARBOUR
BALLYDAVID
SYBIL HEAD
BALLYFERRITER
CONNOR PASS
DUNQUIN
VENTRY
VENTRY HARBOUR
DINGLE
DINGLE HARBOUR
ANASCAUL
INCH
CASTLEMAINE
CASTLEMAINE HARBOUR
GREAT BLASKET ISL.
SLEA HEAD
Dingle Bay
BULL'S HEAD
CROMANE
KILLORGLIN
GLENBEIGH

About three miles (4.8 km) west of Inch [IFT Map (44)], the Annascaul River enters the sea and there is spinning for bass and sea trout at its mouth. Bass can be taken bottom fishing here, but the ground is not very clean.

At Minard, there is some shore fishing for thornback ray on a small shingle beach. At high water, there is a bank of shingle, well within casting range, on which the ray feed. The occasional bass is caught as well. There are a few rock fishing marks about a mile west (1.6 km) of the beach for pollack and good sized wrasse, but access is rather difficult.

Four miles (6.4 km) east of Dingle town is a large land-locked salt lake which enters the sea at Trabeg. Immediately east of the outflow [IFT Map (42)], there is a very nice steep-to beach on which there is good bass fishing, mostly when there is a gentle south west wind blowing. Ray are often taken here as well. From the rocky outcrop at the western end of this beach there is spinning for bass, pollack and sea trout. On the western side of the inlet, you can spin in the channel for bass and sea trout for a few hours on either side of low water. On the seaward side of this beach [IFT Map (41)] there is surf fishing for bass, flounder and thornback ray. A lighthouse stands on the eastern side of the mouth of Dingle harbour. Spinning and float fishing for small pollack, mackerel and wrasse from the ledge just south of the light can be very pleasant on a summer's evening. Just inside Beenbane Head there is more rock fishing for pollack and wrasse.

In Dingle town there is a pier from which a lot of commercial fishing boats work. When the boats come in, they invariably throw out some little bits of fish offal and this acts as ground bait for mullet.

These mullet can be taken on small hooks with tiny bits of fish bait from the end of the pier. A plentiful supply of lugworm and shore crab can be had at Milltown Bridge. At extreme low water sping tides, there are razorfish to be had in the harbour.

Five miles west (8 km) of Dingle lies Ventry harbour, which is in fact a south east facing bay. The northern and western shoreline [IFT Map (38)] is a long shallow beach from which dogfish, flounder and the odd bass are taken. It is best fished in a howling south or south east gale, particularly near one of the many streams which flow onto the beach. I have never come away from this beach fishless.

The Old Fort is a prehistoric construction about midway between Ventry and Slea Head; the fort itself is not visible from the road but immediately to the east, there is an obvious rocky ledge to which access is fairly easy. Good fishing can be had from this spot, particularly on the western side of the rock, for pollack, wrasse and small conger in about five fathoms (9.1 metres) of water. Only the very agile will gain access to the water around Slea Head, but for amateur mountain climbers there is excellent fishing for wrasse, pollack and in high summer the occasional red bream, directly below the religious monument and a little to the east.

About a mile north (1.6 km) of Slea Head is tiny Coomeenoole beach [IFT Map (36)], probably the most beautiful stretch of sand in the country, but not the most productive angling spot. A tremendous surf comes crashing in here in a south west wind; the only fish reported is the odd big bass, usually over 8 lbs (3.6 kg).

The beach is protected from the north by Dunmore Head. There is very good spinning and bottom fishing for pollack, wrasse and mackerel from the very western tip of this headland. Access is by way of a half mile (0.8 km) walk along the northern brow of a 300 ft (91.4 metres) hill, but the fishing can be well worth the effort. About a mile to the north is Dunquin Pier, from which there are some good conger to be taken, particularly at high water. From the rocks just north of the pier, there is spinning for pollack and mackerel and float fishing for wrasse up to 5 lbs (2.3 kg).

The first turn left after Dunquin village brings you down to a car park near a stream. Walking a quarter of a mile (0.4 km) to the north west you reach an old unused pier. Immediately north of this, there is a ridge of rock running out to sea. From about two hours before high water there can be excellent pollack fishing on the northern side of this ridge. Pollack of 4 and 5 lbs (1.8–2.3 kg) are common and the water is three or four fathoms (5.4–7.3 metres) deep.

About three quarters of a mile (1.2 km) further north again is what looks like an old school house perched on the cliff top. It is in fact the school which David Lean built for the filming of his epic, 'Ryan's Daughter'. Directly below the school, amid the most magnificent scenery, is pollack and wrasse territory. The clamber down the cliff face is not too steep, but be careful, especially when the rocks are wet.

Good sized wrasse are numerous here and there is also good pollack and mackerel fishing. If you are prepared to lose a fair amount of tackle, try the bottom for conger. Catches of forty to fifty wrasse and pollack are possible.

Clogher beach [IFT Map (35)] is largely unproductive except for the odd ray, but from the rocks on the northern tip there is spinning for pollack, mackerel and garfish, as well as bottom fishing for wrasse and conger. The rock strata is vertical here and very rugged. The best and most consistent wrasse fishing in the entire area is to be had on the southern side of Clogher beach about half a mile (0.8 km) out on the headland, but access is very difficult and should not be attempted without a local guide who knows the track down. About half a mile (0.8 km) further north, towards Ferriter's Cove [IFT Map (34)], there are a number of prominent rocky platforms where wrasse and pollack can be taken. From the rocks on the southern fringe of Ferriter's Cove, bass can be taken spinning from time to time. Good sized flounder can be numerous in autumn on the beach itself around high water where a small stream flows in.

After Sybil Head the coast falls back eastwards to Tralee and the steep cliffs make rock fishing impossible. However, there are two large sandy bays, the first of which is Smerwick Harbour, a large and in places deep (up to 10 fathoms—18.2 metres) north-facing bay which fishes best in a north or north west wind. There are three fine beaches running along the inner section of the bay, the Black Strand, the Wine Strand and Ballinrannig Strand [IFT Maps (30–32)].

Ballinrannig is the most consistent of the three strands for bass and flatfish when there is a good surf. Lugworm are plentiful at the western end. Some specimen sized flounders are taken regularly towards the eastern end of the beach near the freshwater culvert.

If you are fishing the Black Strand and come across the odd human skull, don't be too alarmed. In 1580, at nearby Dun An Oir fort, there was a massacre of over six hundred Spanish and Irish soldiers and the poor creatures were simply dumped into the sea. Even now the odd skeleton is uncovered by the shifting sand dunes.

Conger to 15 lbs (6.8 kg) can be taken from the pier at Ballydavid [IFT Map (29)] and from Brandon Creek, locally called 'Cuas', from which St Brendan the Navigator is reputed to have sailed on his voyage of discovery to America.

On the eastern side of Mount Brandon lies magnificent Brandon Bay, some ten unbroken miles (16 km) of what must surely be the best bass beach in the British Isles though of late stocks appear to be declining. At the eastern end of the beach lies Cloghane estuary, which is really a large back water into which two small streams flow. There is nice fishing for school bass and specimen sized flounders in the estuary just below Cloghane School [IFT Map (24)] from just before low water through the first two to three hours of the flood. Soft crab are numerous among the rocks here. You can spin and bottom fish this estuary; bottom fishing with lugworm is the most productive.

The main beach is crescent shaped, stretching from the Black Rock [IFT Map (23)] to Faghamore. There can be some nice spinning for bass on the north western face of the Black Rock around low water. There are as many theories as there are anglers about the best locations and the best times to fish on the beach itself. One suggestion is, given a good surf, to fish the beach just east of the Black Rock for an hour on either side of low water and at Fermoyle [IFT Map (22)] for two hours either side of high water. The main period of flood and ebb is best fished at Kilcummin [IFT Map (21)] where there are a few streams running onto the beach. The north eastern end of the beach can also be good, particularly behind the grotto near Fagamore [IFT Map (18)], but anywhere along this beach will produce bass and flounder in certain conditions. Lugworm and clam are the most used baits and there is a plentiful supply of these in the back strand at Fermoyle and Cloghane.

Scraggane Bay [IFT Map (17)] at the northern tip of the Magharee's Peninsula has a north facing beach from which bass and flatfish and the occasional ray can be taken. There is some rock fishing on the western tip of the bay for pollack and wrasse. On the eastern side of the peninsula there is another long crescent-shaped beach roughly facing north east. It does not often have a surf, but when there is you can have some nice bass fishing at the mouth of the stream which flows out of Lough Gill [IFT Map (14)] and particularly about two miles (3.2 km) further east [IFT Map (13)], where another stream flows in.
There is excellent deep sea and inshore fishing available around the Dingle

Peninsula from Dingle, Smerwick and Scraggane Pier near Castlegregory. From Dingle there are plenty of blue shark during the summer months and general bottom fishing, particularly on the reefs which are plentiful around the Blasket Islands. Regularly caught are very big pollack and coalfish, ling, bream, conger, various rays, haddock and common skate. The same type of fishing is available from Smerwick and the occasional porbeagle shark and halibut have been reported. The best fishing in this area is to be had on the mark known locally as 'Green Fields'. From Scraggane Pier you can fish the highly recommended Tralee Bay described in the next section. Inshore fishing in Dingle Harbour and just outside will produce ray, small pollack and dabs. In Smerwick there are bass, ray, flounder and dabs.

FENIT AND BALLYBUNION

The town of Fenit is about nine miles west (14.4 km) of Tralee on the northern shore of Tralee Bay. A large portion of the inner bay (east of a line between Fenit and Derrymore Island) dries out, but at Fenit itself an ocean pier juts out almost half a mile (0.8 km) into deep water. The bay is well known in the angling world for its excellent inshore fishing and well-run boats can be hired locally.

The bay provides large numbers of specimen sized ray (particularly undulates), common skate, tope and monkfish, but there is also reasonable pollack and conger fishing. A large number of cartilaginous fish have been tagged in this area as part of the IFT's investigations into marine sport fishes, so if you come across a tagged fish, please record the number, release the fish, unharmed if possible and report it.

From the pier itself [IFT Map] there is really good fishing. Not only are bass, pollack, ray, conger and dogfish regularly taken, but also tope, the occasional monkfish and common skate well over 100 lbs (45 kg). The latter are taken from the extreme end at the southern side. It is well worth spending a few hours here; the pier is ideal for the lazy angler, who can drive his car right to the end.

Shore angling in the area is also quite good. There is some surf fishing for bass on the western side of the causeway running out to Fenit Island [Map 14 (1)]. To the east of the island lies Barrow Harbour, which dries out except for small streams. Bass, flounder, tope and small turbot can be taken from either side of the narrow mouth [Map 14 (2, 3)]. From the rocks at the northern end of the island [Map 14 (4)], pollack, mackerel and wrasse are plentiful in summer. Just north of the entrance to Barrow Harbour, there is a north west facing beach [Map 14 (5) about a mile long (1.6 km) which offers surf fishing for bass and flatfish. Carrahane Sands is another inlet with a narrow mouth at which bass and flatfish can be taken at low water [Map 14 (6)].

Just inside the mouth, there is a deep pool which holds bass, flatfish and occasionally tope. Turbot can be plentiful at times. Lugworm can be collected at Carrahane Sands, Barrow Harbour and at Fenit itself. Immediately west of the pier, there is a small beach on which sandeel can be collected at low water. These are important for turbot fishing.

From Carrahane the coast runs north to Ballyheigue, a distance of about five miles (8 km). It is mostly a westerly-facing surf beach with the odd patch of rough ground. One such place is the Black Rock [Map 14 (8)] (about two miles—3.2 km—south of Ballyheigue) where bass can be taken spinning on the seaward side, particularly around low water. Bass and flatfish can be caught in the surf almost anywhere along this beach, but mainly just south of the Black Rock, where there is also lug available [Map 14 (7)].

North of Ballyheigue Bay lies Kerry Head, an area I have fished only once, for just a few hours. I fished strictly for wrasse and myself and a few friends landed about sixty, up to 4 lbs (1.8 kg). The north western side of the headland looks like having enormous potential for quality rock fishing, but access is by way of a dirt track which could be difficult in wet conditions.

The next point north of here of interest to anglers is the Cashen River mouth [Map 15 (1)] about three miles (4.8 km) south of Ballybunion. At either side of the mouth, on the beach itself bass can be taken spinning and bottom fishing. It fishes best either side of low water.

At both sides of the narrow entrance, particularly at the most southerly tip of the golf course, there can at times be excellent spinning and bottom fishing for bass. Just opposite, on the southern side, is a good place for flounder.

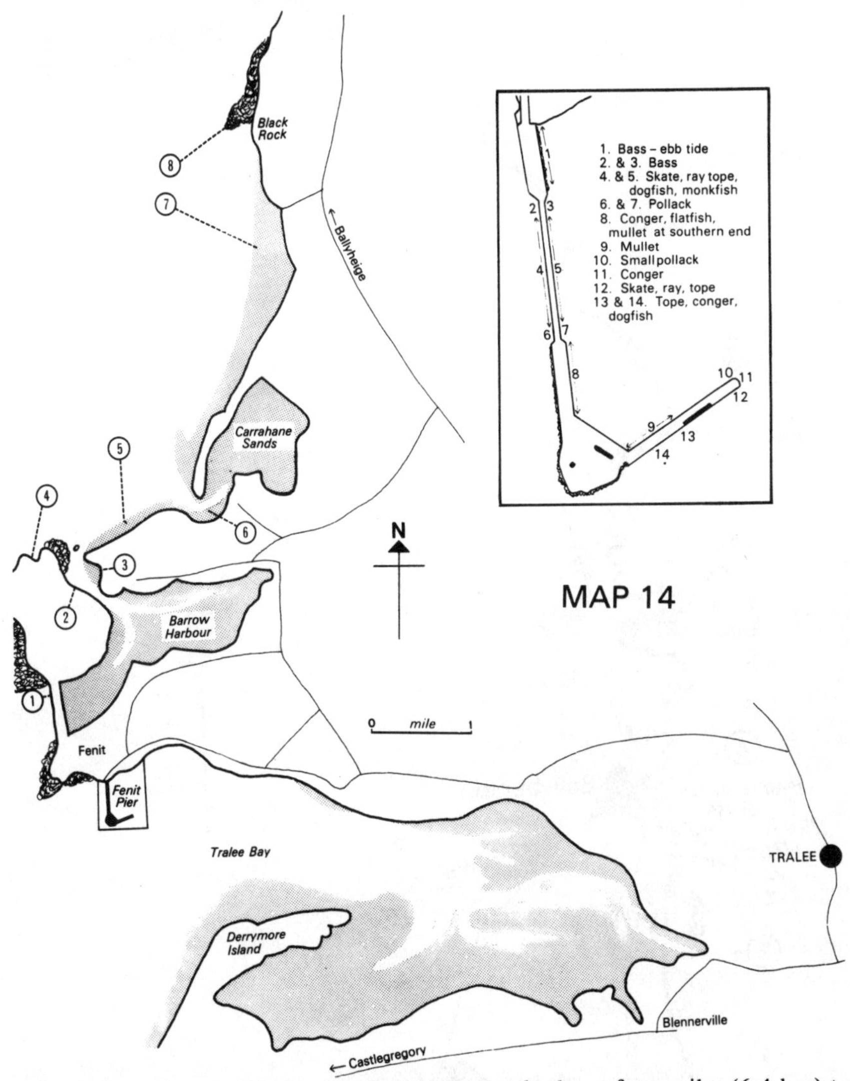

From the Cashen River, the shore runs north about four miles (6.4 km) to Leck Point in a series of beaches and rocky headlands. The first beach [Map 15 (2)], about two miles long (3.2 km), ends at Black Rock just south of Ballybunion town. It is a fine surf beach which offers good bass fishing almost everywhere but particularly just south of the Black Rock [Map 15 (3)] where flounder and small turbot are also taken. If the dedicated angler can tear himself away from the

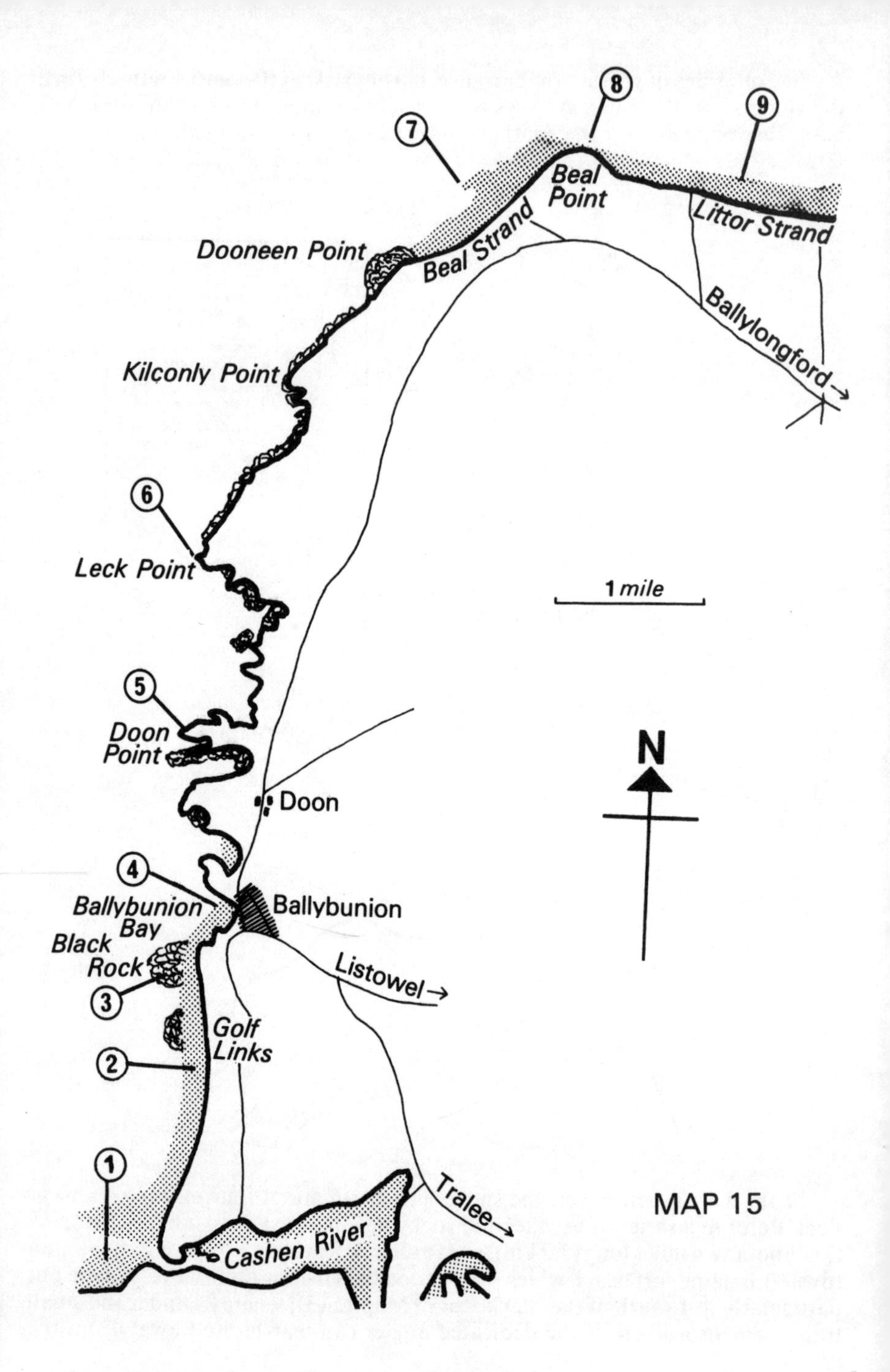
8
9
7
Beal
Point
Littor Strand
Beal Strand
Dooneen Point
Ballylongford→
Kilconly Point
6
Leck Point
1 mile
5
Doon
Point
N
Doon
4
Ballybunion
Bay
Ballybunion
Black
Rock
3
Listowel→
Golf
Links
2
1
Tralee→
Cashen River
MAP 15

hilarious carnival atmosphere of Ballybunion in summer and bring himself down to the beach, especially near the caves [Map 15 (4)], he will be rewarded with nice bass and flounder fishing. From the Black Rock itself and further north, at Doon and Leck Points [Map 15 (5, 6)], there is some good rock fishing for pollack, mackerel, wrasse, conger and dogfish during the summer months.

North of Leck Point, the land slopes away to the east into the Shannon estuary, where there is very little angling apart from Beal Strand and Littor Strand [Map 15 (7, 9)] at the mouth, both of which can be quite good for bass and flatfish. Between these two beaches, at Beal Point [Map 15 (8)], the channel comes close in to the shore and there are bass, turbot, flounder and plaice in the deep water. The Shannon east of this has little of interest to anglers, except at Tarbert. If you have to wait for the ferry across to Clare, a pleasant hour can be spent spinning for bass at the ferry pier or bottom or float fishing in the nearby power station hot water outlet.

4. CLARE

The small pier of Cappagh [Map 16 (1)] is on the Clare side of the Shannon estuary near Kilrush. Fishing from it can be quite good on the flood tide. Conger up to 40 lbs (18 kg) are regularly taken from the back of the pier (i.e. the western side) and from the southern end, conger, dogfish and sometimes monkfish can be caught. The large inlet of Poulnasherry is just west of Kilrush. On the western side of the narrow mouth [Map 16 (2)] (on Querrin Strand) there is really good fishing at low water and early flood for bass, flatfish, ray and the odd tope and monkfish. In a howling gale from the west and north west, this is frequently the only place fishable on the Clare coast and it is under such conditions that it fishes best.

The coast from Loop Head to Kilkee consists for the most part of high steep cliffs and is mostly unfishable, except by mountain climbers. However at the Bridges of Ross [Map 16 (3)], well worth seeing for its beauty alone, there is rock fishing for pollack, mackerel and big wrasse. At Kilkee [Map 16 (4)], a small rock rimmed bay protects a small strand from which some big bass have been taken, mostly at night. Pollack, mackerel and wrasse can be caught from the rocks just south of the bay.

The next point of interest north of here is the noted rock fishing mark of Baltard [Map 16 (5)], locally called the 'Blue Pool', about three miles (4.8 km) west of Doonbeg. Access is not easy and fishing space limited, but the angling is superb. But be careful: it is an extremely dangerous place when there is a heavy swell running. There are 20 fathoms (36.5 metres) of water straight off the rocks and the bottom is a mixture of sand and stone. Excellent pollack, mackerel, wrasse and conger fishing can be had here. On a few occasions porbeagle shark have been landed, and they are frequently encountered in July and August. An indication of the reliability of the fishing in this locality is that the local commercial mackerel fishermen use it each morning during the summer, selling their catch in the local towns and villages.

From Doonbeg to Seafield Pier (just inside Mutton Island) the coast runs almost due north for about five miles (8 km). There are four westerly facing surf beaches on this stretch, separated by patches of low rough. The most southerly is

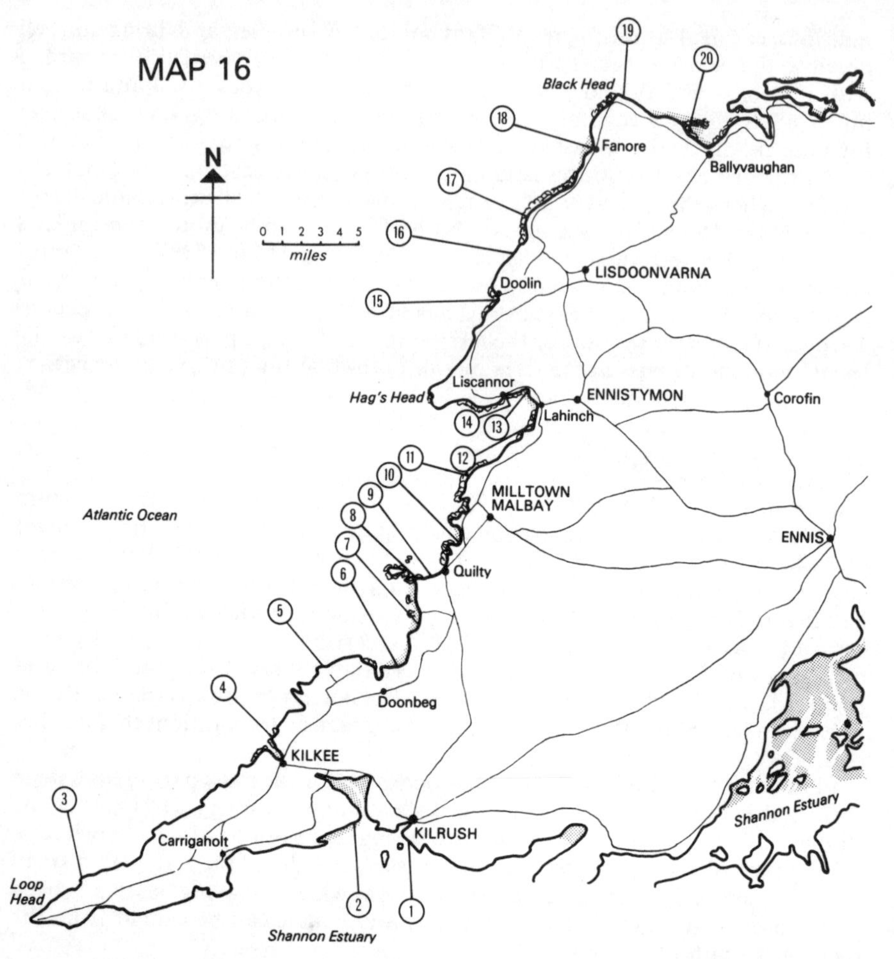

Doughmore Strand [Map 16 (6)], which is a long, curved steep beach; it is a good surf beach for bass, flatfish and ray, particularly at the southern end where a stream flows on to the beach. The other beaches are also quite good for bass and flatfish, particularly at Lough Donnell [Map 16 (7)] near the culvert; it fishes best before and after high water.

Just west of Seafield Pier [Map 16 (8)] a ridge of low rough runs straight west and small pollack and bass can be caught spinning off the northern side. To the east of the pier there is a sheltered north facing bay with low rough fronting the beach [Map 16 (9)]. This beach in a northerly wind can be good for bass, taken spinning and bottom fishing. Lugworm can be dug easily at the pier itself.

At Spanish Point [Map 16 (10)], there is a beautiful west-facing surf beach which can be quite good for bass and flatfish. At the southern end of the beach the Bealaclugga River flows in and at the northern end lies the Black Rock, off which there can be excellent spinning for bass. Tope are often encountered in this area as well. Some sea trout can be taken spinning around the mouth of the Bealaclugga River.

Green Island [Map 16 (11)], the south western tip of Liscannor Bay, is probably the most famous rock fishing mark in the British Isles, since it was here that, a few years ago, a local creamery manager, Jack Shine, regularly took porbeagle shark from the rocks. His largest, a shark of 145 lbs (65.3 kg) was taken in August, 1967 on 31 lbs (14.5 kg) monofilament, a feat which has yet to be surpassed. If anyone has the time and patience to try this type of fishing, then Green Island is the place and July and August the time of year.

Apart from shark there is very pleasant fishing for mackerel, pollack, wrasse and conger in about six fathoms (10.9 metres) with a very rough bottom.

On the inner margin of Liscannor Bay, there are two beaches at Lahinch and Cregg, both of which can be quite good for bass and flatfish. Cregg [Map 16 (12)] on the southern end is a rather calm, shallow beach, never getting much surf. It can be excellent for flounder fishing.

Lahinch fishes well along its length but particularly at either side of the mouth of the Inagh River [Map 16 (13)] which flows into the northern end of the beach. Mullet can be plentiful at times in Liscannor Harbour [Map 16 (14)] and are taken on bread and fish baits. There are lugworm immediately east of the harbour, on the northern side of the mouth of the Inagh River and at Cregg Strand. It was in Liscannor village that John P. Holland (1841–1914), inventor of the submarine, was born.

North of Liscannor Bay stand the magnificent Cliffs of Moher. These 700 ft (210 metres) high cliffs are of enormous interest to the tourist, but not to the angler, although I did hear of one man trying to fish from the top. I can only conlude that he was short-sighted and could not see the bottom, but I never heard if he caught a fish!

At Doolin [Map 16 (15)], apart from a famous pub which offers fine traditional and folk music to holiday makers, there is a very steep beach with bass, flatfish and dogfish. It is a beach which, even in the calmest conditions, always has a good surf running. There is some spinning for bass and pollack off the rocks at the northern end. From here to Fanore, a distance of ten miles (16 km), the shoreline is rocky and good rock fishing marks are scattered all along it, notably at Ard-na-Glaise [Map 16 (16)] and Ballyreen [Map 16 (17)], where mackerel, garfish, wrasse, pollack, dogfish and the occasional tope and porbeagle are taken.

At Fanore itself [Map 16 (18)], there is a very nice gently sloping beach on which bass and flatfish are taken in the surf and also from the rocks at the southern end. Ray are also taken from the rocks, particularly at night.

Black Head, near the lighthouse [Map 16 (19)], has good rock fishing for mackerel, pollack, wrasse, dogfish and conger. The local angling club holds regular weekend competitions here. From Black Head the coast turns east into Galway Bay and apart from some bass and flatfish near Ballyvaughan [Map 16 (20)], very little angling has been done in the inner reaches of the bay.

Deep sea angling is available all along the Clare coast, notably from Liscannor, Seafield and Ballyvaughan where there are boats and tackle for hire. The chief quarry is the porbeagle shark and there is also excellent fishing for blue shark, tope, pollack and general bottom fish.

5. GALWAY BAY TO SLIGO BAY

When an angler sees the sun go down in Galway Bay from the northern shore he is most likely a deep sea angler, for there appears to be very little on this stretch of coastline to interest the shore angler.

At Salthill, just west of the Galway City, there is a frenzy of activity each time the shoals of mackerel come close to the promenade. Sometimes bass are taken here too. At Galway docks, large numbers of mullet are regularly taken on breadcrust and fish bait and about one mile (1.6 km) east of Spiddal there is some rock fishing for good sized wrasse and small pollack.

The deep sea angling, however, can be quite good. The main quarry, once again, is the porbeagle shark, but blue shark, tope, ray and common skate are also taken. A deep sea angling festival is held each September and it can be fished from either Galway City or Spiddal, which lies eight miles (12.8 km) west of the city.

About twenty miles (32.1 km) west of Galway the Connemara coast breaks up into a complex system of bays, islands and peninsulas. It is very beautiful but for the most part unfishable because of the wide belts of bladder-wrack which fringe the shores. Gorumna is one of these islands and is accessible by road. On it there is a beautiful little harbour at the mouth of Greatman's Bay called Trawbawn.

From the pier wall and from the rock opposite, there is some good flounder and plaice fishing. The bottom has very clean white sand, and in calm conditions it is possible to see the flatfish fluttering along the bottom after the bait—something that is always delightful to watch.

Roundstone is a little village about ten miles (16 km) south of Clifden, and about two miles (3.2 km) south west of it there are some prominent rocks on the northern shore of Gorteen Bay, from which pollack, mackerel and wrasse are caught. In Ballyconneely Bay, further west, there are some nice sandy patches with flounder and the odd big bass. From the harbour at Bunowen, two miles (3.2 km) west of Ballyconneely, small conger, flounder and ray can be taken. Just west of the golf course, on the Ballyconneely Peninsula, there are a series of beaches, all of which hold flounder, but they are small and not very plentiful. From the golf course, around Slyne Head and up to Dunloughan, the shore line is mostly inaccessible, but at Dunloughan itself and north for about two miles (3.2 km), there is a series of three small beaches, separated by rocky headlands. Small wrasse and pollack are taken from the rocks, but the beaches have nice flounder, turbot and the occasional plaice. Lugworm are plentiful and large at the extreme end of the road at Dunloughan.

Mannin Bay is about four miles (6.4 km) south of Clifden, and on the southern shore there are long sandy stretches, all of which are easily accessible.

On the most western of these beaches (after driving across the sand dunes and taking care to avoid the numerous burrows and rabbits), there are occasional ray and dogfish to be taken. The northern shore is mostly unfishable, but just around the corner, on the Errislannan Peninsula, there are some interesting rock marks. From the rocks beside Boat Harbour some good wrasse can be caught and the same species are abundant west of the White Lady, a large white concrete bollard marking the entrance to Clifden Bay. Just north of the White Lady, and for a short distance east as far as the 'Hawks Nest', there are a number of rocky outcrops off which large numbers of thornback ray can be taken.

About a mile (1.6 km) to the south of Clifden, on the Ballyconneely road, a road bridge crosses the entrance to Salt Lake. As its name suggests, it is an entirely salt water lake. From the rocks on the southern side, just east of the bridge, there can be good fishing for pollack, coalfish, codling and conger.

Going west from Clifden, skirting the bay, is the Sky road. This is a truly magnificent drive, and below it are two places, Slopers Cliff and Beleek, offering rock fishing for wrasse, pollack and mackerel. They fish best in a flowing tide. Omey Island is about seven miles (11.2 km) north west of Clifden and it is possible to drive onto the island across a half mile (0.8 km) stretch of beach when the tide is out. A road runs across the island to its extreme western end; at the south western tip of a little sandy bay there is a good rock mark for pollack, wrasse and conger.

The next point of interest north of here is just west of Aughrusbeg Lake, three miles (4.8 km) west of Cleggan. There is a ledge of rocks about a quarter of a mile (0.4 km) south of some concrete holding ponds from which excellent fishing can be enjoyed for wrasse and pollack. From the pier at Cleggan some very big conger have been taken and flounder and mullet are sometimes plentiful.

Deep sea angling out of Clifden is first class from June right through to late October. Blue shark are numerous and large catches of pollack, cod, conger, ling, bream and flatfish are common. The odd porbeagle can also be taken. Even when the weather is extremely bad, it is possible to fish Mannin Bay where there are numerous ray and dogfish and the odd monkfish and big common skate. The deep sea angling out of Cleggan is mostly for pollack, but recently there have been some good catches of turbot and ray. There are some excellent angling boats in this area, particularly in Clifden, which is fast becoming one of the country's major deep sea angling centres.

CLEW BAY

Clew Bay faces due west; it is twelve miles long and seven wide (19.2 × 11.2 km). The inner portion is a maze of peninsulas and islands—there are reputed to be 365, or one for every day of the year. There are two major 'inner bays'—Westport Bay in the south east and Newport Bay in the north east.

Beautifully situated right in the middle of the mouth of Clew Bay is Clare Island with its access point, Roonagh Quay at the south western tip of the bay.

South of Roonagh Point there are about six miles (9.6 km) of fine surf beaches, most of them easy to reach. Flounder are taken on all these beaches as well as the odd big bass and tope. Flounder and the occasional bass are also caught on Louisburgh beach, and at Old Head and Lecanvey there is a little rock and pier fishing. Further east a long neck of land runs out to Bertraw Island. On the western side of this neck of land the shore is steep and stoney and some bass are taken spinning from it. A very fast tide rips past the end of the island and bass, ray and the odd monkfish have been taken from the shore here. On the northern side of the bay a road runs close along the shoreline of the Curraun Peninsula, and almost everywhere along this five mile (8 km) stretch of coast you can take wrasse, mackerel and small pollack. In many places the rock slopes gently down to the sea giving easy access.

The deep sea angling in Clew Bay is legendary and festivals and competitions are held very frequently during the spring and summer. An interesting fact about these competitions is that many of them do not weigh in a single fish; in the interests of conservation all fish are returned alive to the water and points are allotted according to the schedule. The quantities of fish caught may not be what they were, but there is still good fishing for ray, common and white skate, monkfish, tope and dogfish.

Newport offers the same type of fishing and from Clare Island you can fish Clew Bay and also the open Atlantic for blue shark, cod, pollack, ling and bream. One of the best known marks in this area is the 'Bill Rocks', pinnacles of granite rising up from 40 fathoms (73.1 metres). Well run charter boats and gear are available for hire at Westport, Newport and Clare Island.

ACHILL

Achill Island is roughly triangular in shape and is reached by a road bridge across Achill Sound. It is a very beautiful and rugged land of mountains, beaches, cliffs, folklore and a deserted village, and although it has very little known shore fishing its deep sea angling is well known and of excellent quality.

The road south from Achill Sound towards Achillbeg Island skirts the sea out as far as Dooeg. The landscape is marvellous as, I am sure, is the rock fishing, although the cliffs look very dangerous. Keel strand, about half way along the island and about two miles long (3.2 km), facing south west, holds some fair flounder and the occasional bass. Frequently encountered on this beach are sea trout; the present Irish record of 14 lbs 3 ozs (6.4 kg) was caught here.

About five miles further west is tiny Keem Strand, reached by way of a breathtaking road carved out of the side of an 800 ft (246 metres) high cliff. There are flounder on this beach and also turbot, notably in September. If you can scramble out to Moyteoge Point at the south eastern tip of the bay, there is good rock fishing for pollack, mackerel, wrasse and, I believe, red sea bream at times. There is still commercial fishing in this bay for the huge 20 to 30 feet (5.9–9.1 metres) basking sharks and this operation is well worth watching from the top of the cliffs if you have the opportunity.

Boats take anglers out from three harbours on the island—two on the south side—Purteen Harbour near Keel and Darby's Point just inside Achillbeg Island at the mouth of Achill Sound, and one on the north side at Bullsmouth. The boat fishing off Achill Head, Saddle Head and the Dysaghy Rocks offers a great variety of quality fish of very large average size. Pollack are plentiful, as are conger, cod, ling, tope, whiting, gurnards, bull huss, wrasse and many other species. Blue shark are numerous in summer and the Irish blue shark record (206 lbs—92.7 kg) and the porbeagle shark record (365 lbs—169.3 kg) were both taken off Achill.

BELMULLET AREA

Belmullet is also recognised as having some of the finest deep sea angling grounds in the British Isles. It too has a number of Irish records to its credit, including a halibut of 156 lbs (69.9 kg).

Like Achill, the Mullet Peninsula is really an island reached by bridge from Belmullet town. The island is about fifteen miles long (24.1 km) and behind it are two large shallow bays—Broadhaven in the north and Blacksod in the south.

There is a limited amount of known shore fishing in the area. Rock fishing on the southern side of Annagh Head produces mackerel, wrasse and pollack, while the rocks on either side of Broadhaven lighthouse yield pollack, mackerel, ray and conger. The western side of the peninsula is fringed with about eight miles (12.8 km) of untried surf beaches. I only fished them once, and for a short spell only, but on one mackerel bait I had ray of 8 lbs (3.6 kg), a bull huss of 10 lbs (4.5 kg) and a sea trout of 5½ lbs (2.55 kg).

On the southern end, boat fishing out of Blacksod Pier, there is really excellent quality fishing to be had—pollack, cod, ling, bream and tope are all plentiful around the isolated and lonely Black Rock, eleven miles (17.7 km) straight west. The same type of fishing is available inside and outside the deserted Iniskea Islands, now a wild goose sanctuary. On the northern side, in inner Broadhaven Bay, there is excellent small boat fishing. Three friends and I once took, in a single day, almost a ton (1024 kg) of fish made up of 16 different species from 12 feet (3.6 metres) of water.

The deep sea angling out of Broadhaven is first class for pollack, cod, ling, haddock, large coalfish, whiting, conger, gurnards, turbot, brill and many other species. Among the better known fishing grounds are the Erris Race, Eagle Island, Kid Island and the 'Haddock Mark'. Also included in this area are the ports of Porturlin and Portacloy on the northern mainland, from which another famous mark, the Stags of Broadhaven, is fished. It was in this area that the record halibut was landed.

KILLALA BAY

From Benwee Head the coast runs due east for fifty miles (80.4 km) to Sligo Bay. Killala Bay is situated right in the middle of this stretch, facing due north. The inner reaches of this bay are sandy and a line of sandy islands separates the bay from the Moy estuary, which is tidal to Ballina. In the last few years the area has gained a reputation for quite good deep sea angling, with charter boats available for hire at Killala on the western side of the bay and Enniscrone on the eastern side.

There is top quality fishing out of either of these ports for blue shark in summer, as well as pollack, cod, ling, gurnard, conger, ray and common skate. Among the best fishing grounds in the area are Kilcummin Head on the north western end of the bay and Downpatrick Head a little further west. Catches are usually impressive with a good variety of quality fish. There is also excellent fishing for sea trout from small boats in the Moy estuary itself.

The shore angling in this area is not very well known, but on the eastern side of Downpatrick Head is a rock mark, or rather a cliff mark. The fishing is from a ledge about 100 feet (30.1 metres) high, so it can be rather difficult to land fish, but in the water below are fine pollack, wrasse, mackerel, conger and I believe, tope. Just west of Kilcummin Head is Lacken Bay, which has a short beach with a river flowing into it at the western end. There are some flounder and turbot in the surf and numerous sandeels can be collected at the river mouth.

Immediately west of the beach is a small pier from which mullet and conger are caught; about 300 yards (274 metres) further west again is a ledge of rock from which pollack, wrasse and mackerel are taken. This is the only place where I have seen wrasse jumping out of the water after sandeel. There are numerous small flatfish on the beaches in Killala Bay itself, particularly Enniscrone beach, and an occasional bass is encountered. Some conger and flatfish are caught from the pier at Enniscrone and from the rocks beneath the bath house.

The coastline from Lenadoon to Sligo Bay is mostly rocky and does not appear to have much to offer the shore angler, but at Strandhill, five miles (8 km) west of Sligo, there is a west-facing surf beach with some flounder. The narrow entrance to Ballisodare Bay is at the western end of this beach and tope are taken in the entrance in early summer.

There is some spinning for mackerel and pollack from Deadman's Point, just west of Rosses Point, but in general there is very little shore angling in the area. For the deep sea angler the 'Ledge', a ridge of rock rising five fathoms (9.1 metres) in the mouth of Sligo Bay, holds good pollack, conger and ling. The three inner sections of Sligo Bay—Ballisodare, Drumcliff and Sligo itself, all have first class tope angling in season. At times the tope can be very plentiful.

6. DONEGAL BAY TO MOVILLE

North of Ballyconnell Point, the land slides away to the north east for about thirty miles (48.2 km) to Donegal town, the ancient home of the O'Donnells. It then turns west again for about the same distance to the wild and beautiful Rathlin O'Beirne Island.

There is a little pollack fishing from the rocks about two miles (3.2 km) east of Ballyconnell Point on the southern side of Cloonagh Bay. About six miles (9.6 km) south west of Bundoran, on the eastern side of a small headland, is Mullaghmore village; in the harbour are good sized conger and small wrasse. On the north western side of the headland pollack, mackerel and wrasse are caught from the rocks in summer.

The deep sea angling out of Mullaghmore is mainly for good sized pollack and tope, both of which can be numerous. Innishmurray Island is a noted local mark for pollack, conger, ling, wrasse and tope. Blue shark are also taken at times, but they are not often fished for. Off Bundoran there is good fishing for pollack and tope. Also in the area are cod, ling, conger and rays. Rossnowlagh beach, north of Ballyshannon, is not fished often but there are reports of flounder, dabs and the odd bass being taken.

On the northern shore of Donegal Bay a long narrow headland, St John's Point, separates Inver Bay from McSwyne's Bay. A road runs all the way down to the lighthouse on the Point and from the rocks around it there is excellent shore fishing for good sized pollock, mackerel, wrasse and conger. A word of caution, however. Look for a safe fishing platform because the swell can be fierce. A little to the east is the large commercial fishing port of Killybegs. Conger and mullet are caught from the various piers in the harbour, and in summer mackerel come right in and can be caught spinning.

Deep sea angling boats can sometimes be difficult to hire in Killybegs because of commercial fishing. A competition is held every year and excellent catches have been recorded. Many specimen sized pollack and coalfish have been landed, together with good cod, ling, bream, conger, ray, tope and the occasional blue shark. Fish baits are never difficult to obtain in Killybegs. About ten miles (16 km) to the west of the town, at the little port of Teelin, conger can be caught from the pier wall.

WEST AND NORTH DONEGAL

Donegal's angling reputation is, without doubt, based on its quality deep sea fishing rather than its shore angling. In fact very little is known about the shore angling as it is for the most part untried.

One interesting form of fishing is known, however—the magnificent beach fishing for sea trout. They are taken spinning in the surf around the numerous sandy inlets and bays. I have only done a little of this fishing on the beaches around Sheephaven Bay and can recommend it. I believe sea trout are also available in some of the beautiful creeks and inlets on the west coast.

Burtonport and Bunbeg are two ports on the western side of Donegal, only eight miles apart (12.8 km), from which a fair amount of boat angling is done. The fishing can be very good, most of all around Aranmore Island, Owey Island, Gola Island and the Stag Rocks. The latter are about six miles (9.6 km) west of Bunbeg and provide first class fishing, mostly over rough pinnacle ground for pollack, ling and cod. Off Aranmore, cod, pollack, haddock and whiting are caught, as well as numerous coalfish which can be a nuisance at times. The ground around Gola is a mixture of rock, sand and shingle, and produces haddock, pollack, cod, ling, gurnard and ray.

Tory Island can be fished from either Downings or Port Na Blagh, two small harbours in Sheephaven Bay. Cod fishing to the north of the island can be particularly good, but double-figure coalfish, pollack, ling and good haddock are plentiful both here and in Tory Sound to the south.

Off Horn Head, on the eastern side of Sheephaven, there is a mark for ray, haddock, pollack and small coalfish. The most famous mark in this area is the 'Garden'. I do not know how it got its name, but it produces good fishing for cod, ling, pollack, haddock and gurnard. Tope can be plentiful in this area during the summer. Most of Sheephaven Bay is clear sand and there is good fishing to be had for a variety of flatfish, including ray, turbot, plaice, dabs and flounder. A few blue shark have been taken from Downings in high summer, but the numbers are small compared with the south west of Ireland.

Lough Swilly is an inlet twenty miles long and two miles wide (32.1 × 3.2 km), facing due north. For years it has been renowned for its tope fishing, particularly out of Rathmullen. Over the years thousands of these fine fish have been killed and their numbers appear to be dropping, so if you are fishing the area please be conscious of conservation. Around Fanad Head and in the mouth of Lough Swilly, in addition to the tope, there can be good fishing for cod, haddock, pollack, whiting and numerous large spurdogs. There is some rock fishing for pollack, coalfish, wrasse and the occasional sea trout around Fanad Head. Flatfish are taken in some of the sandy bays. Lugworm are available in Rathmullen Harbour.

On the eastern side of the Inishowen Peninsula, there are three ports from which there is some boat fishing: Culdaff, Greencastle and in Lough Foyle, Moville. The grounds around Malin Head, the most northerly point in Ireland, and Culdaff, produce excellent fishing for cod, haddock, whiting, pollack, coalfish and tope. In addition, a few skate of over 100 lbs (45 kg) have been taken. Dogfish are also plentiful, including specimen sized bull huss. Around Dunagree Point, the main species are pollack, coalfish, wrasse and on the clean ground, ray, haddock and some common skate.

Moville is situated a few miles inside the mouth of Lough Foyle, which is about fourteen miles long and seven miles wide (22.4 × 11.2 km). The mouth itself is very narrow and a deep channel runs out past Magilligan Point as far as Inishowen Head. In the channel there can be good fishing for flounder, tope, dabs, thornback ray, dogfish and gurnard, especially red gurnards. On the McKinney Bank, opposite Moville, are skate, ray, tope and plaice.

Not much shore fishing is done is this area, but at Dunagree Point, there is a rock mark for mackerel, pollack and coalfish. There is a little float fishing for wrasse south of Moville between Brown Shoulder and Carrowkeel.

7. DERRY, ANTRIM AND DOWN

CO. DERRY

On the eastern side of Lough Foyle between Bellarena and Magilligan Point, there is reasonable shore fishing for flounder, dabs and dogfish, particularly just inside Magilligan Point. Lugworm and clam are plentiful. A road now runs all the way down to Magilligan Point; flounder and the occasional big bass are taken in the surf on Magilligan strand itself, just below the Martello Tower.

From Magilligan Point to Downhill is a long north-facing beach on which there are flounder and a few bass, mainly after a storm. Clam locally called "geegawn" is reputed to be the best bait in the area. Small turbot are best taken at night. A small stream runs onto the beach about halfway along and this is a good spot for flounder, notably after rain. On the beach below Downhill Post Office flounder and sometimes bass are encountered.

There is a wall on either side of the River Bann where it flows onto Castlerock strand and flounder and sometimes bass are taken from it at all stages of the tide. Sea trout are fairly plentiful and are taken spinning, while conger to 16 lbs (7.3 kg) are caught, particularly at night. Fishing is best on the Portstewart side of the estuary, but a word of warning—it is very dangerous place in a north or north west gale. Up river from the beach, sea trout, flounder, dabs and odd plaice are taken.

CO. ANTRIM

Portstewart strand is to the east of the Bann and many coalfish and flounder are taken in the surf on lugworm and ragworm by night. Sea trout can also be taken on mackerel strips.

There are two deep sea-angling ports in this area: Portstewart, and three miles (4.8 km) to the east, Portrush. Although fishing the same general area, they offer between them probably the best boat angling in Northern Ireland. The main marks are the Causeway Bank and the Skerries. The bank is simply a sandy ridge in 20 fathoms (36.5 metres) which runs all along the coast from the mouth of the Bann to Bushmills. On it are thornback, homelyn, cuckoo and small blonde rays. Off Ramore Head, haddock and conger are taken and just outside the Skerries, there are good cod to 30 lbs (14 kg). Just west of the Skerries are plaice, dab, flounder, gurnards, dogfish and numerous whiting. Around the Skerries themselves are conger and tope a little to the east.

Fishing from both sides of the pier in Portrush, especially in winter, you can have good fun with whiting and small coalfish. There are some fine conger in the inner harbour, but it is best to ground bait for these. Some ragworm can be dug

Sea angling at Portrush, Co. Antrim

in the harbour. Below the coastguard lookout station on Ramore Head, there is rock fishing for wrasse, conger, dogfish, pollack and the occasional cod. On the east strand at Portrush, just below the Arcadia Ballroom, are conger, big flounder and the odd bass and sea trout. At the Blue Pool Rocks, west of the Arcadia, and just east of Ramore Head, there is some mixed ground where wrasse, pollack, conger, dogfish, thornback rays and the occasional big plaice are taken.

A very strong tide runs through Rathlin Sound and boat fishing in the area is only possible in slack water. On a boat from Ballycastle it is possible to fish Church Bay in Rathlin Island, where the wreck of the Drake lies. It was torpedoed during World War I and made for Rathlin, but sank in 15 fathoms (27.4 metres). There are big conger in the wreck, along with pollack, wrasse and pouting. In 50 fathoms (91.4 metres) off Bull Point and off the lighthouse on Rathlin, there is a very rough bottom on which are good conger and ling. North east of the island stand the Shamrock Pinnacles, which rise up from 100 fathoms (182.8 metres) to a peak of 30 fathoms (54.8 metres). Drifting over the peaks can provide fun, with good wrasse, pollack and coalfish. In Rathlin Sound itself, when it is possible to fish, there are good cod and gurnards.

From Fair Head to Torr Head is mostly steep cliff; access is very difficult. For the mountaineering enthusiast there is some rock fishing near Fair Head for pollack, wrasse and conger and likewise at Torr Head for pollack and wrasse. Midway between the two lies a small beach in Murlough Bay, and just below the monument to Roger Casement is some winter fishing for whiting, codling, small coalfish and flatfish, particularly at night. In Red Bay, below Cushendall, good night fishing can be had, especially around high water, for cod, coalfish, plaice and the odd bass. There is boat angling out of Waterfoot in Red Bay for flatfish, especially plaice, cod, haddock, whiting, conger, dabs and gurnards.

On the south side of Garron Point, a recognised rock fishing mark provides good wrasse, pollack and the occasional rock cod. The 'Klondyke' is a rocky pinnacle rising from 100 fathoms (182.8 metres) about twelve miles (19.2 km) out from Carnlough. On it are pollack, coalfish, ballan wrasse and the occasional very big cuckoo wrasse. Tope can be plentiful at times during the summer. The 'Klondyke' is usually fished from Carnlough.

The boat fishing in the Larne area is quite good, although most of the fishing is done from Ballylumford, a small port on the eastern side of the north facing narrow inlet, in which there is a plentiful supply of ragworm. A regular ferry runs between Larne and Ballylumford. About ten miles (16 km) east of Larne are the Maiden Rocks, a number of pinnacles with a lighthouse on top. There are large coalfish and wrasse in this area, but the currents are very dangerous; only fish here with a local boatman.

The 'Gobbins' off Portmuck (locally called the 'Measured Mile') is a bank of shingle in 20 to 30 fathoms (36.5–54.8 metres) close inshore. It is a noted mark for cod, turbot and whiting. There is some unusual fishing in this area during late May and early June each year. Herring, locally called 'black gut herring', come close in and a certain carnival atmosphere prevails as local boats go out just before dusk and catch, on rod and line, anything up to 12 dozen herring per angler. They are caught on feathers and even bare hooks.

The 'take' lasts only a very short time, usually between dusk and dark, and is very concentrated. Occasionally some big cod are encountered below the feeding herring. The fishing in Belfast Lough has deteriorated recently, probably due to pollution, but the occasional big hake and cod are still taken in deep water at the mouth of the Lough. Lugworm and clam are available on all shores.

CO. DOWN

About three miles (4.8 km) north of Donaghadee is Orlock Point, a rocky headland on the southern corner of the mouth of Belfast Lough, just inside Copeland Island. On the rocks immediately below the coastguard station is a good mark for specimen sized lesser spotted dogfish, wrasse, codling and small coalfish, locally called 'Blockin'. It is a good place at dusk to try spinning for fair sized sea trout or, if it gets too dark, to try for conger. On Copeland Island there is some good rock fishing for big wrasse, conger, codling, coalfish and pollack up to 6 lbs (2.7 kg), but access is only by boat from Bangor, Groomsport or Donaghadee. A considerable amount of boat fishing is done from these three ports. In Groomsport Bay there are thornback ray and dogfish and during September and October occasional tope are caught at Brigg's Buoy.

Three miles (4.8 km) east of Donaghadee is the Rigg Bank, a bank of sand varying in depth from 8 to 14 fathoms (11.6–25.5 metres) that runs roughly north-south for about four miles (6.4 km). On it are plaice, dabs, codling, whiting, gurnard and pollack. At the southern end is the 'Pimple' which, as the name suggests, is a small mark where coalfish and numerous whiting to 2½ lbs (1.1 kg) are caught in August and September. At the back of the Rigg, in 30 to 40 fathoms (54.8–73.1 metres) there are some very big bull huss.

Strangford Lough is a large inlet about fifteen miles long and five miles wide (24.1 × 8 km), with a very narrow inlet between Portaferry on the northern side and Strangford in the south. Much of the northern end of the Lough dries out, but there are some deep holes and channels, particularly at the southern end. A considerable amount of boat fishing is done from Portaferry in the entrance and Killyleagh on the western shore for common skate, big tope, thornback ray and dogfish, especially spur dogfish. Very little shore angling is known in the area, but at the northern end of the Lough, at Islandhill, in the estuary of the Comber River, there are flounder and sea trout. Mullet have been taken here on bread. Lugworm and clam are plentiful on all shores of the Lough.

Around Gun's Island, particularly on the south side, a clean, sandy bottom holds thornback ray and turbot. Drifting south towards Ardglass, there are patches of rough ground on which there are conger, wrasse and cod.

If you want to catch short spined sea scorpions, this is the place, because they are here in their hundreds and big too—up to 12 inches (30 cm). This area is fished by boat from Ardglass as is Dundrum Bay around the corner to the south. Here turbot, flounder, dabs, thornback rays and small angler fish are taken. Lugworm are plentiful on the beach.

Warrenpoint is in the inner reaches of Carlingford Lough and there is some boat fishing for spurdog, lesser spotted dogfish, thornback ray and some tope, especially round the mouth of the lough, between Greencastle and Greenore.

8. THE EAST COAST

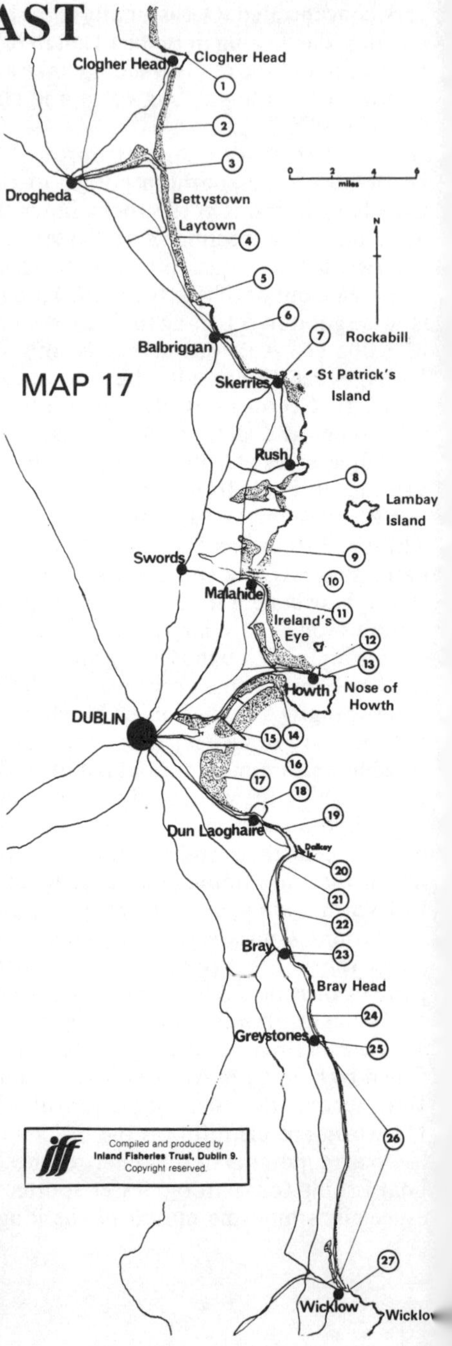

Dundalk Bay faces east and is very shallow. As a result, the tide strips out a long way, and the fishing is not very good. Some flatfish, however, are taken at Annagassan on the southern end and sometimes a small bass.

Clogher Head [Map 17 (1)] is fifteen miles (24.1 km) south of Dundalk and five miles (8 km) north of the Boyne estuary. It is about the only rocky outcrop on a long stretch of sandy coast between Dundalk and Balbriggan. Port Oriel is a small harbour on the northern side of the head and in summer, mackerel, dabs, small pollack and the odd codling are taken from the pier wall. Small pollack, coalfish and codling are taken from the rocks east of the pier on the extreme end of the headland. A little boat fishing is carried out from Port Oriel for codling, dogfish, whiting and some flatfish.

The beach between Clogher Head and Drogheda is not fished much, but it holds the occasional bass and flounder. The mouth of the Boyne [IFT Map (3)] is fished fairly regularly, both from the north shore and the south shore at Mornington. Bass fishing can be good here, particularly with peeler crabs which are collected in the estuary, or with sandeel, plentiful in the sand bars around the mouth. At Mornington, there is a fishmeal factory and mullet are taken at the outflow pipe.

Bass have occasionally been known to go right up the estuary to Drogheda, where flounder are also taken. At Laytown, about three miles (4.8 km) south of Mornington, the River Nanny [Map (4)] flows onto the beach. Bass and flounder are taken here, both on the beach and in the pool below the railway bridge. The odd sea trout is encountered as well.

About three miles (4.8 km) further south again, the Delvin River flows into the sea just north of Balbriggan [Map 17 (5)]. Here again, there is some beach fishing for bass, flounder and the odd sea trout. During the summer months, when the commercial boats are landing fish in Balbriggan Harbour [Map 17 (6)], there is some very good fishing for mullet on small fish baits. Boat fishing out of Balbriggan is rather poor, with little to offer except codling, whiting, dogfish and the occasional good dab. The entire area is clean sand except for Cardy Rocks, just north of Balbriggan, which hold some pollack to about 5 lbs (2.3 kg), wrasse and in spring, small coalfish.

SKERRIES

The commercial fishing port of Skerries is about five miles (8 km) south east of Balbriggan [Map 17 (7)]. There is a little shore fishing at the pier in summer for mackerel, small pollack and coalfish and occasionally mullet on fish bait. From the swimming place on Red Island, mackerel and the odd wrasse are taken. A fair amount of boat fishing is carried on out of Skerries.

Around the islands, pollack, whiting, coalfish, small codling, tiny ling, plaice and dogfish are taken. There are occasionally quite a lot of spur dogfish in the area. The best fishing is to be had drifting between Schenicks Island and St Patrick's Island. The Plough Rocks just south of St Patrick's Island are the best place for pollack, and outside the island tope are often encountered. Fishing half a mile to one mile (0.8–1.6 km) north of the harbour can provide dabs and small whiting. Four miles (6.4 km) east of Skerries stands the Rockabill lighthouse on a rock coming up from about 15 fathoms (27.4 metres). Fishing close in to the light can be good at times for pollack, coalfish, codling, large wrasse and sometimes conger and small ling. Off the rocks, on the sand, whiting and spur dogfish are plentiful.

South of Skerries are two small piers, at Loughshinny and Rush, and in summer mackerel come close in. Just south of Rush is the Rogerstown estuary [Map 17 (8)] and there can be some good bass fishing on the bar in the mouth, using crabs or sandeel, both of which are readily available. On the southern side, at the back of the sand dunes, the channel comes close inshore. As the tide fills, there can be nice bass fishing using crab or sandeel. South of Portrane on Donabate strand [Map 17 (9)], codling are often taken.

Lambay Island is about three miles (4.8 km) east of Portrane. Around Carrickdorish Rock on the north eastern side, pollack, wrasse, coalfish and small conger are taken. About half a mile (0.8 km) north on the sand are thornback rays and dogfish, especially spurdogs and the odd tope. Further out, tope and ray can be taken sometimes. All along the coast from Loughshinny to Lambay and inside Lambay itself there are some ray, and about quarter of a mile (0.4 km) north of the island good dabs are sometimes plentiful.

The Malahide estuary is about nine miles (14.4 km) north of Dublin. A railway line cuts off a large inner portion of this estuary, which forms Broadmeadow water. Mullet are plentiful in the lagoon and can be taken at the Malahide end on bread. On the seaward side of the railway [Map 17 (10)], a large pool is formed by the outflow where there are flounder and a few bass. Flounder and sometimes bass are also taken in the estuary itself, particularly where it enters the sea and at the back of the Island golf course.

Under the Martello Tower at Portmarnock and off the rocks just south of it, bass and flounder are caught on peeler crab. Crab, mussel and ragworm can be collected behind the church in Baldoyle. Howth Pier [Map 17 (12)], although fished consistently during summer, rarely produces anything other than mackerel, small pollack and the poisonous lesser weaver. In summer, mackerel and some flatfish are taken from the rocks near the Martello Tower east of Howth Harbour [Map 17 (13)].

The channel running behind Dollymount enters the sea at Red Rock [Map 17 (14)] on the western side of Howth. The shoreline is rocky but for an hour or two either side of low water, particularly in autumn, bass and flatfish are caught in the channel. It is best about 300 yards (274 metres) north of the Martello Tower or at the steps. Bass and occasionally plaice are taken on Dollymount beach itself, east of the new road. It fishes best at high water from June to September and there are small pollack, codling, whiting, bass and flounder around the bridge on the Bull Wall, particularly from October to December. Bass and flounder are sometimes taken at the end of the Bull Wall [Map 17 (15)].

On the southern side of the Liffey there are a few fishing marks around the Poolbeg. One such mark is the hot water outflow from the ESB Pigeon House station [Map 17 (16)]. Mullet and sometimes bass can be taken here from time to time in great numbers. At the Half Moon swimming club there are bass, flounder, small conger and the odd mackerel, conger and small pollack. South of the Poolbeg is the shallow Sandymount beach running down almost to Dun Laoghaire. In the "Cockle Lake" [Map 17 (17)] at Sandymount, bass and flounder are sometimes taken, as they are at the back of the dump. This area fishes best from half flood to high water in a southerly wind. Bass and flounder are taken on the flood tide at Blackrock baths.

Dun Laoghaire [Map 17 (18)] has two long piers, the West and the East. Fishing north from the West pier, plaice, codling, small pouting, whiting and conger are taken, usually at night. At the end, below the lighthouse, there are conger and the odd plaice, codling and whiting. At the end of the East pier are codling, small pollack and the odd flounder and, very close to the pier itself, conger. Again this location is best fished at night. At the bend on the East pier, fishing south, are some codling bass, conger and very occasionally, tope. Whiting can be numerous in winter. Mullet can be plentiful at times in Dun Laoghaire Harbour, particularly off the West pier; they can be taken on bread.

A few miles to the south east is little Bullock Harbour [Map 17 (19)]. Just east of the harbour are some massive rocks from which wrasse are taken. Further south again, at Colliemore, there is some fishing off the pier into the rough for conger, small pollack and codling. Killiney Bay [Map 17 (21)] is not very productive, but for long casters there are some fine plaice well out. Close in, there is only the very occasional bass and small pollock, but codling can be plentiful. At the end of Corbawn Lane [Map 17 (22)] in Shankill there is quite good fishing for bass, flounder, codling, plaice, dabs and lesser spotted dogfish. It fishes best during the flood. Just offshore is a sandbank and most fish are taken in the channel between this bank and the shore. Lugworm can be collected just north of Corbawn Lane. Crab Island, a few hundred yards south of Corbawn Lane, can be good for codling.

Both piers in Bray [Map 17 (23)] are fished for codling, pollack, lesser spotted dogfish, lesser weavers and occasionally conger. The first quarter of a mile (0.4 km) of strand south of the pier, below the promenade, holds bass, plaice, flounder and codling. At Bray Head, small conger and pollack are taken from the rocks, although access is dangerous.

Boat fishing in the Dublin area is not very good, but there is a reasonable amount of angling out of Dun Laoghaire, Bulloch Harbour and Bray. Off Dun Laoghaire, codling, small pollack, plaice, whiting, conger, dogfish and occasionally tope are caught. The fishing is best during summer months. On the clean Kish Bank, seven miles (11.2 km) out, there are plaice, turbot, dogfish and dabs. Off Bulloch and Colliemore, there are codling, small pollack, whiting, plaice and wrasse. The most fished marks are Carrig Rock, the Muglins, Dalkey Sound, and Jack's Hole at the back of Dalkey Island (best at low water) and the White Rock for plaice. Wrasse and whiting can be plentiful at the back of the convent. In Killiney Bay, there are ray and codling well out, and off Bray Head conger, ray, codling, pollack and all types of dogfish. Small boats can be hired at Bray, Greystones, Killiney, Bulloch Harbour and Colliemore.

GREYSTONES

Greystones, sixteen miles (25.7 km) south of Dublin, is a popular area for boat and shore fishing. From boats, cod, ray, pollack, plaice, dabs, wrasse, flounder, tope and gurnards as well as dogfish, are taken. The best fishing is on the ridge between the Moulditch Buoy and Red Barn on the south beach. On Reilly's Ridge off Kilcoole, plaice are plentiful from June onwards and there are good cod in the shipping lane. One of the best areas for ray is about three miles (4.8 km) out; some very big thornback can be found.

To the north of Greystones, a shingle beach, locally called the North Beach [Map 17 (24)], is best fished by night for dogfish and the occasional dab, plaice, black sole, bass, turbot, tope and conger. The best part is the first 400 yards (365 metres) south of Bray Head. Access is by way of Redford Lane, leaving the car at the railway crossing. Some codling, small pollack and the odd bass and plaice are taken on the seaward side of Greystones pier, and from the rocks south of the pier (locally called the 'Flat Rock'). At Carrigeden, below the hotel, codling, pollack, small flatfish and the odd bass are taken.

Between Greystones and Wicklow, there is an eleven mile long (17.6 km) stretch of steeply shelving beach of coarse sand and fine gravel [Map 17 (26)]. It is extensively fished and offers what is considered the best shore angling on the east coast. Tides are very strong all along it and on the ebb it runs south from half an hour after high water to two hours before low water. All along this beach, where there is access, codling, pollack, plaice, flounder, gurnards, occasional tope, ray and of course dogfish can be taken. It fishes best by night in early autumn, but is quite good from May onwards; the best times are two hours either side of low water and, for codling, one hour either side of high water. The recognised locations are the 'Point', Kilcoole, Newcastle and the Breeches. Lemon sole are often taken at the latter.

Just north of Wicklow at Broad Lough, there are lugworm, ragworm and mussel, but waders are necessary to get out to the bait beds. There are also flounder in Broad Lough, which is really a long tidal lake formed by the Vartry River.

WICKLOW

Wicklow Harbour [Map 17 (27)] is at the entrance to Broad Lough and there is fishing off the east pier for pollack, codling, flounder, good conger and small thornback ray. There are some plaice right in the mouth of the harbour. Wicklow Head is very rocky and the tides are severe off it, but just south on the Silver Strand [Map 18 (1)] are bass, flounder, lesser spotted dogfish and the occasional plaice. Spur dogfish can be numerous by night. In Brittas Bay [Map 18 (2)], just north of Mizen Head, there are bass, dogfish, codling and whiting at night particularly in rough conditions.

South of Mizen Head, there is another long steep beach at Pennycomequick Bridge [Map 18 (3)], the River Redcross (locally called 'Ennareilly River') flows onto it. There is good fishing from May onwards at the river mouth, 400 yards (365 metres) south to the rocks and on the beach. Bass, flounder, whiting, codling, dogfish and the occasional plaice and eel are taken. It fishes best at night for three hours either side of high water.

ARKLOW

Just north of Arklow is a caravan park near Porter's Rocks [Map 18 (4)]. Off the rocks and the beach to the south are bass, codling, dabs and dogfish.

From here south to Arklow, along the back of Ferry Bank, is mostly flounder and codling country. About three miles (4.8 km) south of Arklow at Clogga Beach, also known as Nun's Beach [Map 18 (5)],

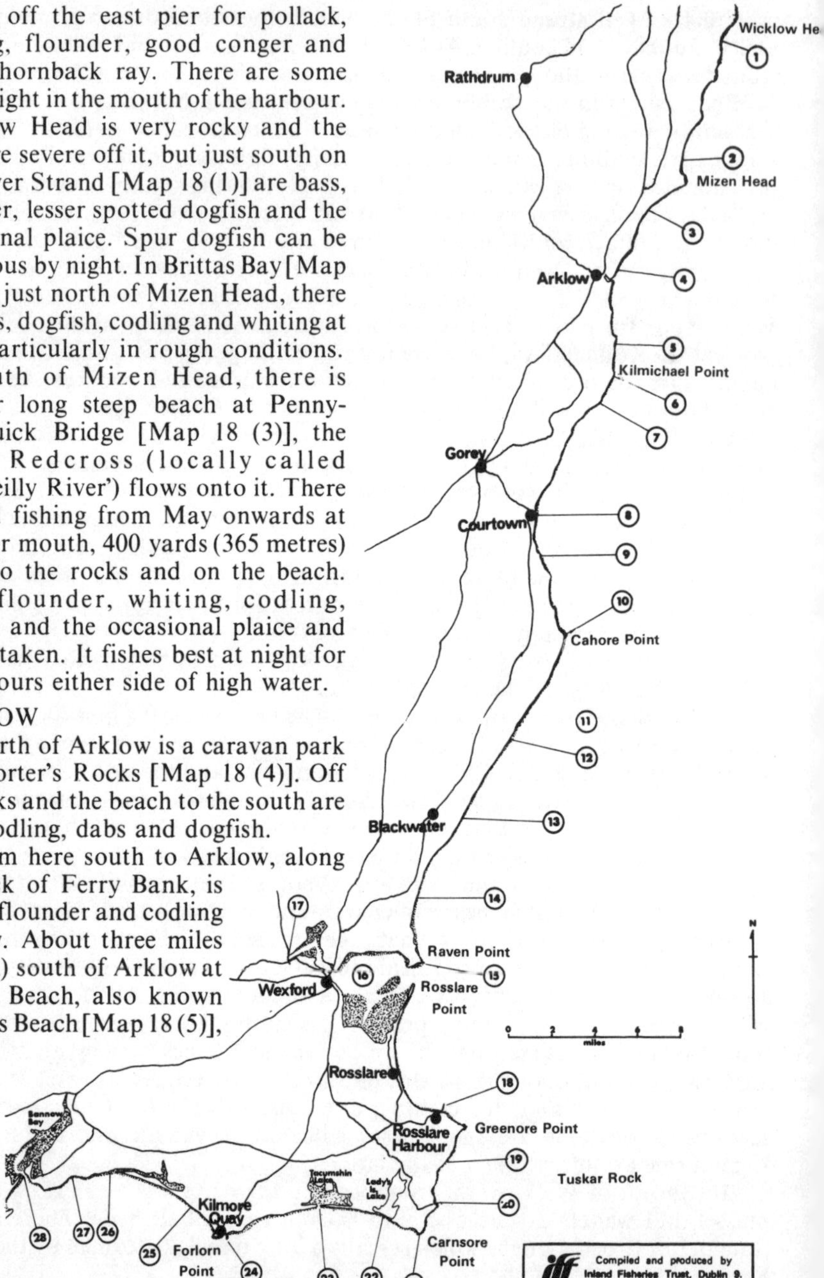

MAP 18

are some bass and flounder. Just south of this location, there is float fishing for good bass into a rocky patch. On Kilmichael Point [Map 18 (6)], five miles (8 km) south of Arklow, are some rocks from which bass and mackerel are taken, and off the north east corner of these rocks are some good plaice. Just south of the point at Clones Strand [Map 18 (7)] there is summer fishing for bass, codling, whiting and the odd tope, particularly on the flood tide. In winter, codling, whiting and medium sized flounder are plentiful. The occasional lemon sole is also taken here. From this point to Courtown is all steep beach, with dogfish, flatfish and occasional bass.

COURTOWN

The occasional bass and flounder are caught from the beach at Courtown [Map 18 (8)], but in Courtown Harbour mullet can be plentiful. They can be taken on bread crust, but watch out for ducks and swans, for they can be hooked by mistake, even by most cautious of anglers. At Pollshone Head [Map 18 (9)], there are some rocks on the south of the beach where bass, flounder, plaice, dabs and gurnards are taken, but south of this, the bottom is rather rough and can be good for bass.

At Cahore [Map 18 (10)], flatfish are taken from the beach and pier and bass from the rocks at the back of the pier. Four miles (6.4 km) south of Cahore is Mauricecastle Strand [Map 18 (11)] to the east of Kilmuckridge. During March, April and May, there are bass and flounder here, but at the end of April and all through May, tope come close in, sometimes in good numbers. There is a sandbank offshore and most fish are caught in the channel between the bank and the shore. Thornback and the odd sting ray are also taken, so pay attention before grabbing any ray-like fish by the tail.

At Tinnabearna [Map 18 (12)], south of Kilmuckridge, are bass, flounder, lesser spotted dogfish and the occasional tope and at night, particularly in winter, bull huss. About a mile (1.6 km) further south at Ballynamona bass and bull huss are again caught at night. Further north, at Blackwater on the mouth of the Blackwater River [Map 18 (13)], bass, flounder and the occasional tope and small angler fish are taken. At the Blue Pool south of Cush Gap, tope fishing can be very good in May. Two miles (3.2 km) north of Raven Point, at Curracloe [Map 18 (14)], night fishing for flounder, bass and tope can be quite good.

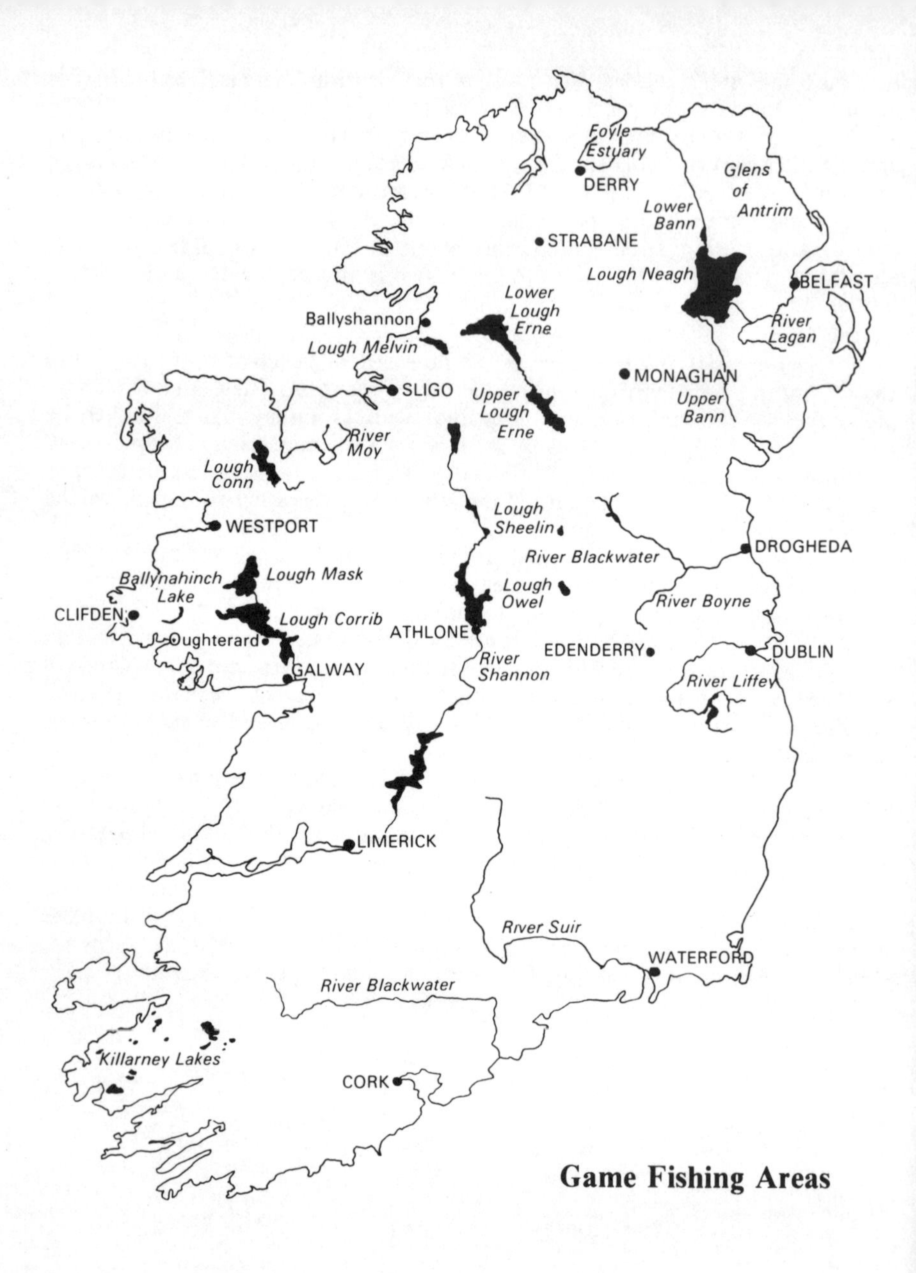

Game Fishing Areas

GAME FISHING
Peter R. Brown

INTRODUCTION

Ireland's reputation for good quality game fishing is sometimes justified, despite the problems caused by over-fishing, pollution, poaching and drainage works. In most parts of the country, the game fishing is nothing spectacular, but in numerous streams and lakes there is pleasant, entertaining but unexceptional fishing for brown trout. The charges are small or non-existent. There is also a great deal of little known and little fished water, some of fair quality. Uncertainty and great expectations are part of the sport of angling. Disappointment can be bitter. In this section of the book, I will try to remove some of the uncertainties and encourage only those justifiable expectations.

Game fishing requires skill; experience and local knowledge are both an advantage. This section, within the limitations of its size, can supply some of the local knowledge; it can be supplemented by talking to fellow anglers, tackle dealers, local tourist office staff and others. I have occasionally met visitors who, lured by colourful tourist brochures, have brought a rod and expected to catch fish, including shy and difficult trout, without difficulty.

This seldom happens, and to avoid disappointment, the novice should study his subject carefully beforehand. Then he should go out in the company of an experienced angler a few times before fishing alone. The most convenient way to do so in Ireland, if one has no experienced companion, is to hire a boatman on one of the better known lake fisheries. The boatman will know the best localities in the prevailing conditions and should be able to give detailed advice on tackle and

WHEN TO FISH

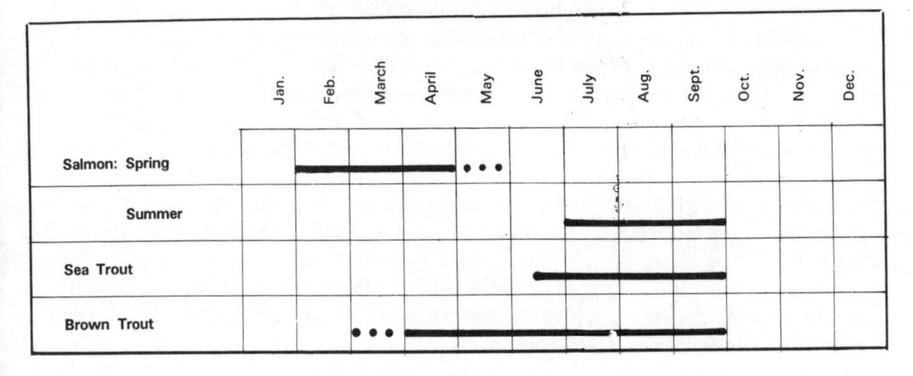

method. Even a novice may catch excellent trout by dapping or trolling from a boat and may also learn to cast a fly in less demanding conditions than river or shore.

SALMON AND SEA TROUT

Salmon and sea trout are migratory species that spend most of their feeding lives in salt water. They ascend all rivers and many streams that directly enter the sea; they may be caught in fresh water by fly fishing, by spinning or by using a worm or other bait. Fly fishing is the most attractive as well as the most productive method, especially for sea trout. Bait fishing may be necessary in waters that are high and discoloured after rain, or in very low water. Visiting anglers may be restricted to fly fishing only in some fisheries.

The mountain river and lake systems of the west and south west probably provide the best all round fishing for salmon and sea trout in Ireland. Lakes may be fished all day, preferably from a boat, provided for anglers on all the better waters. Rivers fish best in the mornings and evenings, but if a river is high after rain, daytime fishing can also be very good.

Spring salmon may be caught as early as January in some waters, but the best months are March and April. Summer salmon and grilse are caught from June to September. The best sea trout runs are from June to September, but some localities have quite good early runs, which are usually of bigger fish, in April and May.

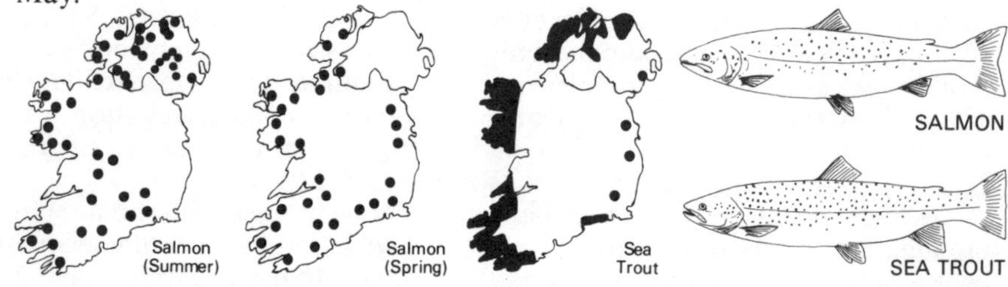

Salmon fishing in Ireland in under great pressure at present as the salmon is a valuable commercial species, netted at sea and in the river estuaries. Poaching is common in some districts and may even interfere with angling at times, but despite this, there still seems to be some good salmon fishing available. The serious salmon angler may fish for the bigger Spring fish in a large river such as the Blackwater, Nore or Slaney, but he should only expect to average a fish every two or three days. The best way of catching a salmon or two without taking too long is to combine salmon with sea trout fishing in summer on one of the noted western waters. Many of these are open to visitors for a charge that varies with the quality of the sport to be expected; some are preserved by hotels for their guests, while others are let by the period. Hotels often offer special facilities to their guests and also offer day or evening period permits to others. The sea trout fishing can be extremely good and is not so subject to suitable weather and water conditions as is salmon fishing. Sport can be fast and furious, with the possibility of a salmon ever present.

A licence is required to fish for salmon and sea trout. The charge varies with the period and the district, a typical one at the time of writing being about £3 a week or about £10 for a season. (See appendix).

Licence holders require a permit to fish in privately owned waters; this may cost from about 50p to about £10 per day, depending on the quality of the sport. Some fishery owners also issue permits for an evening's fishing. On a recent occasion, I took out one such permit from the Newport House Hotel in Co. Mayo and went to fish the Newport River from 9.30 until 11.30 that July evening. In this time, I took thirteen sea trout and met with a salmon. This was excellent sport, but not exceptional for an evening's fly fishing in good conditions. There is some salmon and sea trout fishing that is free to licence holders, notably in Loughs Conn and Corrib, as well as in Lough Currane in Co. Kerry and in many small streams of little interest that receive runs of sea trout and the odd salmon after rain.

Salmon and sea trout flies are lures that are designed to catch the attention of fish rather than to imitate any natural insect. Many of them suggest tiny fish that may have formed part of the quarry's diet in the sea. Salmon flies are divided into Spring and Summer sizes, and into bright, dark and yellow patterns. Some traditional patterns are very fancy and consequently rather expensive. Spring patterns are Thunder and Lightning, Silver Blue, Golden Olive, Hairy Mary, Silver Doctor, Black Goldfinch. Summer patterns are Black Doctor, Connemara Black, Silver March Brown, Yellow Dog and Blue Charm. The best sea trout flies are slim bright patterns with some blue or black, and a mallard or teal wing seems to be attractive. Popular patterns are Teal and Blue, Alexandra, Peter Ross, Invicta, Butcher, Mallard and Jay, March Brown and Silver.

BROWN TROUT

Brown trout are present in most running waters in Ireland as well as in many lakes; they are highly regarded both for their sport and as table fish. The quality of the brown trout fishing depends largely on the nature and the geology of the country in which the waters are situated. Those waters rising from and flowing through limestone produce the heaviest trout, but extensive mountain streams are more prolific. A combination of these two factors, in which a mountain stream system drains into a limestone river or lake, produces a good number of trout that should grow to a satisfactory size. Some limestone systems have insufficient spawning areas to produce a heavy stock of trout, and such waters may provide fishing for a small number of heavy trout. Many mountain rivers flowing largely over granite provide such poor feeding that they yield only stunted brown trout, although in most of these waters sea trout and salmon are likely to be found in their season.

Much of the better brown trout fishing in Ireland is in the hands of angling clubs. Most of it is leased to the clubs by the Land Commission or private owners. It follows that any visiting angler wishing to fish in a particular locality should first find out if there is a local club. If there is, he should obtain permission to fish. In some cases, he may be granted free fishing; in others, he may be asked to become a

member or he may buy a day or week permit. Pressure on brown trout fishing resources has greatly increased in recent years and there is not much free fishing.

As a rule, however, there is still plenty of water. A licence is not required for trout fishing in the Republic, but one must be purchased in Northern Ireland. Club membership costs from 50p to a few pounds. A day ticket on the better trout waters costs about 50p and club membership is usually about £3 a year.

There are some free brown trout waters; many of these are of little account but some of the lakes are excellent. The most notable are the great lakes on the western edge of the limestone plain, Loughs Corrib, Mask, Conn, Cullen and Arrow. These lakes are possibly unique in Europe for providing superb free fly fishing for trout of good average size as well as producing some very heavy fish of up to 20 lbs in weight (9.0 kg) every year. Although they are free fisheries, these lakes are carefully managed by the State through the Inland Fisheries Trust. There are also many other lakes, especially in the west and north, some of which occur over limestone and which give good trout fishing.

The main difference between trout fishing in Ireland and in most European countries is that most Irish trout are wild fish, produced by wild parents and hatched in the wild. There are some hatchery stocks, but these are largely confined to the waters managed by the Inland Fisheries Trust. In my opinion, there is a big difference in behaviour and feeding habits between wild and hatchery fish.

The wild fish have been accustomed to natural feeding all their lives and so they are most active when natural foods are in greatest abundance, that is during the day in spring and at the ends of the day in summer. Hatchery trout will have been kept in a fish farm for a year or more; this is a quarter of the average life expectancy and has a marked effect on feeding habits. As hatchery fish are fed at regular intervals during the day, and all day, they grow accustomed to looking for food near the surface in daytime. It follows that hatchery trout are liable to grab at anything that looks like food at any time of day, and so they are more easily caught than wild fish. Wild trout are most likely to be caught when feeding during their natural feeding times, on an imitation of the actual food. Thus fishing for them is more demanding; catching them is a greater achievement.

Most Irish fisheries are very natural in appearance. River and lake shores tend to be wild and sometimes overgrown, as cultivation seldom extends right up to the waterside. As a rule there is plenty of cover for the angler, and ample shelter for emerged aquatic insects. Weeds are seldom cut in rivers and lakes and heavy weed growth in summer is a characteristic of some waters. This may be a drawback in some respects, but it also holds back the flow and maintains the depth, provides cover for fish in low water and provides a good and well oxygenated environment for insect life. Birds and wild animals may also be seen taking advantage of the undisturbed areas.

An exception to these remarks is the case of rivers that have been the subject of arterial drainage schemes. These devastate the river bed and banks and do a great deal of damage to the fishing. River systems that have been subject to drainage will be named in the following notes; visiting anglers are advised to avoid them.

The most common method of fishing for brown trout is by using an artificial fly or nymph which imitates the insect on the water and casting to fish that are seen feeding, or into waters they are known to frequent. Trout may also be caught with float or ledger tackle using worms, slugs or other baits, or by spinning a natural or artificial fish. A popular fishing method used on large lakes is dapping with a natural insect. The insect, usually a mayfly, daddy long legs or grasshopper, is impaled on a fine hook and allowed to blow out from a drifting boat and skip over the water. A long rod and light line must be used and a good breeze is required. This method is entrancing, simple enough to be tried by a novice, and it produces some very big trout. Trout of over 10 lbs in weight (4.5 kg) have been caught occasionally by dapping in lakes such as Corrib and Mask.

Very large trout, of 5 to 20 lbs (2.3–9.0 kg) are usually caught by trolling a large spoon bait behind a boat. Corrib, Mask and Conn are the most likely lakes for a very big fish and salmon may also be caught by trolling on Corrib and Conn.

Artificial fly fishing with conventional tackle is probably the most productive as well as the most entertaining way of catching trout on lake or river. The traditional method of lake fishing is to cast a team of wet flies from a drifting boat, covering the maximum amount of water. If a particular pattern of fly is more effective, two or more of that pattern may be used. In this way, catches of from two to ten or more fish may be expected in an average day's fishing in the better waters. The more experienced angler will try to imitate the fly on the water, and cast to rising fish. This method is most interesting and productive on summer evenings or during the emergence of mayflies or large black midges in spring. Dry fly fishing from boat or shore in summer, when big sedges are hatching, can be very exciting.

River fishing for trout with an artificial fly is perhaps the most exacting and interesting method of fishing for game fish. Skill and experience are desirable, as well as some knowledge of insect life. Although the average size of catch is likely to be smaller than that of lake trout, fish of 1 lb (0.5 kg) and over are common enough on the better limestone waters. Fish of over 8 lbs (3.6 kg) have been taken. It should be noted that where such large trout occur in rivers, good numbers of fish are less likely to be found. The majority of the river angler's catch is likely to be about 6 to 12 ozs (0.16–0.34 kg) in weight on an average day.

River trout may also be caught on bait. Worms are very killing at times but in general bait fishing is a waiting game and not as deadly as many anglers would imagine.

The spinning minnow will take large bags at times, and some big fish, but it is difficult to spin in many good trout waters because of weed and snags. Many baits may be lost for each trout that is caught. Fishing with worm, grub or slug baits is usually most effective early in the season, during floods, and when trout are not observed rising to fly.

The trout season is from mid-February to mid-October and varies slightly in different areas. The best daytime fly fishing is from mid-March to the end of May, and in September. In summer, early morning and late evening fishing is best.

More exact details of each water and of the fish and fly life to be expected, will be given in the sections on each water.

The Inland Fisheries Trust is a State sponsored body which manages a number of brown trout waters in the Republic and promotes all angling interests. The Trust has fish farms for restocking its waters and also sells stock to angling clubs. Valuable research work is done by Trust scientists and other staff.

The main Trust waters are the midland lakes and rivers in the Shannon drainage system. It also manages a number of smaller lakes and the great lakes of the west that are free fisheries. In general the Trust waters, especially their lakes, are well managed and well stocked. The rivers are not all exceptional trout waters as they have been subject to drainage and other disturbances and they are only localised trout waters. Frequent electrical fishing operations have to be carried out to control predators and these also upset the trout.

1. DUBLIN TO WEXFORD

The principal river in the Dublin area is the Liffey. It rises in the Wicklow Mountains and flows south, then in a broad loop into Co. Kildare, then north and east through Dublin City to Dublin Bay. A dam at Poulaphouca, on the Wicklow-Kildare border, has created a large hydro-electric reservoir. Above this lake, the Liffey is a rapid stony mountain stream holding mostly very small trout, as is the other main stream entering the lake, the King's River. Poulaphouca Lake holds trout, including a few big fish, but is subject to frequent and great changes of level, has poor fly life and is of little account as a trout fishery.

Below Poulaphouca Lake, the Liffey flows through the limestone plain of Co. Kildare and is a good trout river. It is pretty and well sheltered with trees, meandering through park-like farmland. There are long pools separated by broad weedy shadows and a few stony rapids. Much of the water is weedy glides. There is not a great deal of natural spawning in the lowest parts and trout are bigger but rather scarce below Straffan. Above and through Newbridge, there are good stocks. The average size of Liffey trout is small above Poulaphouca—about ½ lb (0.25 kg) in the upper middle reaches and ¾ lb (0.375 kg) in the lower middle. 1 lb (0.5 kg) trout are common enough, and fish of up to 4½ lbs (2.05 kg) are caught each year. Trout of over 2¾ lbs (1.2 kg) are seldom caught on fly.

Fly life is prolific and typical of an Irish limestone water. As it is much the same as for other limestone rivers, it will be described in some detail. The first fly to appear is the Large Dark Olive of March and early April. It is a big fly which hatches on fine days between noon and mid-afternoon. Later in April and early May, the smaller Olives appear round midday, but the trout often take little interest in them if the Iron Blue Dun, a small blackish fly, is hatching. Also reed smuts appear in fine weather and may be present in some numbers until midsummer. The smuts are small and black, and trout often take them in preference to larger flies.

Later in May, yellow stone flies appear on the stony stretches, and the Yellow May Dun hatches at dusk. The May fly is a large and conspicuous insect, of only local importance on the Liffey. It appears in late May and early June, the best hatches being at midday and at 7 p.m. On calm June evenings, the spent May flies, which fall on the water after depositing their eggs, sometimes provide a feast for the trout and a good opportunity for the angler to take some really fine fish. After the May fly, daytime fishing is not so good and evening fishing is recommended. Small Olives and sedge flies are the most important insects and dry fly fishing is the best method.

Sedges are moth-like insects, some of which are of large size, that emerge at dusk and after dark. From July to September, the most important fly is the Blue Winged Olive and its imago, the Sherry Spinner. Sedges and smuts are also present, along with small Olives.

In September, when the Large Olives and Iron Blues reappear, daytime fishing is once again worthwhile, and small sedges are important. In August and September, land insects may fall on to the water and be eaten by trout; the most common are probably ants but even a single daddy long legs is usually snapped up very quickly. It is beyond the scope of this book to describe the insects and artificial fly patterns in detail, and those interested should consult one of the many specialist books on the subject. The following patterns may, however, be of some help:

A good Olive imitation such as the Imperial in sizes 14, 16 and 18 will suffice for all the Olives; a Cinnamon Sedge and a Black Sedge, also an Alder in sizes 8 to 14, for the sedges; a Red Spinner in sizes 14 and 16, a Reed Smut, a Black Gnat, sizes 16 and 18, a Yellow Fly size 14 and some May flies and spent gnats, for the dry fly selection. Nymph-like patterns are better than traditional wet flies on limestone rivers: the Sawyer nymphs are good.

Other wet flies are the Partridge and Orange, Partridge and Yellow, Waterhen Blue and Black Spider. It is important that artificial flies are the correct size—similar to that of the natural. Most artificials sold in shops are far too big.

All the best fishing in the Liffey is in the hands of angling clubs. Day and season tickets may obtained in the Dublin tackle shops as well as in local centres like Naas and Newbridge. The Liffey is polluted for a short stretch in Dublin City, but despite this, spring salmon manage to ascend each year. It is a very early river; the salmon season starts on January 1 and the fishing continues until April. The first salmon of 1980 was caught at Islandbridge on January 1 and weighed 10 lbs (4.5 kg). In general, it is only of local interest.

Liffey clubs are as follows:

Dublin Trout Anglers' Association. About 12 miles, moderate stock. 25p per day, £5 annual (1979). Hon. Sec.: M. Donohoe, Clonkeen Road, Deansgrange, Co. Dublin.

North Kildare Trout and Salmon A.A. 30 miles, good stock, heavily fished. £1 per day, £3 per week (visitors—1978). Hon. Sec.: P. Byrne, 33 College Park, Newbridge, Co. Kildare.

Clane and Kilcock A. A. 50p per week (1979). M. Casey, Firmount, Clane.

Rory's tackle shop, Temple Bar, Garnett and Keegan, Parliament Street, and Moorkens, Upper Abbey Street, Dublin, all sell permits.

Dublin Salmon A. A. has the salmon fishing rights on the lower reaches. Charges £5 per day, £15 per annum. From tackle shops or C. Mew, Rose Cottage, Chapelizod Co. Dublin.

CO. WICKLOW—SMALL STREAMS

The Wicklow Mountains are granite, and in general the waters hold only small trout. A number of small streams drain east to the Irish Sea.

The main ones are the Dargle, which runs through Enniskerry to the sea at Bray, the Vartry at Ashford, the Inch River, and the Owenavorragh, which enters the sea at Courtown. All these rivers are rapid, rocky spate streams, holding small trout. They also have runs of sea trout and occasional salmon. The Dargle and the Owenavorragh can be good for sea trout after a summer flood. The Roundwood reservoirs are on the headwaters of the Vartry. They are pleasant mountain lakes holding a good stock of small trout of 4 to 8 ozs (0.11–0.22 kg) with occasional bigger ones to 2 lbs (0.9 kg).

The Dodder is a rocky stream flowing through the south Dublin suburbs and entering the tidal portion of the Liffey. It holds trout, but has been subject to intermittent pollution. The Bohernabreena reservoirs are lovely wooded lakes of natural appearance at the head of the Dodder. They hold a lot of trout; the average size in the lower lake is about 8 ozs (0.22 kg) and in the upper one, 5 ozs (0.14 kg). Trout of over ¾ lb (0.34 kg) are rare. Fly fishing only is allowed and permits are issued by the Dublin Corporation Water Works. Members of Dublin T.A.A. and the Dodder A.A. may fish free. Charges 25p a day, £1 per week.

The Avoca River system, comprising the Avonmore and Avonbeg, which combine to form the Avoca near Arklow, is an extensive system of mountain rivers. Again, the trout are small because of the nature of the country. However, the fishing is very enjoyable and the scenery is magnificent. There are fish farms on both rivers and the frequent escapes liven up the fishing in the vicinity of Woodenbridge and Rathdrum. Fly hatches are adequate and wet fly fishing is the most popular method on these rapid and stony waters. Seepage from old mine workings has polluted the lower Avoca, so there are few migratory fish.

Roundwood reservoir permits from Vartry Lodge, Roundwood. 25p per day or £1 per week. Two boats available at £1 per day (1978).

Avonmore River: Aughrim and District A.A. 50p per week (1978) D. M. Byrne, Aughrim Post Office.

Dargle River: Owens tackle shop, Bray. £1 per week (1979).

Owenavorragh River: Gorey Angling Club; Hon. Sec.: E. Lacey, 22 Main Street, Gorey. Also free to guests of Bayview and Courtown Hotels.

There is some free fishing in the Co. Wicklow rivers.

THE SLANEY VALLEY

The Slaney is a rapid river which rises in the Wicklow Mountains and flows generally south to Enniscorthy, where it meets the tide. It has a stony bed throughout its length, but there are good growths of ranunculus weed in many places. It contains large numbers of rather small trout and is a major salmon river. The opening day for salmon angling on the Slaney at the end of February (1980) produced the best catches for at least ten years. Over 150 fish were taken, a welcome boost for anglers who had been somewhat starved of catches in the river over the last five or six years. Some anglers went home with as many as eight fish.

Despite the small size of the fish, the Slaney is a pleasant and picturesque river and is of some account as a trout fishery in its upper and middle reaches. In the vicinity of Rathvilly and Tullow, it touches the limestone plain and the fly fishing can be very good at times, with occasional trout of over 1 lb (0.5 kg). The average size is about 6–8 ozs (0.16–0.22 kg). The fly life of a rocky river is slightly different from that of a limestone stream. The Large Olive and Iron Blue Dun are still important, as is the Yellow May Dun on May evenings. There are fewer small Olives, and Stone Flies are numerous between March and late May. Reed

Smut and the small black sedge flies known as needle flies are important day flying species.

Both of these may be seen on any day in late spring or summer, but the smuts are the more important in spring and the Needles in summer. The May fly does not occur. Different species of ephemeroptera are to be seen, but this is of marginal value to the angler as the various species are similar in general appearance and one imitation in suitable sizes will do for them all. The Blue Winged Olive is important. Land-born insects such as ants, beetles and Crane Flies are more important in the diet of trout in a spate river such as the Slaney than in limestone streams. During a spate, slugs and worms washed off the banks are readily accepted by the fish.

The Slaney is a good spring salmon river and is largely preserved for salmon fishing below Tullow. Salmon runs have decreased considerably in recent years, probably because of netting in the estuary and the sea. Sea trout also ascend the river and the best fishing for them is between Enniscorthy and Bunclody; they also ascend the tributary Rivers Bann and Boro.

Much of the salmon fishing in the Slaney is in private hands, but permission may occasionally be obtained by anglers staying in the locality. Sea trout fishing is free to licence holders below Enniscorthy Bridge. There is club water as follows:

Tullow A.A. 12 miles of water, good trout fishing, some salmon. 25p per day, £1 per week (trout). £2 per day for salmon (1978) W. Ward, The Square, Tullow.

Enniscorthy and District A.A. 2 miles of Slaney and River Boro. £4 per day for salmon; River Boro, £1 per year (1978). P. Courtney, 5 Weafer St, Enniscorthy, Co. Wexford. Also Slaney Hotel, Tullow.

2. WATERFORD TO KINSALE

The Rivers Barrow, Nore and Suir flow from the south midlands to the south coast; together they drain the Galtee and Slieve Bloom Mountains, as well as large areas of limestone plains. They have many tributaries and they unite to enter the sea at Waterford harbour.

The Barrow is a large river rising in the Bog of Allen near Mountmellick and it flows generally south to Waterford. Much of the Barrow is sluggish, especially the upper portion, and there is a number of towns along its length which pollute the river. In consequence, much of what used to be good fishing water is now poor or useless. There is some trout fishing in the upper reaches above Monasterevan, in the main river and in the tributaries Slate and Figile. This fishing is quite good at times; it is limestone water flowing through peat bog and rather featureless farmland.

Below Monasterevan is mostly coarse fishing water, more or less polluted as far as Milford Mills below Carlow, where there is a rapid stretch. From here, the condition of the river gradually improves, and it becomes a mixed fishery until it reaches the influence of the tide at St Mullins. The character of the Barrow changes completely where it runs through the Blackstairs Mountains in its lower course. Although it is a big river, it is rapid and rocky in places with some weirs and some long deep pools. The valley is steep sided and well wooded, and there is some excellent trout water.

This is limestone water and some big fish may be caught. Hatches of fly are good, especially just above St Mullins. There are many small tributaries running from the mountains providing good spawning. The casual angler may receive the impression that the average size of trout is small because of the large number of young fish, but there are many good trout for the careful and selective angler. The fly life has something of the nature of both limestone and acid rivers.

The Barrow in this area is a first class mixed fishery and is popular with coarse anglers for the size and variety of its fish. The fly fisher may occasionally catch large rudd and there is also salmon and a few sea trout.

The principal tributaries of the Barrow, apart from those already mentioned, are the Bog River (Athy A.A.—good for trout) and the Greese, Lerr and Graney (small limestone streams, good trout fishing—Carlow A.A.).

Barrow clubs:

Monasterevan and District A.A. 8 miles, 25p per day (1978). Paul Cullen, Main Street, Athy.

Athy and District A.A. 50p per year (1978). P. Mulhall, 20 Emily Square, Athy.

Barrow A.C. £1 per year (1978). D. Rea, tackle dealer, Dublin Street, Carlow.

Also small local clubs at Graiguenamanagh, Borris, Goresbridge, Muine Bheag, Stradbally, Portarlington. Also New Ross A.A.

The River Nore rises in the Slieve Bloom Mountains and runs generally SSE to join the Barrow at New Ross. It is very different in character to the Barrow, despite their close proximity. The Nore is rapid and stony from its source to Inistioge, where it meets the tide. The normal character of the Nore is a succession of stream and pool. Some of the pools are long, but it is all trout water. It is also an important salmon river.

Locally, the Nore is held to be a mediocre trout fishery when compared with some of its tributaries, which are limestone in character and hold trout of rather better than average size than the main river. These tributaries, although small, are excellent trout fisheries. They are the Mountrath or White Horse River, the Erkina and Gayle, which join the Nore at Durrow, the Dinan, which flows from the NE via Castlecomer and the King's River, which flows through Callan. All of them hold good stocks of trout averaging perhaps half a pound (0.25 kg) or a little over, with some excellent fish of up to and over 5 lbs (2.3 kg). Some drainage work has been carried out on the Erkina and Gayle.

The best trout fishing on the main river is between Kilkenny and Thomastown. There are some long pools and flats near Bennetsbridge, where there is a local May fly hatch, and trout over 6 lbs (2.7 kg) have been taken on fly. There are some sea trout in the vicinity of Inistioge. Fly life is generally excellent, more in the character of a mountain river, but the tributaries have excellent B.W.O. and sedges. The Nore gives good spring salmon fishing and has some summer fish. Catches have declined recently due to netting in common with all the SE rivers. Much of the salmon fishing is in private hands. The trout fishing in the Nore and tributaries is worth attention; much is in the hands of the clubs listed below and information may be had from the Kilkenny tackle shops.

Abbeyleix A.A.-H.A. Bardon, Abbeyleix.

Stradbally and Mountrath A.A., Nore and Mountrath Rivers.

Castlecomer A.A.—Dinan River, good trout.

Durrow A.C., and Rathdowney A.A.—Nore, Erkina and Gayle. Good trout.

Kilkenny A.A.—P. A. Troy, College Road, Kilkenny. 10 miles, Nore and Dinan Rivers. Fly only. £3 per week (1979).

Also Kilkenny City and County A.A., 11 miles of water. £1 per day. £3 per week. Fly only. Bennettsbridge A.A., Thomastown A.A.

THE RIVER SUIR

The River Suir rises in the Devil's Bit Mountain, runs south to Cahir and thence east to Waterford Harbour. It's an excellent limestone trout river from near its source to where it meets the tide at Carrick-on-Suir. It holds a heavy stock of fish and has several tributaries which also provide good trout fishing. In some places, the stock is heavy, to the detriment of the average size, but in others, especially in the lower reaches, there are good numbers of heavier trout. The general character of the river is a long series of rather shallow gravelly glides with a very rich weed growth; there are occasional stony runs and some deep pools. It flows through rich farmland and it is well sheltered by waterside trees. The banks are rush-grown in many places. Wading is generally easy and there is plenty of cover but the trees do not interfere too much with angling.

The main tributaries are the Tar, Neir, Annagh, Clodiagh, Multeen and Aherlow. All are good trout rivers; the Neir is rapid and rocky, while the others have more weedy glides and long shallow pools as well as some stony runs. In recent years, there has been a great deal of localised pollution of the Suir, the worst caused by untreated town sewage. At the time of writing, all angling clubs have declined to issue visitors' tickets. The worst affected areas are Thurles, Cahir and Clonmel. Preventive measures have had little effect to date.

In my opinion, the Suir is still a very good trout river, although one effect of pollution is a very heavy growth of weed which makes fishing difficult in summer. Much of the fishing is in the hands of angling clubs and some is in private hands. Where visitors' tickets are issued, fly fishing only is frequently the rule; fly life is very rich. See the 'Liffey' section for details of a limestone river. The Blue-Winged Olive and Sherry Spinner fishing is especially good. A favourite stretch is the water of the Cashel and Golden Angling Association in the vicinity of Athassal Abbey, below Cashel. Although the average size of the catch may not be large, at around 6 to 7 ozs (0.16–0.19 kg), fish are nearly always found to be rising. There is a variety of water, and the evening rise, when larger trout take the fly, can be very exciting. The fish are very quick risers and are difficult to hook, but if the imitation is a good one they take very readily. Locally tied flies are well proven and may be bought in the riverside towns. There are information centres and tackle dealers in Thurles, Cashel, Cahir, Clonmel and Carrick. There are runs of spring and summer salmon, but they have decreased in recent years in common with other Irish rivers. Much of the salmon fishing is in private hands but permission may be obtained in some cases. There is some association water at Clonmel and Kilsheelan.

The Suir is a highly regarded fishery and permission must be sought before the visitor wets a line. The pollution situation should be ascertained in advance.

Suir Angling Associations:

Carrick-on-Suir A.A.; Kilsheelan A.C.; Clonmel Salmon A.C.; Cahir and

District A.A.; Ardfinnan A.A.; Cashel, Golden and S. Tipperary A.A.; Goatenbridge A.A. (River Tar).

GALTEE MOUNTAINS

There are a few lakes in the Galtees, some of which are reputed to provide quite good trout fishing. The fishing is free, but ask the farmer's permission first.

SOUTH COASTAL STREAMS

A number of streams run into the sea from the Comeragh Mountains; the main ones are the Mahon, at Bunmahon, the Tay at Stradbally, the Dalligan and the Colligan at Dungarvan. All of these streams hold some trout and sea trout. The sea trout fishing can be quite good at times during the summer nights, but all of these are small streams and are only of local interest. Before fishing, permission should be obtained from John Casey, tackle dealer, Dungarvan, Co. Waterford.

THE MUNSTER BLACKWATER

The Blackwater rises in the mountains east of Killarney and flows east to Lismore, entering the sea at Youghal. It is a major salmon river which also holds a lot of trout. Dace and roach are numerous in the middle and lower stretches, and may be a nuisance to the trout fly fisher. The Blackwater flows over sandstone, and is a swift and rocky spate river in its upper reaches. It has a stony bed in most places, but in the middle and lower reaches, the nature is stream and pool, with some weed and long sandy flats. It is a big river in the lower parts.

There are trout throughout its length; the average size is not large, being ¼ to ½ lb (0.12–0.25 kg). On a good day, the discerning angler's bag may average a little over the half pound (0.25 kg).

Some of the Blackwater's tributaries, principally the Bride, the Awbeg and the Funshion, provide rather better trout fishing than the main river.

The Blackwater is best known as a salmon river and it receives good runs of spring, summer and late salmon. Some sea trout ascend the lower reaches and the Bride. Much of the salmon fishing is private but beats may be rented from the local owners. There are many angling clubs along this river, probably more than in any other part of Ireland. Some of these clubs have salmon as well as trout fishing rights, while others have their waters on the condition that they give salmon anglers first preference on the water. The river has the fly life to be expected on a stony water—March Brown, Olives, Stone Flies, Black Midge and small sedges are the more important flies. The Needle Fly and August Dun are to be expected. A description of the Cork Blackwater would be incomplete without mention of the Lower Blackwater fisheries at Ballyduff, Co. Waterford.

The Blackwater Lodge Hotel maintains about 25 miles (40 km) of the Blackwater and two miles (3.2 km) of the South Bride for guests of the hotel and adjacent holiday bungalows. This is a carefully maintained fishery, divided into beats of ample size to ensure unspoiled angling, well keepered and carefully regulated. The fishery is best known for salmon fishing, which is possibly the best in the country.

Spring fishing starts in February and continues until April, and this is the best time for catching a big salmon of 20 lbs (9.0 kg) or over. Smaller summer fish comprise the bulk of the run from mid-April until August, when the late runs of big salmon come in. There is a great variety of water and beats are rotated so that all guests have a chance on all parts of the fishery. I would repeat that salmon fishing requires some skill, but the desirable local knowledge is provided by the staff of this fishery, giving visiting anglers a much better chance of success.

Figures of catches speak for themselves and the average catch on this fishery is about one salmon per rod per day. If there is good water in the summer, this average may rise to two per day, but summer fishing is somewhat dependent on a good flow. Guests have taken up to six salmon in a day in recent seasons (1976 and 1977). As well as salmon, there are sea trout which run the Lower Blackwater and the Bride. About a thousand sea trout are taken each season from the latter river by guests of Blackwater Lodge. There is also fair brown trout fishing and excellent coarse fishing and sea angling in the area, so even if the salmon are not running well, there is plenty to interest the angler. The annual catch of salmon to guests of the hotel is around five hundred fish in recent years. This is a first class fishery and is highly recommended to visitors.

The charge for fishing is from £1 a day, £6 per week on the Bride, to £6 a day and £45 a week on the best Blackwater beats (1978). Tuition and ghillies are available. Boats available on some beats at £12 per day for 2 rods. Ghillies £7 to £8 per day. Anglers are advised to book well in advance, as quality fishing like this is in great demand. Day permits may be available, if all the beats are not taken up, on enquiry at the Blackwater Lodge Hotel and Sporting Centre, Ballyduff, Co. Waterford.

Cork Blackwater—Angling associations and fisheries:

Salmon fishing: Lismore Estates, Lismore, Co. Waterford.

Cappoquin Estates. Cappoquin Angling Club—W. Deavy, Richmond House, Cappoquin.

Peter Demster, Carrigeen, Conna, Co. Cork. Twenty named pools and nine miles (14.48 km) of water. Ghillies, tackle, instruction and advice available. Charges from £6 to £9 a day and from £35 a week (1979).

S. H. Martin, Blackwater Lodge (see text).

Fermoy Salmon A.A.—Jack O'Sullivan, 41 Patrick Street, Fermoy.

R. Wallis, Bridge Street Bar, Mallow. 1 mile (1.6 km) of water.

Trout fishing: All parts of the river and tributaries are controlled by angling clubs. The above salmon fisheries will issue permits to genuine trout anglers if the water is not occupied.

There are trout angling clubs at Cappoquin, Ballyduff, Mallow, Fermoy, Banteer, Kanturk, Kilworth, Doneraile, Mitchelstown, Kildorerry and other locations.

THE RIVER LEE

The Lee is a sandstone river rising in the Caha Mountains and running east to Cork Harbour. It is a lovely river, flowing through a deep valley and a series of lakes. The lower portion has been dammed in two places to make two hydroelectric reservoirs.

There is good fishing for rather small trout in the Lee. The reservoirs also hold trout and the lower one is maintained as a trout fishery by the Inland Fisheries Trust. They also hold a lot of coarse fish, and the trout angling is not particularly good.

The tributaries Sullance and Laney are small stony rivers with heavy stocks of small trout and occasional bigger fish that ascend from the reservoirs. The trout average 4 to 5 ozs (0.11–0.14 kg) in the rivers. The river fishing is very pleasant and some stretches of the Lee hold better fish. Much of the fishing in the Lee and its tributaries above the reservoirs is reputed to be free. The reservoirs are owned by the ESB and Inland Fishery Trust members may fish them. Below the reservoirs, the Lee is preserved. The Cork Salmon A.A. has some water. Permits from the Cork Fishing Centre, MacCurtain Street. There is also the Macroom Angling Association; B. Baker, South Square, Macroom.

The River Bandon rises in west Cork and flows east to Kinsale Harbour. The Bandon is like a miniature of the Cork Blackwater; it is swift and streamy with a stony bed, but it may fall very low and become weedy in summer. In its lower reaches, there are plenty of small trout, but salmon and sea trout are more important. The best fishing is after rain in summer. At such times, the sea trout fishing can be very good. Higher up, in the vicinity of Enniskeane, the trout fishing is rather better. There are some good pools but low water reduces the fishing.

Bandon Salmon and Trout A.A. Permits £1 per day, obtainable in Bandon.

Ballineen and Enniskean A.C. Permits £1 per day (salmon and sea trout), 25p per day (trout). Fly fishing only. Mr P. Fehilly, Ballineen.

3. THE SOUTH-WEST AND WEST

In the mountainous regions of the south west and west, as well as in Donegal, the terrain is rugged and well watered. There are many small streams and some considerable river and lake systems. Most of the rivers are rather short and rapid, but some achieve considerable volume.

The rugged nature of the mountains, with large areas of bare granite, shallow soils and peat bog, affords little feeding for fish, but provides plenty of ideal spawning ground. Consequently, this is salmon and sea trout country. These migratory fish feed in the rich waters of the sea and ascend the rivers and lakes in the late spring, summer and autumn. Salmon runs have been affected by netting at sea, but in some of the best preserved waters, salmon netting is controlled and there is some good spring and summer fishing.

Most waters have runs of sea trout or white trout, as they are known locally. These fish are the migratory strain of brown trout, and they ascend the rivers in very large numbers in summer. In the better fisheries, where the rivers run directly into the sea over rocks, and there are good holding pools and lakes on the system, the runs of sea trout are not dependent on rain and good fishing may be expected even during dry periods. Other fisheries are dependent on rain to some extent. Sea trout take the fly very freely, but like all fish, they have their taking times and their resting times.

Much fishing is done from boats on lakes. Anglers fish all day and take advantage of the rise when it occurs. Others prefer to fish in the early mornings and evenings, when sport is more dependable and may be very fast.

Most of the rivers are of much the same nature, with bare rocky bottoms, rapid runs and deep dark pools. The banks are open rough pasture or bog land, with the occasional alder, gorse or thorn bushes. Some of the best rivers have frequent artificial dams along them which provide holding pools and resting places for the ascending fish.

Many of these mountain river and lake systems are privately owned and carefully managed fisheries. Some are leased to hotels. They are well keepered and the number of rods is regulated to maintain the quality of the fishing. Boats are maintained on the lakes and boatmen are normally available. In fact, everything possible is done to ensure the comfort and success of the angler. The various hotels and guesthouses that cater especially for the angler often arrange boats and allocate beats in advance so that their guests may have a chance at all parts of their waters. At the end of the day, the various catches are frequently displayed in the hall of the hotel or in the fishing lodge, and great dishes of silvery sea trout and salmon may be seen.

Quality fishing is in demand and anglers wishing to avail of it should apply in good time, especially for salmon fishing, as the number of rods on any water is usually limited. Charges for fishing are not as high as one might expect.

Good salmon fishing is expensive as a rule, but sea trout fishing is often very cheap. Some hotels do not charge anything extra for their guests on their own waters. Normal charges are from about £1 to £6 or more a day, depending on the quality of the sport to be expected. This charge may include the use of a boat and engine, but an extra charge is made if a boatman is required. There is some free salmon and sea trout fishing and some Association water. The free fishing is not necessarily of poor quality. For example, Lough Currane at Waterville in Co. Kerry is free but it is possibly the best sea trout water in the west, and a good salmon lake too. On one occasion I took six good sea trout in an hour, fishing from the shore of Lough Currane. Most small streams that enter the sea directly receive a few sea trout and the odd salmon after rain. These are frequently free, but they may also be popular with local anglers.

The most common method of fishing for sea trout in rivers and lakes is with conventional fly tackle, casting from a drifting boat or over known lies from the shores of lake, and where fish are observed to be active in rivers. Fly patterns used are not imitative as a rule; successful patterns such as Peter Ross or Teal and Silver are attractive lures, barely resembling any insect. Dapping a live insect or a bushy artificial frequently attracts good sea trout on lakes in warm weather, and when rivers are low, small brown trout flies can be successful.

Migratory fish usually take very freely during their best taking times. In fact, they appear to be attacking the fly rather than just eating it, but like all fish they may also be very dour. Generally speaking, migratory fish take best in fresh water when they have just ascended from the sea and are resting. They do not take well when they are running, but they may do so during short rests in pools between spells of running. The best catches are made at any time of day after rain, especially when the raised water levels are just beginning to recede. If there has been no rain, very early mornings and late evenings are the best times, although many lakes fish well all day as long as there is enough wind to keep the surface layers well oxygenated. When fish are taking well, fly patterns may not be important, but most localities have their traditional favourites.

Sea trout may also be caught with spinner, worm or slug baits. Salmon also are caught with fly, spinner or worm. Salmon seem to take best in full daylight, although fairly early mornings can be a good time if the fish have been in fresh water for some time.

4. SOUTH-WEST CORK & KERRY

BANTRY BAY AND THE KENMARE RIVER

A large number of short rivers drain into these two deep inlets from the surrounding mountains. All receive runs of sea trout and some salmon after floods in summer. Some of these rivers are fished very hard by local anglers and it is customary, at times, to reserve a spot for the evening's fishing! Some fishing is available for visitors. The main waters are the Ilen River (Ilen Anglers Club, Skibbereen) and the Ardrigole River (Land Commission).

There are many trout lakes in south west Co. Cork. Among them are the Shepperton Lakes, near Skibbereen. They comprise a cluster of five spring-fed lakes which hold plenty of quite nice trout of fair average size. In one of them, the most difficult to fish, the average is nearly ¾ lb (0.34 kg). These lakes are managed by the Inland Fisheries Trust. Some of the numerous lakes scattered about the plateau of the Caha Mountains are rich and weedy; they hold small numbers of big trout. Others hold many smaller fish and local knowledge is needed to select the right lake! These lakes are a stiff climb from Glengarriff. Barley Lake, near Glengarriff, is a good lake for smallish trout and occasional fish up to 1 lb (0.5 kg) and a little over. These are free fisheries situated in magnificent mountain scenery.

There are a number of spate rivers flowing into Kenmare Bay. The main ones are the Blackwater and Skreen Rivers. They hold sea trout and a few salmon after summer and autumn floods. Parts of them are preserved and advice should be obtained locally before fishing. The Kenmare Estate Office preserves a number of sea trout and salmon lakes in the Kenmare area and permits to fish in some parts of them may be obtained from the estate office in the town. The main waters are the Cloon River and Cloon Lakes, the Dawros River and the Roughty River. It is advisable to enquire in advance, as some of these waters, especially the rivers, may be let in advance, by the period or the season. They provide good fishing at times.

Kenmare A.C. has fishing on the R. Roughty. 1½ miles of salmon and sea trout. £3 per day, £10 per week.

SOUTH WEST KERRY

The Waterville or Currane River is a short stream connecting Lough Currane with the sea. The river below the road bridge, containing the famous Butler's Pool, is preserved by the Lake Hotel, although I believe occasional days may be had on it for about £20. Above the bridge, a short stretch of river and the whole of Lough Currane is free fishing. Currane is a large lake; access is easy and it may be fished from the shore. The usual method of fishing is wet fly from a drifting boat. The local boatmen know the best drifts and lies of salmon and sea trout, so a stranger may be better advised to hire a boat, at least until some local knowledge is acquired.

Lough Currane is one of the best sea trout waters in the country and has excellent runs of fish from May to October. The fish are of better average size than the usual Irish sea trout. Average size is around 1¼ to 1½ lbs (0.61–0.75 kg). Two pounders (0.9 kg) are common and fish of 5 and 6 lbs (2.3–2.7 kg) are not infrequent. Good bags are frequently taken, a typical recent one being 110 trout to one rod in five days' fly fishing and eight salmon to one rod in one morning. This lake is famous, but not over-fished.

The inflowing rivers, the Cummeragh and Coppal, and Loughs Derriana and Cloonaghlin and others, are preserved by the Butler Arms, Waterville Lake and Bayview Hotels for the use of their guests. All are good sea trout waters. The higher waters are more dependent on recent rain. Charges are £4 per day. Boat with engine and boatman on Lough Currane now the charge is £17.50 per day, including lunch (1979).

Lough Currane also holds some respectable brown trout and fish of 10 ozs to 1 lb (0.28–0.5 kg) are common enough. All these lakes and rivers are set in magnificent, rather severe mountain scenery.

The Inny River is a fair sized salmon river flowing into Ballinskelligs Bay near Waterville. Most of it is preserved for guests of the Waterville hotels. There are a number of lesser streams in the vicinity of Waterville and Cahirciveen with runs of sea trout and the odd salmon. Visiting anglers are advised to join the Angling Association at Waterville, or make a small contribution, as they will receive some good advice on the locality.

It is important to realise that local knowledge is needed to get the best out of large lakes such as Currane, both for brown trout and migratory fish. Fish have established lies, follow certain routes and take better in certain areas. The local anglers and boatmen know the best areas.

CAHIRCIVEEN TO GLENBEIGH

The Carhan and Terta Rivers run into Valentia Harbour near Cahirciveen; they receive runs of sea trout after summer rain, but are of only local importance.

The Behy River is another small, rapid mountain river. It receives good runs of sea trout at times, but does not have many good pools. A lake at the head of it—the water belongs to the Glenbeigh Hotel—is worth fishing. The Caragh River is a big but short river draining Caragh Lake. The Upper Caragh, Meelagh, Brida and Owenroe run into the lake. There is good salmon fishing in these rivers and the lake, and in several small lakes in the area. There are also good runs of sea trout and small brown trout. Most of the fishing is preserved by the Glencar Hotel, Glencar, for guests only, but permits may be obtained for some other waters. Boats are available.

The Lower Caragh River is an excellent early salmon and summer sea trout river, which flows from Caragh to the sea near Glenbeigh. March is the best month, followed by April and February. In summer the river is normally low but brown trout and sea trout may be caught. Salmon and sea trout may be caught in Caragh Lake.

The Caragh is preserved by the Towers and Glenbeigh Hotels, which also have several miles of fishing for salmon, sea trout and brown trout, including some of the best named salmon pools and the Muckross Trust water, in the River Laune and in the Feale. Boats are provided by the hotels when required and boatmen and ghillies are also available.

THE RIVER LAUNE AND KILLARNEY LAKES

The Laune flows via Lough Leane, the largest of the Killarney Lakes, into the head of Dingle Bay at Killorglin. It is a completely different river in its lower reaches from most of the other rivers in Co. Kerry. It has long pools and weedy glides over a bed of small stones and gravel and holds a heavy stock of brown trout as well as receiving good runs of salmon and sea trout. The brown trout are very numerous and rise well to the fly.

It is an ideal spawning water, so there are a lot of small fish. There is a good sprinkling of excellent brown trout over 1 lb (0.5 kg) that may be caught on fly by the careful angler. Laune trout are beautifully marked and are very hard fighters. Fish of over 5 lbs (2.3 kg) have been caught in the tidal waters in the vicinity of Killorglin. The Lower Laune is well wooded and flows through rich pasture land; it has some of the appearance of a limestone river.

A good reach is in the hands of the Milltown and District Trout and Salmon Angling Association and permits may be obtained in Killorglin and Milltown. There is a little free fishing in the vicinity of Killorglin Bridge. Other parts of the river are in the hands of various private owners. Apply to Earl of Desmond Hotel, Tralee.

The Killarney Lakes, famous for their beauty, also provide free fishing for trout. Lough Leane is probably the best, and although the fish are rather small, on a good day they may average over ½ lb (0.25 kg). They are very free rising. Some large ferox trout are taken from Lough Leane by trolling. All these lakes may be fished from a boat or from the shore. Most of the mountain lakes in the vicinity of Killarney hold good numbers of small trout. One of them, Kilbrean Lake, is managed by the Inland Fisheries Trust and holds some better fish. It is occasionally restocked with rainbows as well as brown trout.

The Flesk is a stony river with streams and pools, which runs into Lough Leane at Killarney. It is a good trout river, although the fish are rather small. The local angling association, the Lough Leane A.A. has rights on this river and members also fish the lakes in the area. Visiting anglers are advised to join. Apply to Joan Fleming, 25 High Street, Killarney. £1 annual membership.

DINGLE PENINSULA WATERS

A number of streams drain this mountainous area, most of them of little account for fishing. The Annascaul River is rapid and rocky, draining Annascaul Lake. It holds small trout and has good runs of sea trout and some salmon after summer rain. Apply locally before fishing.

The Owenmore River runs into Brandon Bay and has good runs of migratory fish; it is private. The River Maine flows into the head of Dingle Bay and is reputed to provide fair brown trout fishing as well as sea trout and occasional salmon. Said to be free fishing, but local advice should be sought. These rivers are heavily poached.

There are several lakes on the Dingle Peninsula. The mountain ones hold some small trout, but are of little account for fishing. One of them is said to hold char. Lough Gill at Castlegregory is a large shallow lake separated from Brandon Bay by a sand bar. It is surrounded by dense reed beds, but it can be fished from a boat or with some difficulty by wading. It holds excellent trout which average about 12 ozs (0.34 kg) and fish of up to 1¾ lbs (0.84 kg) are commonly caught on the fly. The water is shallow and clear over a sandy bottom with chara weed, and the fish must be approached with care, but it is most entertaining fishing. There are many wildfowl. The fishing is free and a farm/guesthouse on the lake side has some boats for hire.

The River Maine, which enters the head of Dingle Bay near Castlemaine, is a trout river which has good runs of sea trout, including some large early fish in

May and early June.

THE RIVER FEALE AND TRIBUTARIES

The Feale rises in the Mullaghkirke Mountains and runs generally north west through Abbeyfeale and Listowel into the Shannon estuary. It is a big spate river system running through mostly rather poor rocky country; it used to receive very heavy runs of salmon and sea trout. Salmon runs are now reduced by netting but the sea trout runs are still good. The river is quite heavily fished by local anglers.

The Feale system was the subject of a drainage scheme some years ago; it ruined the appearance of some parts of the river and made the banks difficult in places. The river has recovered somewhat, but it is still not pretty and is subject to violent spates. The sea trout fishing can be very good; much of it is in the hands of local angling associations. However, there was a local pollution problem recently.

Tralee and District A.A. 2 miles of water. £2 per day, £10 per week. T. Hennebery, Castle Countess, Tralee, Co. Kerry.

North Kerry Salmon A.A. 15 miles of water. £3 per day. North County Guesthouse, 67 Church Street, Listowel.

THE DEEL AND MAIGUE RIVERS

These rivers are limestone trout streams and both used to provide first class fly fishing for big trout. Unfortunately, the Deel was the subject of a drainage scheme some years ago, from which it has only partially recovered. The Maigue is now undergoing the same treatment. The Office of Public Works carries out these drainage schemes, which are supposed to improve the agricultural potential of the river basins by removing the risk of flooding and by lowering the water table to make bog land available for farming. In practice, they usually do severe damage to the ecology of the river, create water shortages in the summer, cause severe spates and destroy as much land as they reclaim with spoil heaps. They also destroy the fishing and although some attempt may be made to restock, the food supply is so upset that it takes years for any real recovery.

Visitors should beware of fishing in any river that has had recent drainage works. The Deel drainage scheme was completed more than ten years ago; the river has somewhat recovered. An occasional good trout may be caught on the fly. There are angling clubs at Rathkeale, Newcastle West and Askeaton. There is some salmon fishing; some of the water is privately owned.

5. THE SHANNON, TRIBUTARIES, WESTMEATH & WEST CLARE

The Shannon and its tributaries drain a large proportion of central Ireland. The main river is sluggish with a number of large lakes along its course and is navigable by small craft. It is of little interest to the game fisherman, but there are trout in the Shannon; because it is limestone water, they grow to a large size. Some of the Shannon tributaries are in themselves quite big rivers, and most of them have been the subject of drainage schemes, justified by the boggy nature of the central plain. The fishing in the Shannon is owned by the Electricity Supply Board and much of it is managed by the Inland Fisheries Trust.

On the main river trout fishing is very localised, in the vicinity of the weirs and the few rapids. Some large trout of up to nearly 20 lbs (9.0 kg) have been caught on spinning baits intended for pike and a few of over 5 lbs (2.3 kg) have come to fly. The areas for trout are below the weirs, especially at Jamestown, Tarmonbarry and Athlone, the rapids at Meelick and Castleconnell and near Limerick City. Some parts, especially at Castleconnell, are preserved for salmon fishing.

The Mulcaire River is a limestone stream of moderate size that enters the Shannon from the south east above Limerick. It is a salmon river and also holds trout that average about ½ lb (0.25 kg); it is good fly water.

The Nenagh River is a similar stream, holding good trout and suitable for dry fly. It flows through Nenagh to Lough Derg and is subject to slight pollution at Nenagh. The Little Brosna River is a limestone trout stream managed by the Inland Fisheries Trust. It has a heavy stock of rather small trout and a few big ones; the river also receives a few salmon. Large trout from Lough Derg ascend it in the late summer and autumn. The river is affected by slight pollution from Roscrea and other sources which cause a heavy weed growth in the summer and fishing becomes difficult in the large pools which hold the better trout. Even so, it provides quite good fly fishing. There are good hatches of Olives and smuts, good May fly at times and excellent sedges. The most attractive parts of the Little Brosna are in the vicinity of Birr, where the trout average 6 or 7 ozs (0.16–0.19 kg) and occasional pounders (0.5 kg) may be caught. The best places for big fish are the Monastery Flats near Roscrea, the rather featureless water below Brosna Bridge and the lower parts well below the Angler's Rest.

The Little Brosna is a typical Irish bog stream. It has a gentle flow with weedy glides and deep, rather dull looking flats. The headwaters have some streams and rapids; the banks are rather bare and open. The fishing is very demanding; the water is well fished by locals. There are pike and other coarse fish; the IFT uses electrical fishing to control these, possibly to the detriment of the larger trout.

The Big Brosna drains Lough Ennell in Co. Westmeath and flows via Kilbeggan and Clara to the Shannon at Lough Ree. It is a limestone river and was subject to a drainage scheme some years ago. It is fairly well recovered but the banks are steep and the bottom somewhat unstable in places. It is a sluggish river with a few glides and rapids where trout may be caught. It holds a lot of pike and coarse fish and the IFT keeps the trout areas stocked and controls

Salmon fishing at Waterville, Co. Kerry

the pike. The best trout stretches are in the vicinity of Kilbeggan, from below Clara to Ballycumber, at the junction with Clodiagh, around Ferbane and below Belmont Bridge. There is a May fly hatch and good B.W.O. The river holds some excellent trout, but because of the patchy fishing and poor appearance of the banks, it is of mainly local interest.

The Big Brosna tributaries, the Clodiagh and the two Silver Rivers, hold heavy stocks of smallish trout and some good ones, providing good fly fishing. These rivers too have been subject to drainage schemes and in one place, the Big Silver River flows through a commercial peat bog. The banks are steep and the appearance poor. The fish average about six ozs (0.16 kg) and occasional pounders (0.5 kg) are caught.

The Inny River flows through Lough Sheelin and Lough Derravaragh, thence to Ballymahon and the Shannon at Lough Ree. It is a sluggish river, with a lot of coarse fish water, but locally there is quite good fishing for big trout. There seems to be very few small fish and the stock is rather poor; fly hatches are rather unreliable.

Big trout are notoriously uncertain risers and this coupled with the poor stock makes the Inny a most uncertain river for the fly fisher, but it does have a May fly hatch and good B.W.O. If the angler is fortunate enough to find a few trout rising, he may enjoy good sport. The Inny had a drainage scheme some years ago, and the insect life has not yet settled down. There are large numbers of dragonfly larvae which are carnivores, and possibly a reason for the poor fly life in many stretches. The best trout areas are between Lough Derravaragh and Ballinalack—a few trout but most of them over 1 lb (0.5 kg)—and from Abbeyshrule to Ballymahon. There are some trout here and there elsewhere in the Inny, but in general it is a rather dull river for the trout angler, although there is the chance of catching a very large fish. The size limit is 12″ (0.3 metres).

THE WESTMEATH LAKES

There are numerous large lakes on the midland limestone plain, several of which have been developed by the Inland Fisheries Trust as brown trout fisheries. These lakes always held a number of wild trout, but because of limited spawning ground and coarse fish predators, stocks were not heavy. Fishing was confined to times of big fly hatches that made trout easier to locate. In the Trust lakes, the wild stock has been supplemented by hatchery fish. Predators are controlled and natural spawning is encouraged. These lakes now provide excellent fly fishing for trout of good quality and size.

Lough Sheelin is at present the best of these lakes. Situated on the Cavan/Longford/Westmeath border, it is several thousand acres in area and is all shallow limestone water. The shores are wooded and well indented, so nearly the whole lake is holding water. It has excellent hatches of chironomids from April to September, some May fly, good Lake Olives and quite good hatches of small sedges on summer nights. The trout are silvery, red fleshed and quite good fighters. The average size is about 1½ lbs (0.75 kg) and fish of over 2 lbs (0.9 kg) are common. The biggest fish taken on fly each year are usually 5 to 6 lbs (2.3–2.7 kg). There are no "best areas". The whole lake is fishable; the shores are mostly fished. Favourite areas are the bay adjacent to Chambers' farm/guesthouse, Kilnahard Bay and the east shore north of Bog Bay. Boats are available for hire

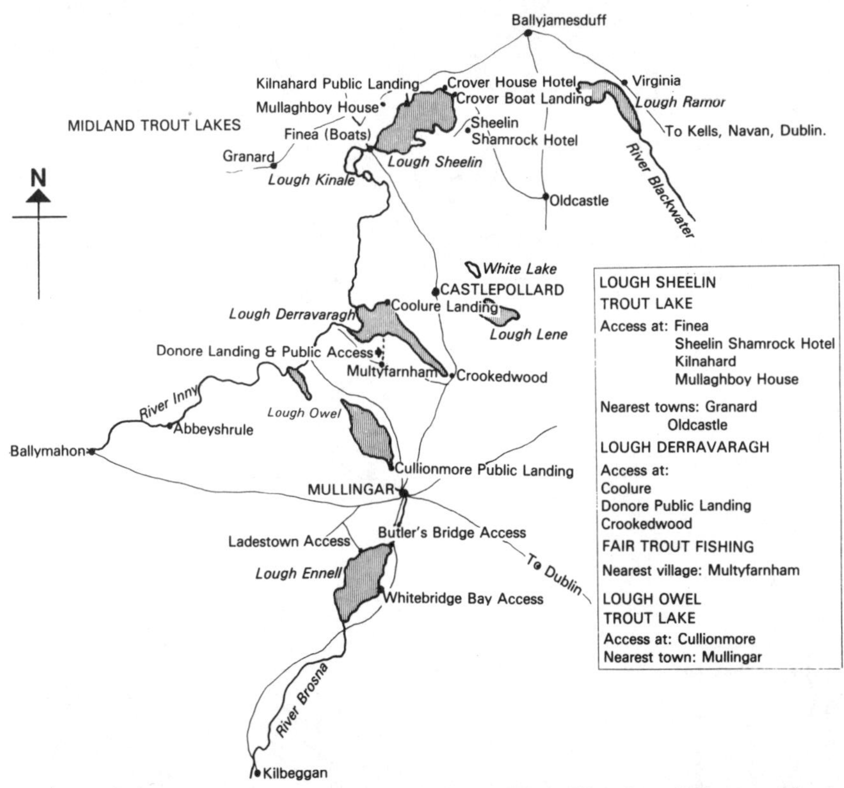

from Chambers' and from the Sheelin Shamrock Hotel and Crover House. These hotels and Chambers' guesthouse cater especially for anglers.

The usual way of fishing the midland lakes is from a drifting boat using wet flies. Shore fishing is possible on Sheelin, the shore from Kilnahard to Chambers' being a likely location. Anglers often fish traditional patterns of wet all day, but the more particular angler will fish the rise. This can be very effective on a summer evening, when a good imitation of a chironomid or sedge pupa fished near the surface can produce excellent catches. The usual bag is about two trout per rod per day; limit catches of eight trout are not unusual. Lough Sheelin is heavily fished and visiting anglers should reserve boats in advance to avoid being disappointed.

Lough Sheelin has been affected by eutrophication due to intensive farming around its shores. At present, this has not adversely affected the fishing and although it may have been the cause of reduced Mayfly hatches, it could also have caused increased chironomids.

Lough Derravaragh is similar in character to Sheelin but at present is not so prolific. It has good Mayfly hatch and the trout are large, averaging about two pounds in weight (0.9 kg). As the stock is not as heavy as Sheelin, shore fishing is not recommended. The average catch is only about one trout per rod/ day and local knowledge is an advantage. The best fishing is at the northern, shallow end

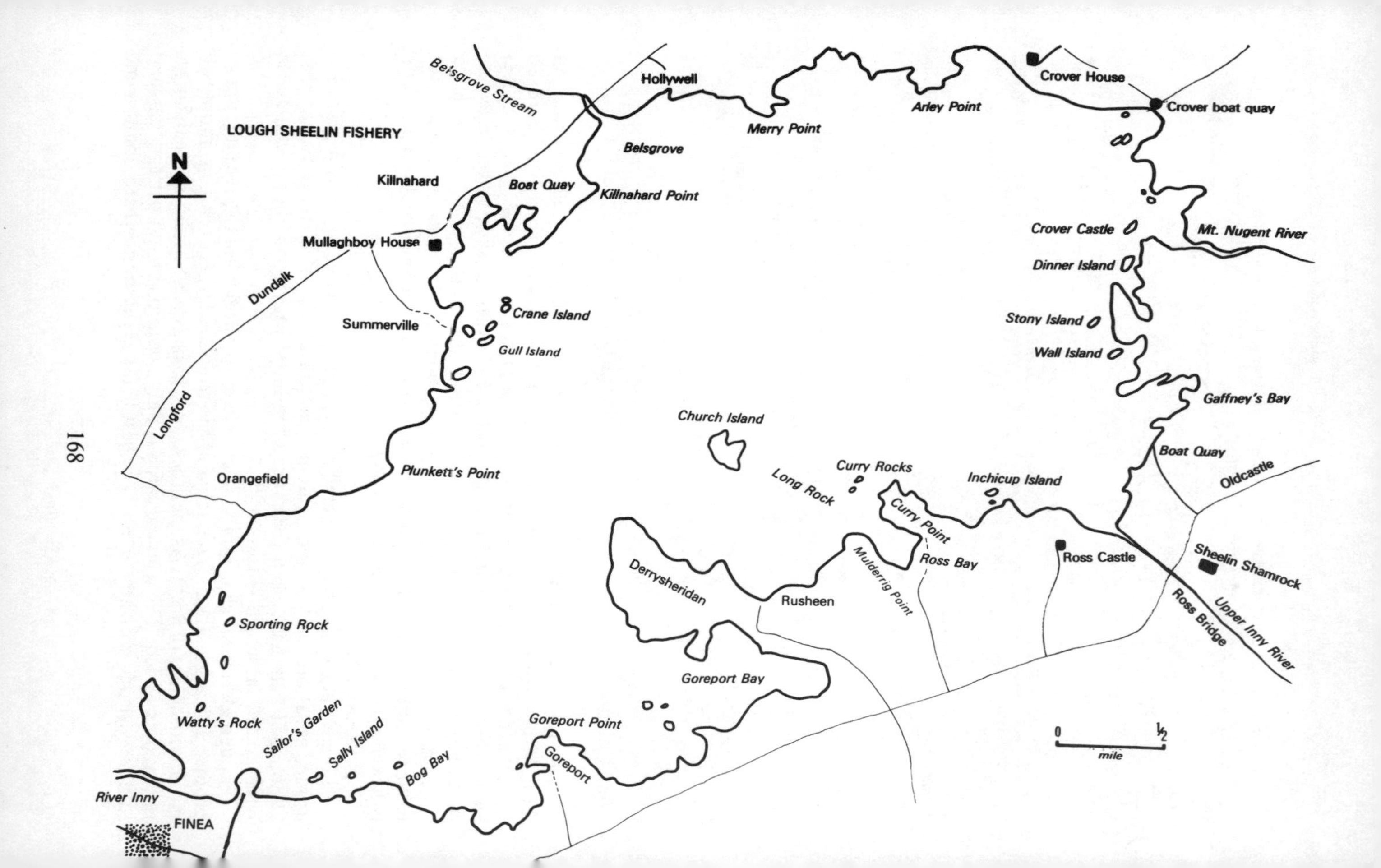
LOUGH SHEELIN FISHERY
N
Belsgrove Stream
Hollywell
Merry Point
Arley Point
Crover House
Crover boat quay
Belsgrove
Killnahard
Boat Quay
Killnahard Point
Mullaghboy House
Crover Castle
Mt. Nugent River
Dinner Island
Dundalk
Crane Island
Summerville
Gull Island
Stony Island
Wall Island
Gaffney's Bay
Church Island
Longford
Boat Quay
Oldcastle
Orangefield
Plunkett's Point
Curry Rocks
Long Rock
Inchicup Island
Curry Point
Ross Castle
Sheelin Shamrock
Derrysheridan
Ross Bay
Mulderrig Point
Rusheen
Ross Bridge
Upper Inny River
Sporting Rock
Goreport Bay
Watty's Rock
Sailor's Garden
Goreport Point
Sally Island
Bog Bay
Goreport
0
½
mile
River Inny
FINEA

of the lake. The long, deep southern extension has some fish but is not such good fishing water. Boats are available; ask in Multyfarnham village.

Lough Owel near Mullingar is a deeper lake, brilliantly clear and so perhaps more difficult to fish than Sheelin or Derravaragh. It also holds a good stock of large trout and is heavily fished by local and Dublin anglers. Owel also has hatches of Mayfly, Olives and chironomids, but is best known for big hatches of large sedges in July and August. Fishing a dry sedge at dusk to trout of up to 5 or 6 lbs (2.3–2.7 kg) is most exciting and two or three fish may be caught in the last hour of the day. Boats are available on Lough Owel through private owners in Mullingar and the Greville Arms and Lakeland Hotels in the town. Enquiries should be made in advance.

All three lakes already mentioned are popular with anglers from many parts of Ireland and competitions are held on them at times. At such times and also at popular fishing times such as during the Mayfly, boats may be difficult or impossible to obtain.

Lough Ennell is another large limestone lake of several thousand acres, close south of Mullingar. It was undoubtedly the best of the midland trout lakes, and possibly the best trout fishery in Ireland. It was polluted by sewage from Mullingar town; at present the fishing in Ennell is poor, but it still holds some very big trout. A new sewage plant has now been installed, but the necessary tertiary treatment had still to go into operation at the time of writing. It is hoped that the installation of such a system would save Lough Ennell. At present, however, it cannot be recommended to visitors.

The smaller lakes, Lough Glore and White Lake, are similar limestone lake trout fisheries. All these lakes are managed by the Inland Fisheries Trust and only members of the Trust are allowed to fish them. On joining, members receive the Trust handbook which contains detailed information on these waters, fishing methods, boat stations, access details—in fact, all the angler needs to know. Trust staff will advise on the best fishing area; returns of catches should be made.

The midland lakes, especially Sheelin, are highly recommended to the skilled visiting angler. Other lakes in the midland limestone plain hold some trout, but have not been developed in the same way as the IFT lakes. Lough Ramor in Co. Cavan is one such lake, also parts of Lough Erne, Lough Oughter and the Shannon lakes Derg and Ree. Lough Derg is the earliest Mayfly lake and provides good Mayfly fishing at times.

OTHER SHANNON TRIBUTARIES

The Suck is a sluggish river draining part of Roscommon and east Galway. It is an important coarse angling river and holds a few very good trout. The trout fishing is very local and not very dependable, but there is some Mayfly. The best areas are above Ballinasloe, near Castlecoote and Castlestrange and at Athleague. There are smaller trout and a few big fish between Ballymoe and Castlereagh, where the Suck is a small stream. The Suck tributaries are rather small streams and fall very low and weedy in summer. They all hold trout and some provide good fishing for big fish at times. The best of them is the Shiven; it has alternating stretches of thin runs and deep, dark pools. The pools hold some excellent trout. There is Mayfly hatch and the fly fishing is best in spring. In summer, low water and heavy weed growth make the approach difficult; fish are

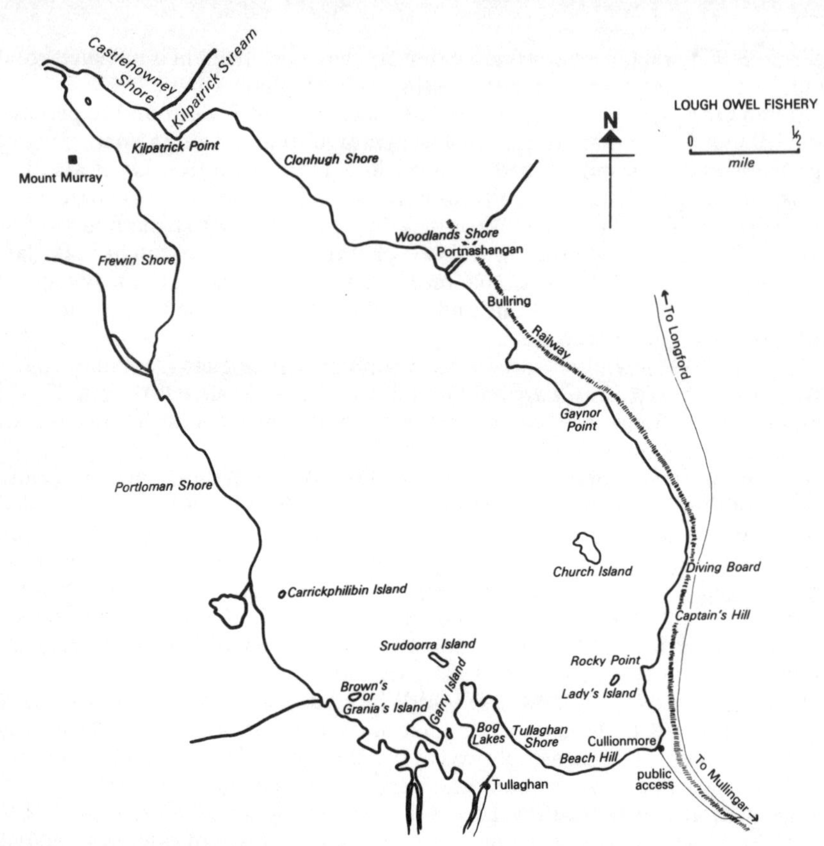

easy to lose. The Bunowen is heavily fished by anglers from Ballinasloe. Trout stretches are rather local and there are a lot of coarse fish. These rivers are controlled by the IFT.

At the headwaters of the Suck, near the village of Ballinlough, is Lough O'Flynn. It is a limestone lake with a good stock of trout averaging about ¾ lb (0.34 kg); occasional fish of up to 6 lbs (2.7 kg) have been caught on the fly. It is a miniature Sheelin, with clear gravelly shallows and weed beds, a good Mayfly hatch and excellent small fly. It is highly recommended to the fly fisher. Some boats may be available for hire. This Lough, which is IFT water, may be fished from the shore on summer evenings when the trout come inshore for caenis or sedges.

The Fergus is a short river connecting a chain of lakes and draining the limestone plateau of Co. Clare. It is a fair sized stream at Ennis, where it meets the tide, and it holds some excellent trout. Above Ennis there are some short stretches that provide some trout fishing; there are trout in all the lakes, as well as coarse fish. The best fishing in the Fergus is in spring, when the river fills its bed and trout are spread out all over it. In summer, the flow is liable to disappear completely, due to the porous nature of the limestone rock, and the trout migrate to the lakes.

The Upper Fergus, above Lough Inchiquin, is a small stream holding a lot of small trout. In the early spring, it still holds some big fish from the lake and is then worth fishing. On a good day the average size of a catch of trout from the Lower Fergus near Ennis may be about a pound (0.5 kg), but in general the average is a little over half that weight. There are some very heavy fish in the vicinity of Ennis town although when the water is low the Fergus is very difficult.

The best Fergus lake is undoubtedly Lough Inchiquin, near Corofin. Ballyteigue, Dromore and Ballyline loughs are also good. All of these lakes are clear limestone waters holding excellent trout and situated in well wooded, rocky country. The average size of Inchiquin trout is 1¼ lbs (0.6 kg) and in the other lakes it is a little larger. The best fishing is from March to May and in September. All these lakes are rather demanding and are not recommended to the novice. The Fergus system is mostly free fishing, managed by the IFT.

Before leaving the Shannon system, mention should be made of Lough Acalla, a small lake near Ballinasloe managed by the IFT as a rainbow trout fishery. It is a rich, shallow and weedy lake; trout in it grow rapidly and feed avidly on the big hatches of small chironomids and sedges. Wet fly fishing with small imitative patterns of pupae can be quite common. Fish of up to 7 lbs (3.2 kg) have been caught. The best fishing on Acalla is from the reedy side of the lake, where access is difficult. The clear sides are fished hard by locals. Summer evening fishing is best. The fishing is not really natural, as rainbows are not an indigenous species and do not breed in Ireland. Annual restocking is required.

There is a number of small lakes in Co. Clare that provide good trout fishing. Two of these are Raha Lake near Ruan and Gortglass Lake near Kildysart. Many of the other lakes in the Fergus system hold some good trout although they are mainly coarse fish waters. Worth trying are Loughs Ballyallea, Atedaun and Bunny.

WEST CLARE

The hills of Clare west of the Fergus are mostly granite, and do not produce good trout. The several short streams running into the Atlantic are spate rivers and are salmon and sea trout waters. The best of them are the Doonbeg River, which is quite a good sea trout river and also receives a few salmon, and the Inagh or Cullenagh, which flows through Ennistymon.

At Ennistymon, there is a magnificent fall which has had a salmon ladder constructed beside it. The Falls Hotel is situated on the riverside close to the falls and guests may fish the adjacent waters. Other parts are preserved by the West Clare A.A.

The granite gives way to limestone at the edge of the Burren plateau and in the porous strata many of the streams run very low, even disappearing underground in summer when the weather is dry. The Kilcolgan River is a small stream that holds some big trout; it enters Galway Bay at Kilcolgan. The best parts of it are preserved. A number of other small rivers in the neighbourhood of Loughrea and Gort hold big trout in their pools, but they are only of local interest. Lough Rea is a limestone lake which is preserved and restocked by the local angling association; it provides good fly fishing for trout of average weight—about 1 lb (0.5 kg).

6. THE WESTERN FISHERIES

The Corrib River enters the Atlantic at Galway City; it drains Loughs Corrib and Mask, two very big limestone lakes that provide first class fishing for wild trout. Together with Loughs Conn and Carra in Co. Mayo, they comprise the western lakes, well known for the quality and variety of their trout fishing.

The Corrib River is also a good salmon river and is now a state fishery. Limited to 5 rods at £20 per day, £10 per half-day. Salmon may be caught from February to August. Advance booking is advisable. Apply to the Salmon Fishery, Nun's Island, Galway. A number of canals and mill races taken off the river flow through the city. All of these hold trout, including some very good ones that can easily be observed from the various bridges and walks in the city. They can be fished in places and although they are very difficult to attract to nymph or fly, when hooked they give excellent sport.

Lough Corrib is a vast lake of 41,600 acres (16,806 hectares). It is mostly shallows and contains many islands. The water is very clear over a bottom of marl, gravel and limestone rock and it holds a good stock of trout which average about 1¼ lbs (0.6 kg). Fish of up to 3 lbs (1.4 kg) are commonly taken by fly fishing and much bigger trout, up to 20 lbs (9.0 kg) are occasionally taken by trolling. Fly fishing is best in spring and autumn, but may be practised throughout the year.

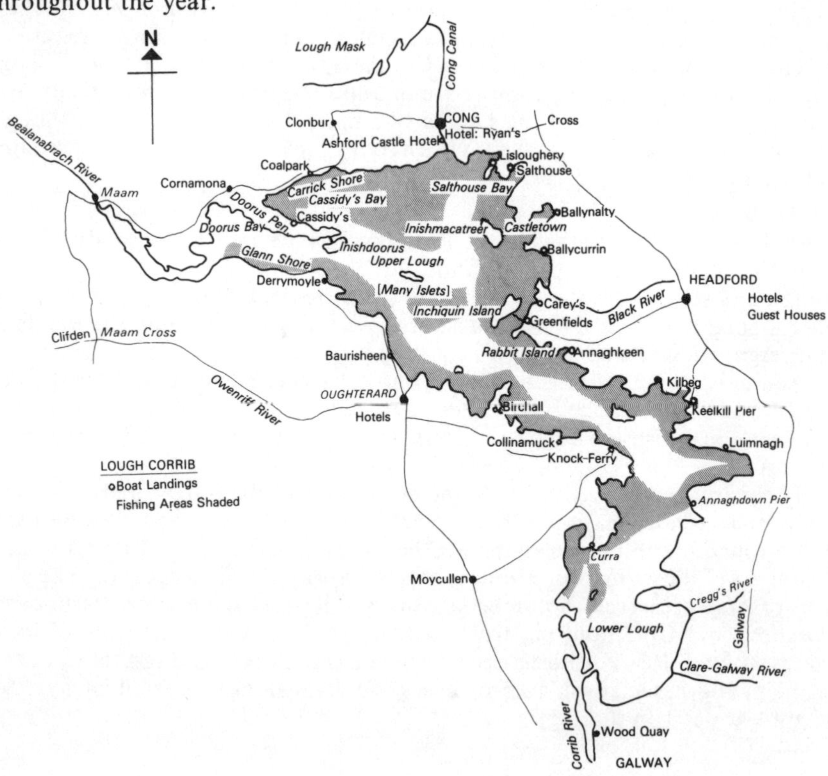

The most popular area for early spring Duck Fly fishing is Salthouse Bay near Cong; on a good day in this area during April, double figure bags are common. The area round Inchiquin Island is also good. The Corrib Mayfly hatch is not very dependable and is somewhat over-rated, but the ordinary wet fly fishing at that time of the year can be really excellent. Dapping is the most productive summer daytime method and during the summer evenings big fish move inshore and especially into the proximity of the island shores to feed on good hatches of midge and sedges. The islands near Oughterard are good at this time. The south end of the lake between Annaghdown and Curra has fished very well in recent years and the average size of trout taken here is rather larger than at the northern end. The normal catch on Lough Corrib for boat fishing is two or three trout per rod per day. A skilled angler could expect to double that. Shore fishing is possible in many places, a notable location being the north shore of Ballynalty Bay, but local knowledge and keen eyesight are required for successful shore fishing. Salmon are also taken. Local knowledge is required to locate the better lies. The best salmon fishing is usually after rain in June, particularly near Oughterard—the whole of the north facing bay into which the Owenriff River flows, especially the north west shore of the bay and between that shore and the offshore islands.

Lough Mask is another very big lake of over 20,000 acres (8,080 hectares) and is joined to Lough Corrib by a river which runs underground for a good distance. For this reason, no salmon reach Mask, but it is a very good trout lake. There is a good deal of deep water in Lough Mask, but there are also extensive shallows along the much indented northern and eastern shores and around the islands. In general, there is more rock and less marl in Mask than in Corrib and the trout are rather darker. Lough Mask holds an excellent stock of fish which average 1 lb 2 ozs (0.55 kg) and also provides most of the specimen trout of over 10 lbs (4.5 kg) caught in Ireland every year. These big fish are caught by trolling along the thermocline at a depth of about 25 feet (7.6 metres) on the edge of the great deeps of the lake.

Lough Mask also provides good wet fly fishing in April and May; there is a Mayfly hatch and good Olives, chironomids and sedges. The east shore provides the most extensive fly fishing, a good centre being Cushlough Bay near Ballinrobe. Castle Bay, where the Cong Canal runs out, is well known for large trout early in the season. The Cong Canal outflow is a popular place for anglers and becomes quite crowded at times. It is a clear, rapid, rocky run that gradually soaks into the limestone. The normal catch on Mask is two or three fish per rod, but the careful and experienced angler, fishing the rise, can easily double this. On one occasion I took four trout of over 2 lbs (0.9 kg) in about an hour, fishing from the shore at Bay of Islands with a dry sedge fly. Shore fishing is not recommended until some local knowledge is gained.

The eastern shore of Mask north of Cushlough Bay public landing is all excellent trout water. A number of dispersed islets and a shoreline with many deep inlets provides shelter so that some fishing is possible in almost any weather. The shores are mostly rocky and in places jagged limestone rocks rise steeply from black depths to within a few inches of the surface. Any angler using a boat should proceed with caution until he knows the locality. Most angling boats head out north of Cushlough to fish these varied waters with wet flies, but

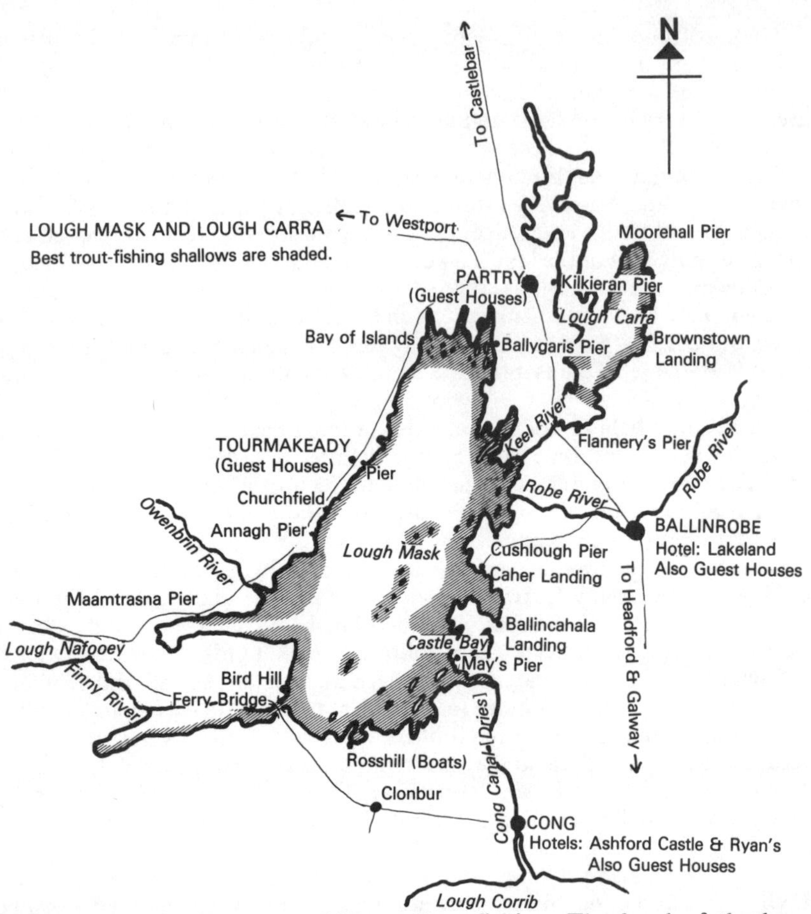

Cushlough Bay itself can provide excellent fishing. The head of the bay is shallow, weedy and mud bottomed, well sheltered by trees and so has excellent hatches of fly. It holds some very good trout. Lake trout in shallow water are notoriously shy and difficult to approach and this is why most anglers leave these fish alone, but they offer an interesting challenge to the keen fly angler.

The normal wet-fly is better modified at times by using a drogue or an anchor weight to hold the boat in a taking area. Insect hatches on these large lakes can be very localised and the trout may be concentrated in the area of emergence or an area where flies are accumulating, such as a weather shore. If such an area is located, sport can be much faster than it is in the normal drift. The shores of the long inlets north of Cushlough and some island shores are particularly suitable for an anchored boat.

If the angler walks the lake shores at dusk on a calm summer evening, he may observe the localities where trout are rising. Large fish move inshore at dusk to feed on the heavy hatches of sedge and midge that come off the marginal shallows. These fish may be caught with a dry sedge or a pupa pattern, and provide most exciting fishing. The catch will be of much better average size than the normal, as fish can be selected to some extent. On being hooked, these inshore trout will run for the deeps and they generally give a much better fight than boat-hooked fish, which try to go down. The best areas are shelving bays with open access to the deeps. Keel Bay, into which flows the Keel River, is a good place for this method.

Lough Carra is a clear, shallow, reedy lake of 4,000 acres (1,616 hectares), joined to Lough Mask by a short river. Carra holds a moderate stock of trout of good size, averaging about 1½ lbs (0.76 kg). The trout are not very free rising, but the Mayfly hatch is good and can provide excellent fishing for very silvery, hard fighting trout. Dapping in late summer and autumn can also be good. Loughs Corrib, Mask and Carra are free fisheries but they are all managed by the IFT.

The western lakes are recommended to visiting anglers. They may be fished by the novice as well as by experienced anglers. Dapping a natural insect from a drifting boat is worth trying as it is interesting, productive and sometimes very exciting. It is also a method that can be used at times when there is no rise to natural fly.

Visitors should try to obtain the services of a boatman, at least for the first few days on any of these lakes, for there are many places where rocks rise from a great depth to within inches of the surface, especially on Lough Mask. Bad weather can raise considerable waves in the most exposed places.

A number of hotels and guesthouses in the district cater especially for anglers and some have their own boats or have arrangements with local boatmen. The accompanying maps show some of the boat landings and the better fishing areas. Visitors are advised to book well in advance, especially at popular fishing periods such as Mayfly time, in order to avoid disappointment.

There is a number of rivers in the Corrib/Mask basin, but they are mostly spawning streams. Those entering Lough Corrib were subject to drainage work some years ago. The Clare-Galway River is recovering from drainage and provides good fly fishing in places for trout that average ½ lb (0.25 kg); fish of over 2 lbs (0.9 kg) are regularly caught. It is also a salmon river, but the salmon fishing is only of local interest. The Black River is a small stream that holds a few big trout. The Robe River enters Lough Mask near Ballinrobe; it is polluted by the town sewage and contains a lot of pike. Parts of it also hold some very good trout. The best trout stretches of the Robe are near Hollymount and immediately above and below Crossboyne Bridge. The Joyces River, which enters the west side of the lake near Tourmakeady, holds only small trout, but big lake fish may be caught in it late in the season when they ascend to spawn.

CONNEMARA AND WEST MAYO

West of Galway and the big lakes is an area of granite mountains containing many lakes and rapid rivers. This area has some of the best sea trout and salmon fisheries in the country, but the brown trout are mostly rather small. A general description of this type of water was given earlier; more particular details of each fishery are as follows:

The Owenriff River, which has many headwater lakes, enters Lough Corrib at Oughterard. It has late salmon, but is preserved. Enquire at the Oughterard hotels.

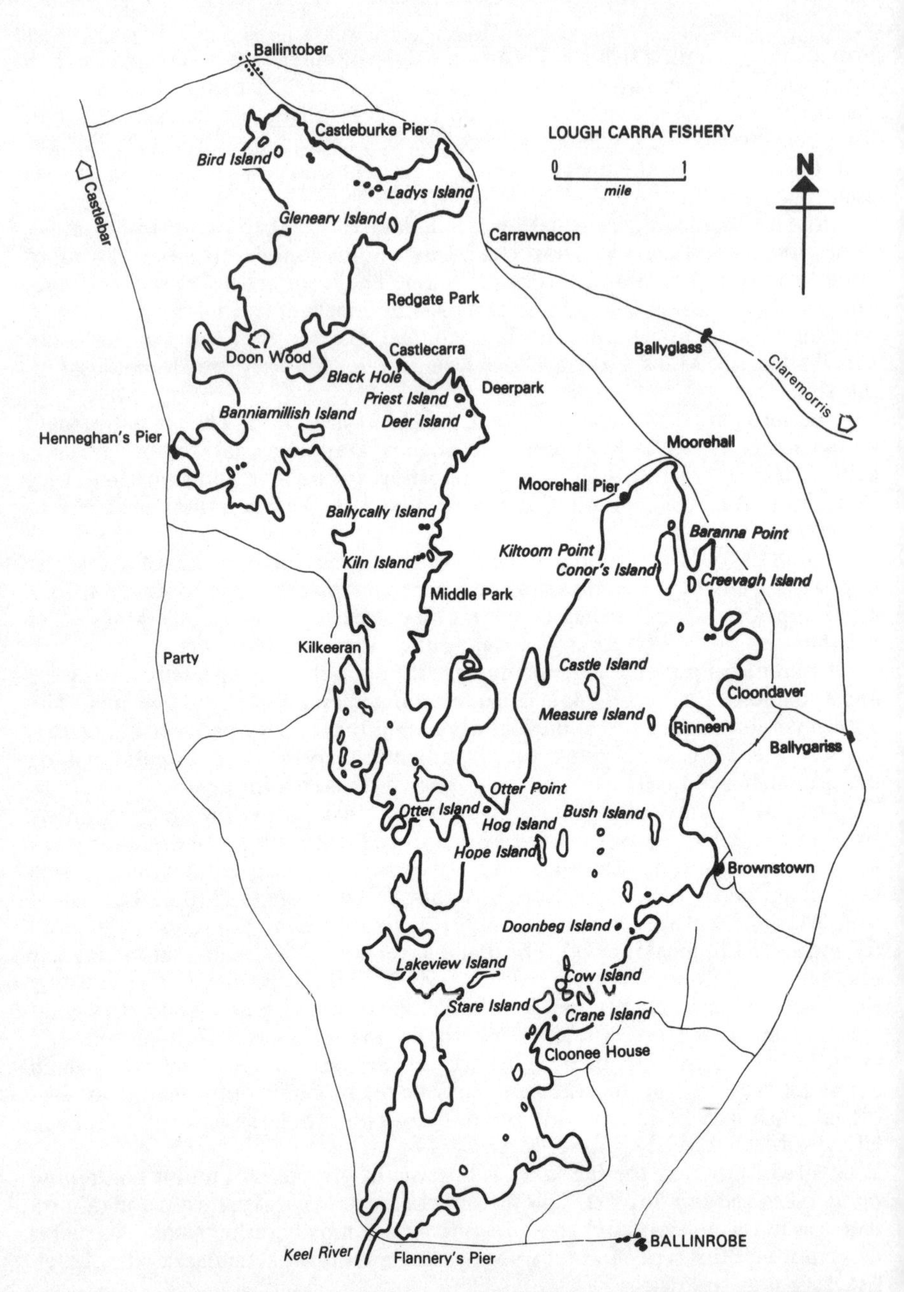

The Spiddal and Crumlin Rivers and their headwater lakes are excellent sea trout fisheries and also hold salmon. The waters are preserved by the owner, Crumlin Lodge, Inverin, Co. Galway.

The Costello and Fermoyle fishery is a first class salmon and sea trout fishery, said to be one of the best in the country. The sea trout fishing is excellent, but salmon catches have been declining in recent years, probably due to overnetting in the sea. The main waters are the Cashla River, which enters the sea at Costello, and connecting lakes Glenicmurrin, Carrick, Clogher and Shanawana. These are wild, open, rocky waters in open and treeless moorland. Sea trout average ¾ lb to 1 lb (0.34–0.5 kg). Two pound (0.9 kg) fish are fairly common and fish up to 4 lbs (1.8 kg) were taken in 1978. The salmon catch was 67 in 1974 and only 25 in 1977. Sea trout catch is 2,000 to 2,500 per annum and the average day's catch five to twenty fish per rod (1978).

Charges in 1978 were £15 per day for the best river beats (2 rods) and £10 per day for lesser beats. Lake fishing cost £24 per boat per day, including boatman. No shore fishing is allowed. This fishery is popular and is mainly for the guests of Costello Lodge. Casual rods can frequently be accommodated. Some parts may be fished by guests of Currarevagh House, Oughterard.

The Furnace fishery is a good summer salmon and excellent sea trout fishery. It is made up of several lakes, the principal ones being Loughs Nagarrivan and na Furnace, draining into Camus Bay. The fishing is private.

The Screebe fishery and Lettermucknoo give good summer salmon and excellent sea trout fishing. A number of lakes drain into Camus Bay at Screebe, the main ones being Screebe, Carnaceeragh, Cornaree, Aisleam and Glentrasna. Mostly open and very rocky waters, but there are some sheltered and partially wooded portions. The catch in 1978 was from three to seventeen sea trout per rod per day, weighing from 11 ozs to 3 lbs 11 ozs (0.3–1.7 kg). Charges were from £10 to £14 per boat for two rods, but not including a boatman. Permits can be obtained from Screebe House, Camus, Co. Galway. Upper Shindilla Lough is preserved for the guests of Currarevagh House, Oughterard.

The Inver fishery consists of two chains of lakes draining into Kilkieran Bay. There is excellent sea trout fishing; the occasional salmon may be taken. Permits from Annilaun House, Cashel, or the Zetland Hotel, Cashel. The Carna system is a chain of good sea trout lakes draining into Bertraghboy Bay. Permits only from Kilkieran Angling Club, Carna, and the Carna A.A. Fly fishing only. £2 per day; £5 per week.

The Gowla fishery has good sea trout with the occasional salmon; it is preserved by the Zetland Hotel, Cashel Bay, Connemara. The fishery comprises the Gowla River and lake and a complex chain of connecting lakes, mostly set in wild and treeless moorland, but there are some sheltered spots on the lower part of the river. The main lakes are Redman's and White Loughs, Lough Annilaun, Invermore, Emlough. Avalley, Curreel, Shanaket and Cushmeg. (Some maps show the lake names in Irish, but the above are the most commonly used versions).

The fishing is nearly all for sea trout. Three and a half miles (5.6 km) of river is divided into four beats and the lakes are also divided into beats with boats provided. The best beats are allocated to hotel guests, but beats are frequently available to casual callers. Previous booking is advised. 1979 charges were £6 per rod per day and £30 per week. The season runs from mid-June until October 12. Fly fishing only is the rule. The average catch in 1978 was three to fifteen sea trout per rod, average weight over ¾ lb (0.375 kg). About one fish in ten weighed over 2 lbs (0.9 kg) and a fair number were over 3 lbs (1.4 kg). The best fish up to August 1979, weighed over 6 lbs (2.05 kg). The use of a boat is included in the lake charge but a boatman, if required, costs extra.

The Ballynahinch fishery comprises the Owenmore River and Ballynahinch Lake and a number of small lakes in the immediate vicinity of Ballynahinch Castle Hotel. It is a first class salmon fishery with a heavy run of sea trout. These waters are very different from the average Connemara waters and merit a separate description.

This is probably the finest fishery in Connemara. The river flows from Ballynahinch Lake generally southward, but with so many meanders that it can be fished in comfort in almost any wind. The valley is deep and heavily wooded in many places, especially in the vicinity of the hotel, with mixed coniferous and deciduous trees, so there is plenty of shelter and the waters are richer than many others in Connemara. The river is rocky with many deep pools and gentle runs, and a few weedy pools and glides. Excellent riverside paths are provided. Good stands and groynes facilitate fishing over all the better salmon lies and most other parts of the water. The banks and grounds are carefully tended to make access without spoiling the natural appearance and wild beauty of the riverside, which surpasses anything else in this area. Many of the walks are private.

Ballynahinch is a salmon fishery and even in 1978 the salmon fishing was still good. One can frequently see salmon rolling in the pools and sea trout are everywhere. There is a spring run of salmon which is little fished as the hotel does not open early. Spring fish were taken in 1978 up to 12 lbs (5.4 kg) and the summer salmon average 6 to 10 lbs (2.7–4.5 kg). In 1975, 453 salmon were taken, in 1977, 160. In 1979 the salmon fishing was improving again. The 1979 charges were £18 per beat (2 rods) but the fishing may be confined to hotel guests.

Sea trout are very numerous in the river and lakes and catches are frequently heavy. Most hotel guests concentrate on the salmon and may try for a few sea trout in the evenings, but even so, the annual catch is about 3,000 fish. An average angler may expect up to a dozen or more fish in an evening, weighing between 1 lb and 3 lbs (0.5–1.4 kg) each.

Loughs Inagh and Derryclare are two large lakes on the Upper Owenmore River and once part of the Ballynahinch fishery; they have good salmon and sea trout fishing and are now owned by Mr Tennant of Inagh Lodge. Rods and boats are available. Apply to Mrs McAuley, Inagh Valley Inn, Recess, Connemara. Angler's Return Hotel at Toombeola on the Ballynahinch River, has fishing for sea trout and occasional salmon in several lakes in the vicinity. This fishing is preserved for hotel guests.

The Dooholla fishery comprises a short river system and several lakes, the main ones being Loughs Emlaghgeeragh and Maumween, draining into Ballyconneely Bay. There are summer salmon and fair sea trout. 1979 charges are from £2 to £5 a day. Permits from Emlaghmore Lodge, Ballyconnelly, Co. Galway.

Clifden is a good centre for visiting anglers. The Clifden A.A. has some sea trout and fair salmon fishing on the Owenglin, Derryborron and Ballinaboy Rivers and on several lakes. Some of their lakes also provide fair brown trout fishing. Permits from P. Stanley, Clifden, Co. Galway. The Celtic Hotel, Clifden, caters especially for anglers and arranges permits, boats and boatmen if required on many of the waters of Connemara and Loughs Corrib and Mask. This hotel also arranges sea angling trips and advises guests on all aspects of angling in the area.

Carraroe, Lettermore and Gorumna—this outlying peninsula and two islands are limestone. The lakes in this small area offer rather better trout fishing than most Connemara waters. The lake in Carraroe village holds trout that average about ½ lb (0.25 kg) and fish of over 1 lb (0.5 kg) are common. The fish are pink fleshed and hard fighting. Two lakes on Gorumna Island, which is joined to the mainland by a causeway, also hold similarly good trout.

The Dawros River and the three Kylemore lakes are a first class salmon and sea trout fishery. Salmon fishing is mostly in summer, but there is a spring run which at present is little fished. The river is swift and rocky but with many good pools, flowing through a steep sided valley. The banks are heavily wooded in many places and so are well sheltered. They are somewhat overgrown, but some clearance was carried out in 1978. There are many named salmon pools, but in 1979, only occasional salmon were being taken. Sea trout fishing is still excellent.

The three Kylemore lakes, Castle Lake, Middle Lake and Top Lake are attractive waters with partly wooded shores and steep rocky slopes rising to high mountains close on either side. Castle lake is well sheltered and wooded and is overlooked by Kylemore Abbey convent.

The river is divided into six beats of two rods each, with a charge of about £4 per rod per day. Lake fishing is also £4 per rod including the use of a boat. The 1978 catch was four to fifteen sea trout per rod per day. Sea trout had an average weight of 1¼ lbs (0.625 kg) and the best fish weighed 3½ lbs (1.65 kg). A fair number of fish over 3 lbs (1.4 kg) were taken. There are some good brown trout in Castle Lake, which has quite good fly hatches. A 2½ lbs (1.15 kg) brown trout was taken here in 1977. Fly fishing only is the rule.

This is an excellent and beautiful fishery; at present, it is not fully utilised. There is plenty of water and opportunities for many more anglers to fish. The river and much of the lake fishing belongs to Kylemore Abbey and permits may be obtained from Mrs Aspell, Kylemore Main Gate, Connemara, Co. Galway. Kylemore House, a comfortable hotel beside Top Lake, has some fishing on each of the three lakes, mainly for house guests but also under-utilised at present. Apply to Mrs Naughton, Kylemore House.

The Louisburgh and District A.A. has some sea trout fishing on the Carrowniskey River and two lakes near Louisburgh. There are summer and late salmon and good sea trout. Permits can be obtained from Mr Philbin, Bridge Street, Louisburgh.

The Westport Estates control a lot of good salmon and sea trout fishing in the vicinity of Westport. The Erriff is a big spate river with many tributaries draining bare and rocky country. Its banks are mostly open, but there are a few sheltered places in the lower reaches. The river, which flows over the Aasleagh Falls and enters Killary Harbour near Leenane, is a good salmon river and also has heavy runs of sea trout. The 1979 returns showed 167 salmon, the largest weighing 16 lbs (7.3 kg) with the average 4½ (2.05 kg) grilse. There were 626 sea trout, the largest weighing 4½ lbs (2.05 kg) and the average ¾ lb (.37 kg).

The fishing is divided into eight beats, on five of which only fly fishing is allowed. On the other three, any legal method may be used. Beats are marked and are easily accessible from the Leenane-Westport road. Tawnyard Lake is at the head of the Erriff and is also a salmon fishery. The fishery was formerly part of the Delphi fishery, but is now privately owned. Permits are available from Mr Jack Stack, fishery officer, Leenane, Co. Mayo. Advance booking is advised as this is a popular fishery.

The Delphi fishery is the Bundorragha River and the connecting lakes Doolough, Finlough and Glencullen, which drain into Killary Harbour. It is a typical western salmon and sea trout fishery situated in remote mountain country. The river provides early salmon fishing from February 1. The early runs may be quite good and efforts are being made to improve them, but it is as a summer sea trout and occasional salmon fishery that Delphi is best known. The sea trout fishing is from late June to October 12, and is excellent. A catch of fifty sea trout to one rod in a day was recorded on Finlough in 1976, by a rod that has fished this water for many years with consistently good catches. The average size of the sea trout varies from 12 ozs (0.34 kg) to nearly 2 lbs (0.9 kg) and an 8 lbs (3.6 kg) sea trout was taken in 1977.

The Bunowen River at Louisburgh is managed by the Westport Estate. It is a late salmon and sea trout fishery which has recently been taken over and is being improved and developed. Charges are from about £2.50 a day and £30 per season on the Bunowen and from about £5 per day on the Delphi fishery. Boats, engines, tackle and ghillies are all available for hire from Delphi Lodge. Evening or short period permits may be issued if the water is available.

Delphi is an excellent fishery at present under-utilised: It is recommended, especially to experienced anglers. Permits from the Estate Office, Westport House, Westport, Co. Mayo and Mr Philbin, Louisburgh.

In the Westport district, a few small streams run into Clew Bay near Westport; they have a few sea trout after rain. The best of them is the Owenwee, but these streams are of little account. There are some good brown trout lakes in this area. Clogher Lough, Black Lough and Lough Moher are the best. On a good day, the average size in Clogher is over ½ lb (0.25 kg) and the trout are very numerous. Westport is not too far from the north end of Lough Mask.

The Newport River and Lough Beltra. The Newport River drains Lough Beltra and enters the north end of Clew Bay at Newport. It is a stony river running through pasture land with plenty of trees and bushes along the lower reaches. The river is divided into holding pools by many weirs and stone dams and is a first class salmon and sea trout water. Spring salmon are caught in February, March and April. There are also fair runs of summer fish, especially after rain, and very heavy runs of sea trout. In July, the river pools are full of sea trout and very large bags can be taken. This is a first class fishery and is carefully preserved for guests of Newport House Hotel. Day or evening permits may be issued and boats are maintained on the lakes. Newport House Hotel also has boats on the Burrishoole fishery, Loughs Furnace and Feeagh, which is a good salmon water as well as having big runs of sea trout. It is partly tidal water. Approximate charges for Newport River are £4 per day or £2 per evening. The weekly charge is about £20, limited to 20 rods. On Lough Belta, the charge is about £12 per day per boat, including engine and fuel (one to three anglers). On Lough Furnace, two rods in a boat with a ghillie cost about £30, or about £150 per week. Information from Newport House Hotel, Newport, Co. Mayo.

The Castlebar Salmon A.A. has four boats on the east side of Lough Beltra. The cost is about £3 per rod per day and an extra £4 for the boat.

Bilberry Lough, between Castlebar and Westport, is a limestone trout lake managed by the IFT. It has a bottom of soft marl and the banks are difficult, so only boat fishing is allowed. The trout average about 12 ozs (0.34 kg) and the average catch is two or three per rod. There is a Mayfly hatch during which fishing can be very good. IFT members only. There is a large number of lakes in the vicinity of Castlebar, many of which hold brown trout and give quite good fishing. Castlebar and Pontoon A.A., Main Street, Castlebar.

West Mayo waters. The Owengarve is a sea trout and salmon river entering the Atlantic north of Newport. Quite good salmon and good sea trout. The water is preserved for guests of Rosturk Castle guesthouse and the Newport Angling Club. Permits are available for about £1 a day and £5 a week.

The Owenduff and Ballaveeny Rivers are similar waters, four miles (6.4 km) of river. They are let by the period to parties, with fishing lodge and housekeeper. The charge for a week for a party of four is about £80.

The Owenmore is a large spate river which receives good runs of spring and summer salmon and excellent sea trout. It is also let by the period. Enquiries to J. Sweeney, Achill Sound, Co. Mayo.

Enquiries for Owenduff to P. J. Handcock, Lagduff Lodge, Ballycroy, Co. Mayo or to F. T. Chambers, Rock House, Ballycroy, Co. Mayo.

Keel Lough, on Achill Island, contains small trout and receives runs of sea trout.

RIVER MOY AND LOUGH CONN

The Moy is an important salmon river, rapid and stony. It suffered a drainage scheme some years ago, and although it has somewhat recovered the scars remain in the form of large and unsightly spoil heaps along the banks. The river falls very low in summer. Despite the drainage works, the salmon runs have continued, but the fishing is not as pleasant as before. Also, the fish tend to run rapidly through the lower reaches. Large fish, whether they are salmon, sea trout, brown trout or any other species, do not like to be exposed to the gaze of man or any other predator. They like cover, and in the case of salmon and large sea trout in fresh water, the best cover is provided by deep water.

Drainage schemes tend to remove deeps and shallows and to widen the bed of the river in order to allow rapid run-off, so the wide bed becomes a great exposed shallow at times of low water and fish will not remain there. Instead, they try to run through and look for a suitable resting place. The spring salmon fishing in the Moy is now poor, partly for this reason, as spring fish have to remain in the river until spawning time; many did not live through the low water periods. Summer salmon fishing can still be very good and in June and July, when conditions are good, catches of up to six fish a day are to be expected. In June, 1977, one angler took seventeen salmon in five days' fishing. The first salmon of the 1980 season weighed 9½ lbs (4.35 kg) and was taken at Ballina.

Mrs Aldridge of Mount Falcon Castle near Ballina has some water and rents some of the best salmon beats on the Moy for her guests. Boats and ghillies are provided on the river and on Lough Conn for about £12 a day on the river and about £7 a day on the lake, inclusive.

Some sea trout ascend the Moy and the nearby Palmerstown River. They are caught from boats in the estuary. There is also some quite good brown trout fishing in the Moy, especially in some of the tributaries and in the upper reaches, which flow over limestone. This too has suffered from the drainage works, but is quite well recovered.

Permits to fish the Moy may be obtained from Mr E. Kennedy, East Mayo A.A., Bridge Street, Swinford and from Mr B. Howley, Market Street, Swinford. Charges in 1979 were £2 per day, £10 per week.

Lough Conn and Lough Cullen are two large limestone lakes separated by a peninsula at Pontoon, with an outflow to the Moy. They provide first class trout fishing and are comparable with Corrib and Mask, although of slightly different character. Salmon also enter Lough Conn and are caught in fair numbers.

Conn, with its margins of rocks and small stones, has more of the character of a mountain lake than Corrib or Mask, but there is sufficient marl to provide habitat for Mayfly, and there is a good hatch. The general wet fly fishing is very good; the best fishing is probably in April and May when there are good hatches of small black chironomids. Dapping is popular on summer days and wet fly fishing in the evenings. There are big hatches of caenis and small sedges in summer. The average size of Conn trout is about 13 ozs (0.36 kg) and the average bag is over three trout per rod. Trout of 6 to 8 lbs (2.7–3.6 kg) are caught on Conn every year, frequently by anglers trolling for salmon, but some big fish of over 5 lbs (2.3 kg) are taken on wet fly or by dapping. Boat landings and fishing areas are indicated on the map. Boats can be hired here. Local hotels also keep boats for their guests. Lough Conn is highly recommended for visiting anglers; it is free fishing, managed by the IFT.

7. SLIGO & DONEGAL WATERS

Sligo is rich in fishing. It contains limestone rivers and lakes which provide good trout fishing. The acid waters are good for salmon and sea trout.

A number of streams flow north into the Atlantic from the Ox Mountains. The biggest of these is the Easky, a good salmon and sea trout river which is preserved locally and is heavily fished by local anglers. Lough Talt, in the Ox Mountains, is a big lake in pleasant surroundings with a good road running along one shore. It holds a good stock of smallish trout and is renowned for the heavy bags that may be taken on wet flies. Boats are available and it can be fished from the shore. Lough Easky, at the head of the Easky River, is similar but the trout are smaller.

The Ballisodare River and its tributaries the Owenmore and Arrow Rivers are limestone waters. The Ballisodare is a broad river of moderate flow with shallow pools and weedy glides. It holds some big trout. On parts of the river owned by the Cooper family, local anglers under the auspices of the local angling club are allowed to fish at certain times of the year. The lower parts of the Owenmore are similar. Both rivers are weedy and overgrown by trees in places. They are good fly fishing waters for the experienced angler. The lower parts are private fishing, but permission may be obtained to fish on some upper parts.

Lough Arrow is a large limestone lake managed by the IFT. It is five miles long by one to two miles wide (8 km × 1.6–3.2 km) and is surrounded by rich, undulating pasture and woodland. It has a gravelly and marl bottom and

Salmon fishing at The Rosses, Co. Donegal

frequent beds of weed and emergent reeds. It is an excellent trout water. The fish average about 1¼ lbs (0.6 kg) and trout of over three pounds (1.4 kg) are regularly taken by fly fishing. There is an excellent hatch of big early chironomids, good Mayfly and Lake Olives as well as good sedges. Arrow is the ideal fly fishing lake. Boats are available. Fishing from the shore is not advisable. Free fishing, managed by the IFT.

The Garavogue River flows from Lough Gill to the sea at Sligo. It is a good trout river and also holds salmon and sea trout. It is preserved locally. Lough Gill is a good trout lake too. Enquiries should be made to the Sligo Angling Association through the local tackle shops or c/o 4 Wolfe Tone Street, Sligo. There are a number of small lakes in the district which provide good trout fishing. Lough na Leibe is a limestone lake and is periodically stocked with rainbow and brown trout by the IFT. Lough Feenagh and Castledargan Lake are similar waters.

North of Sligo Town a number of rivers drain the hills around Ben Bulben. The main ones are the Drumcliff River and the Grange River, both salmon and sea trout waters. Glencar Lake and Lough Colga also hold quite good trout. Permission to fish should be obtained in Sligo; see the local tackle shops.

The Bundrowes River flows five miles (8 km) from Lough Melvin to the sea. It is one of the earliest salmon rivers in Ireland, opening on January 1 when salmon are usually caught! It also holds sea trout and quite good brown trout. It is preserved locally but permits to fish can be obtained from J. G. Phillips, Bundoran A.A., Main Street, Bundoran. Lough Melvin is a large limestone lake holding excellent trout and providing good fly fishing. The average size of the fish is about 12 ozs (0.34 kg). Fish of three and four pounds (1.4–1.8 kg) are fairly common and they have been caught up to 14 lbs (6.4 kg). Melvin is a good wet-fly water and it has a Mayfly hatch. Salmon are also caught in the lake. Parts of Lough Melvin are free fishing, there is some hotel water and some areas are preserved. Part of the lake is in Northern Ireland and a Northern Ireland trout licence is required to fish in these parts. Boats are available at various addresses in Kinlough village—enquire at the local post office.

RIVER ERNE AND LOUGH ERNE

The Erne is a complex system of rivers and lakes draining the north midlands, flowing generally north west and entering the sea at Ballyshannon, Co. Donegal. Part of it is in Northern Ireland. Most of the course of the river is through complex, dispersed lakes with hundreds of islands. It is limestone water with a moderate flow in some parts and little perceptible current in others. The surrounding country, including the peninsulas and islands in the various loughs, consists almost entirely of small glacial drift mounds called 'drumlins'. Much of it is wooded and the whole makes a well sheltered and picturesque fishery.

Most of the Erne system is coarse fish water, renowned for the number and size of its fish. There are some trout and where the flow speeds up, a few are to be found. They grow to a very large size and trout of up to 19½ lbs (8.8 kg) have been caught in recent years, mostly by anglers fishing for pike. Trout may be caught in the river in the vicinity of Belturbet, Co. Cavan. Lough Gowna holds some good trout and has a Mayfly hatch. Fishing in Gowna is good at times, but local knowledge is required to locate the better areas for trout.

Ballyshannon, Co. Donegal, is a good centre for fishing the lower Erne and many other waters in the district. At Ballyshannon, there is a dam which impounds the river for generating hydro-electricity. There is quite good trout fishing in the vicinity of the dam; some very big trout have been caught and there is a Mayfly hatch. Permits are issued by the Electricity Supply Board. Below the dam there is also some trout fishing and sea trout ascend in the summer. The sea trout fishing in the Erne estuary is very good.

Many of the Erne tributaries hold trout, which grow to a good size. Unfortunately they are full of small roach and other coarse fish which are a nuisance to the trout angler, and the best trout areas are very local. Lough Annagh, near Butlersbridge, is a lovely wooded lake which has been stocked with trout by the IFT. It cannot be fished from the shore and the Trust has placed several boats on the lake, which can be hired by the day or half day for a moderate fee.

Annagh gives good fishing for trout which average about 14 ozs (0.39 kg) and which have been caught up to 4 lbs (1.8 kg): It is a completely artificial fishery in that there is no natural spawning, so all the trout are stocked fish. Coarse fish have to be kept down.

In the vicinity of Ballyshannon, there is a large number of small lakes, many of which hold trout and provide excellent free fishing. Some of these lakes hold good fish. The best ones are probably Bradley Lough, Colmcille Lough, Glen Lough, McGlinchey's Lough and the Raths Loughs. This is a pleasant area for the visiting angler to explore, as there is also good sea and coarse fishing available. Visitors are advised to join the Ballyshannon A.A. to obtain the best local advice.

CO. DONEGAL

Nearly all of Donegal is rugged, mountainous country of acid rock peat bog. Most of it is poor country for feeding trout and the best of the game fishing is for sea trout and salmon. There are large numbers of lakes, a few of which offer good trout fishing.

Lough Eske, near Donegal town, is a fair trout lake, preserved locally, but permission to fish in it can be obtained and boats are available. Enquire at Lough Eske Castle estate office.

The Inver fishery is a system of sea trout and salmon waters running into Inver Bay. It is made up of the Eany River and its tributaries and lakes. It costs about 50p per day or £1 per week from C. Doherty, tackle shop, Main Street, Donegal town.

The Oily River, Strager River, Owenwee and Glen Rivers are similar waters holding a few salmon, sea trout and small brown trout.

The best lakes in this area are Lough Adeery, near Killybegs, and Loughs Divna and Geeta.

The Ardara A.A. and the Glenties A.A. have good salmon and sea trout water in the north west Donegal. Salmon runs have been much reduced recently, but sea trout fishing is still good. The main water is the Owentocker River and the Ardara club is active; I believe it still runs a hatchery. Permits from Ardara A.A., Main Street, Ardara, Co. Donegal. About 50p a day or £2.50 per week for sea trout.

The Glenties A.A. has the fishing on the Owenea River system. Permits from C. McDyer, secretary, Glenties A.A., Kilraine, Lifford, Co. Donegal. There is a large number of trout lakes in this district, holding mostly small brown trout. Lough Nacrooey, Lough Anna, Lough Sallagh and Lough Naclogher are reputed to be the better ones. Lough Adoon, Lough Kiltooris, Clooney Lough and Lough Summy give good trout fishing in the vicinity of Rosbeg.

The Gweebarra and Owenwee Rivers and Lough Barra are a good salmon and sea trout fishery controlled by the Letterkenny and District A.A. Permits from P. Macloone, 14 McMahon Villas, Letterkenny.

The Gweedore and Crolly Rivers have been impounded for hydroelectricity, but they still have runs of migratory fish. Permits from the Electricity Supply Board.

The Dungloe River drains a very large area holding many lakes, which are collectively known as the Rosses fishery. Good sea trout fishing and some salmon; some of the lakes are reputed to give fair brown trout fishing. Permits from the Rosses A.A., Dungloe, Co. Donegal. About £1 a day or £5 a week. Boats available, as are boatmen. Recommended to visitors.

Lough Shure, on Aranmore Island, holds rainbow trout and it is the only place in the whole of Ireland at present where rainbows have become a breeding species. Fish, average ½ lb (0.25 kg), are caught up to 1½ lbs (0.75 kg) and the lake can be fished from the shore.

A number of small streams in the Gortahork to Falcarragh area hold small trout and have runs of sea trout, but there are few holding pools and the fish are liable to run through to the lakes. Lough Aluirg, at the head of the Ray River, is a good trout lake.

Lough Sessiagh, at Dunfanaghy, is reputed to be a good trout lake. Permits from Sessiagh Lodge, on the lake shore. Fly fishing only.

Lough Veagh is a long narrow mountain lake which drains into Glenlough via the Owencarrow River and thence to the head of Sheep Haven. A good salmon and sea trout fishery. Letterkenny and District A.A. and also the Rosapenna Hotel, Downings.

The River Lennon drains via Lough Fern and enters Lough Swilly at Ramelton. A good salmon river but recently badly affected by UDN disease. The famous pool a Ramelton is privately preserved. Parts of the Lennon can be fished by members of Letterkenny and District A.A. The Milford Hotel at Milford, near the head of Sheep Haven, caters especially for anglers. This hotel keeps boats on a number of good sea trout waters in the vicinity, especially on Lough Veagh, the tidal head of Sheep Haven and on Lough Fern. Several of the smaller lakes in the vicinity of Milford provide good fishing for trout of average size.

On one of these waters, which is reed fringed and so cannot be fished from the shore, the trout averaged ¾ lb (0.34 kg) in 1977 and trout of up to 2¾ lbs (1.24 kg) were caught by fly fishing. A boat was provided on this lake in 1977 for guests of the Milford Hotel; it was probably unfished before. A few other lakes have been investigated by the management of this hotel and boats are placed where the trout fishing is worthwhile, giving good fishing for guests on little-fished waters. There are many lakes in this district, mostly little known and fished only occasionally, and although some of them hold only small trout, there are a few rich ones that give good fishing.

In the lakes near Rathmullen and Port Salon, there is some quite good brown trout fishing, with trout averaging 10 ozs (0.28 kg); pounders (0.5 kg) are quite common on the fly. The best ones are Lough Kindrum, Lough Kinny and Shannagh Lough. There are some small and unnamed lakes in the area which hold good trout. Ask locally before fishing as some of these lakes are preserved by the Port Salon Hotel and by private owners.

The Mill River and the Crana River enter Lough Swilly near Buncrana and both are preserved salmon and sea trout waters. Guests of Lough Swilly Hotel may fish, and permits may be obtained from the Buncrana A.A., c/o Major L. Spragg, Buncrana. About £2 a day or £5 a week.

The Clonmany River is a small stream which has runs of sea trout and a few salmon. The Culdaff River runs north to the sea at Culdaff and is reputed to hold quite good trout as well as sea trout and some salmon. Culdaff A.A.; ask at Culdaff.

The Foyle system was once the richest salmon fishery in Europe, but it has been so abused by poaching and overfishing by nets that it is no longer worth angling for salmon. Most of the Foyle rivers are rapid and stony and hold only small brown trout. The Strule is a fair trout river of pools and rapid streams, with steep rocky banks in some places. It has excellent hatches of fly and the trout are free rising, averaging about ½ lb (0.25 kg).

8. NORTHERN IRELAND

The Northern Ireland Department of Agriculture controls a great deal of game and coarse fishing which is available to holders of their permits. 1980 permit prices are £11 per season, £4 per 15 days and £1.50 per day. A rod licence is also needed. The Foyle Fisheries Commission licence for salmon, sea trout and freshwater trout cost £5 per season in 1980 or £2.50 for 14 days. The Fisheries Conservancy Board licence for these species cost £6.20 for the season (1980) and £4.20 for 15 days. The Department's game fishing is carefully regulated, with size and bag limits on most waters and some restrictions as to method. Fly only is the rule on a few trout waters.

As in the Republic, salmon runs are much reduced of late. The best salmon water is the Northern Ireland section of Lough Melvin which has a good run of both spring salmon and grilse. In the Foyle basin salmon angling is now only of local interest. The Department of Agriculture runs a salmon hatchery and smolt rearing unit on the River Bush at Bushmills on the north coast. The fishing rights of the entire Bush catchment, except the stretch from the sea to Bushmills, are owned by the Department. Angling is restricted in the reaches around Bushmills, but even so salmon angling returns are disappointing, being only about one fish per five rod-days in 1980. However, salmon runs are said to be improving. There is quite good brown trout fishing in the upper reaches of the Bush system.

The Department of Agriculture publishes an excellent guide to its waters which contains many details of catches, charges, where to buy permits, access to waters and so on. Some waters are jointly managed with local angling associations. Prospective visitors are advised to write to the Northern Ireland Tourist Board, River House, High Street, Belfast 1, for the latest guide.

Most of the remaining game fishing waters in the six counties are in the hands of angling associations, from whom permits should be obtained. A rod licence is required to fish in any of these waters, with some exceptions for those under 16 years.

CO. TYRONE

The Omagh A.A. controls most of the best river fishing in the district. From Newtownstewart to Omagh, a distance of ten miles, (16 km) is the River Strule, a very good trout water with salmon in season. Permission must be obtained from the Omagh A.A.; there are some private stretches near Stone Bridge. From Omagh, the river runs eastwards for 15 miles (24 km) as the Camowen, a good trout water, although the fish are small. Branches from Omagh to the south and west are the Owenragh, Quiggery/Fintona and Drumragh. All are stony rivers in upland country with much good farmland bordering them, but they are not of an excessively acid nature. The salmon fishing is of little account at present, but the brown trout fishing is generally excellent, the fish averaging around ½ lb (0.25 kg), with plenty of better ones. Stocks are very good.

There are good hatches of fly and a variety of very attractive water. Flies are mostly of stony river species, but there is good B.W.O. on parts of the Strule. Some sea trout ascend the lower reaches between Newtownstewart and Strabane known as Mourne. Most of the Mourne is in private ownership, but the Department has stretches at Sion Mills, Victoria Bridge and Liskey. Some farmers allow fishing; there are salmon and sea trout from June/July and some brown trout. East of Omagh there are a group of upland trout lakes controlled by the Omagh A.A. known as the Mountfield lakes. The River Fairywater, which enters the Strule below Omagh, has some trout upstream of Dudgeon Bridge but is better known for roach fishing. Permission must be sought from the landowners.

The Department of Agriculture also manages a number of lake fisheries in Tyrone that are regularly restocked with trout. They are as follows:

Bradan: 12 miles (19.3 km) west of Omagh. Brown trout reservoir.

Lee: a small isolated mountain lake near Drumquin reputed to hold good trout.

Bantry: 5 miles (8 km) from Benburb, a woodland lake annually restocked with brown trout.

Moor Lough and Ash Lake: two small mountain lakes west of Strabane. Brown trout, average size 8 to 12 ozs (0.25–0.34 kg).

Roughan Lough: near Coalisland, is an artifically stocked rainbow trout lake.

A rainbow of 5 lbs 14½ ozs (2.7 kg) was taken in 1976 on worm bait.

CO. DERRY

Derry is mountain country of rapid rivers. The Roe flows north through Dungiven to the Foyle estuary. It is fast and rocky, a salmon and sea trout river also holding small browns. Permission may be had from the Roe A.A. or the Dungiven A.A. The Department of Agriculture has a 1¼ mile stretch (2.0 km) at O'Cahan's Rock Amenity Area, north of Limavady.

The River Faughan flows north for 20 miles (32 km) to enter the Foyle estuary east of Derry City. There is good angling water—sea trout, salmon and brown trout—for some 15 miles (24 km) up to Claudy. Permission: Londonderry and District A.A. The Lower Bann is mostly coarse fish water, but it does hold a few big trout. There is said to be good sea trout fishing in the

Game fishing on the River Bush in Co. Antrim

estuary in the vicinity of Coleraine. Permission from the Bann Fisheries at Coleraine. The Moyola River flows from its source in the south Co. Derry to enter Lough Neagh at the north west corner. There are some good brown trout in the lower reaches, but it is known for dollaghan and salmon from July onwards. Permission from the landowners. Moyola Park above Castledawson is private.

CO. ANTRIM

The Glens of Antrim rivers are rather short, rapid streams draining north and north east. The Bush has previously been mentioned as a salmon river; it is also a fair brown trout water. A tributary, the Dervock, has good trout fishing on the eastern bank flowing through the village of Dervock for two miles (3.2 km).

The other glens rivers are the Dun, the Glenarm, the Glenariff and the Margy/Carey/Glenshesk system. The Dun enters the sea at Cushendall, there is a fair run of sea trout and salmon late in the season. Permission from the Glens A.C. The Glenariff has sea trout and the odd salmon near its mouth at Red Bay; permission from the Glens A.C. The Glenarm River is private. The Margy/Carey/Glenshesk rivers near Ballycastle are controlled by the Department. The sea trout fishing can be very good at times, with occasional salmon in the late season.

The River Main runs south to Lough Neagh south of Randalstown and is a first class trout river including dollaghan in the late season. It also receives a few salmon and large migratory trout from Lough Neagh known as dollaghan. The average size of fly-caught trout is around ½ lb (0.25 kg) and there are plenty of bigger fish. Permits from the Main A.C., the Randalstown A.C. (from Randalstown upstream) and from Gracehill, Galgorm and District A.C. Dungonnell and Killylane reservoirs are both Department fisheries in the Main catchment. Dungonnell reservoir near Ballymena is a moorland lake holding many small trout, some up to 2 lbs (0.9 kg). It is less heavily fished than Killylane, reservoir, another brown trout water at the top of the Kellswater.

The Sixmilewater flows easterly from Ballyclare to enter Lough Neagh on the north eastern corner at Antrim. It is a very good trout water including dollaghan. Permission from the Antrim and District A.C. downstream and landowners upstream.

Woodburn reservoirs near Belfast are Department fisheries and are popular with Belfast anglers. The seven lakes are frequently restocked with brown trout; some are restricted to fly fishing only. Fish up to 7 lbs 5 ozs (3.34 kg) were caught in 1976.

Stoneyford and Leathemstown reservoirs near Lisburn offer good trout fishing; Leathemstown is fly only. Trout up to 4½ lbs (2.05 kg) were taken in 1976. These are Department fisheries.

Some reservoir fisheries are liable to fall low during dry periods. Fishing is normally best when the level is high, early in the season. Reservoirs in the Belfast area tend to be heavily fished.

COUNTIES DOWN AND ARMAGH

The River Lagan runs into Belfast Lough. There are trout from Magheralin, Co. Down, upstream for 12 miles (19.3 km). Permission: Iveagh A.C. and Dromore A.C.

The Upper Bann enters Lough Neagh north of Portadown. The parts nearest the Lough are mainly coarse fish water, but they receive runs of dollaghan from the lake. From the Point of Whitecoat (the junction of the Cusher River and the Newry canal above Portadown) to Hilltown in Co. Down, there is good trout water for 20 miles (32 km). Permission: Gilford A.C., Banbridge A.C. and Rathfriland and District A.C.

The largest of the Lough Neagh tributaries is the Blackwater, which enters the lake at the south west corner. From Blackwatertown to Benburg, a 1¼ mile (2 km) stretch of Department waters has good trout fishing.

Department waters in this area include:

Craigavon lakes—brown trout. A 80 hectare artificial lake in 2 divisions, in the new city which produces good quality fish. Fishing by boat (available to hire) is permitted on the northern lake.

Gentle Owens and Aughnagurgan lakes are both brown trout waters, Tullynawood and Darkley are rainbow trout waters.

These four small lakes are near Keady in Co. Armagh. Permission from Armagh District A.A. except Gentle Owens which is a Department water.

Shaw's Lake—a reservoir near Markethill. Brown and rainbow trout. Good fishing, resticted to fly only. Armagh and District A.A.

Loughbrickland—a Department lake near Banbridge. Good brown trout. Castlewellan lakes—one larger lake and several ponds in Castlewellan Forest Park. Stocked with browns. Good fishing and very popular.

Portavoe reservoir—near Donaghadee. A small coastal lake stocked with browns and rainbows. Falls low in summer. Generally overfished.

Spelga reservoir—in the Mourne Mountains near Newcastle. Small brown trout, average under ½ lb (0.25 kg).

River Shimna—a rocky river that enters the sea at Newcastle. It is a Department fishery noted for late salmon and sea trout. Difficult to fish because of gin clear water. Bag limit is two fish. No Sunday fishing. A section in the lower reaches is controlled by Newcastle A.A. who sell a limited number of day permits.

CO. FERMANAGH

This county, known as the Ulster Lakeland, holds the most and some of the best fishing in Northern Ireland. The long meandering Ernes dominate, bisecting the county from east to west. Together they cover over 15,000 hectares which, with numerous feeder lakes, teem with fish. Upper Lough Erne is a famous coarse fishery. There is however some good trout fishing in Lower Lough Erne and in some smaller lakes and rivers mostly, like the Ernes, in Department control.

Best of these is Lough Melvin already described in Chapter VIII and which is partly in the Republic. It is a Department fishery and the only spring salmon water in Northern Ireland. A good second is the trout areas of Lower Lough Erne in the north-west. There are abundant trout in the 2-3 lbs range and large trout of over 10 lbs (4.5 kg) frequently taken. The big ones are caught mostly by trolling. Dapping in the Mayfly season, once popular, has now diminished but the wet and dry fly in the hands of a skilled angler can reap a rich harvest in the numerous bays and inlets when conditions are right. Trout angling tends to fall off in late June and July when the trout are feasting on the perch fly. Tributaries of the Lower Lough are regularly stocked with trout.

Other trout waters are the Department lakes Bellanaleck and Coolyermer south of Enniskillen; Glencreawan, Meenameen and Achork to the west, Corry and Corranny east of Lisnaskea; a 1 mile stretch of the Ballinamallard river at Riversdale (near St Angelo airport) and Keenaghan lake near Belleek. All are brown trout waters except Corranny which is a small rainbow lake.

In addition to the Department waters there is the Ballinamallard river upstream of Riversdale, some 11 km of good trout fishing, the Tempo, over 11 km from the junction with the Colebrooke river up to Tempo, and the Arney river, 8 km from Arney Old Bridge to Lough McNean, all mixed fishing with good trout stocks. These three rivers by permission of the landowners.

The whole of the Fermanagh area is highly developed for fishing and as a general tourist centre. The access points are well signposted and much work has been done on the provision of roads, car parks, paths, stiles and so on for the convenience of the angler.

Fishing by boat for game fish is permitted on the Ernes, Melvin and Bellanaleck. Boats are available for hire.

9. CAVAN, MONAGHAN & LOUTH

These three counties are drumlin country with many lakes, most of which are good coarse fishing waters. Many of the rivers, although they do hold a few trout, are overrun with small roach. The headwaters of the Erne are here and also Lough Annagh; these have already been described.

Emly Lough, near Monaghan, is a good trout fishing lake which is stocked and managed by the IFT. Trout average about 1¼ lbs (0.6 kg) and fly fishing only is permitted. Boats are available and the lake can also be fished from the shore. IFT members only.

The Blackwater is a fair sized river which drains north through counties Monaghan and Armagh into Lough Neagh. In Co. Monaghan, it is well overgrown with bushes and is stony and gravelly with streams, pools and a few weedy glides. It is a good fly fishing river, holding fair numbers of trout averaging about ½ lb (0.25 kg).

The Castletown River runs into Dundalk harbour. It holds small trout and some sea trout in summer. The River Fane also enters Dundalk Bay, but it falls very low in summer and becomes very weedy. The Fane receives salmon and sea trout. Permits to fish from Dundalk Salmon A.A. Charges about £1 per day or £5 per week, however the river is of little more than local interest. Recent reports are poor.

The rivers Dee and Glyde are limestone streams running into the Irish Sea between Dundalk and Drogheda. They were both subject to drainage works some time ago. Fishing is quite good in spring and when there is sufficient flow, but like many drained streams they tend to fall too low to fish well in summer. Permits to fish for trout from the Dee and Glyde Fishing Development Association. T. O'Callaghan, Newtowndarver, Castlebellingham, Co. Louth, and from the Dundalk and District Brown Trout A.A., G. Elliott, Ann Street, Dundalk. About £1.50 per season.

THE BOYNE SYSTEM

The Boyne is a big river rising near Edenderry, Co. Offaly and flowing north to the Irish Sea at Drogheda. It flows over limestone for most of its course and receives many tributaries. All of the Boyne system was first class trout water as well as receiving excellent runs of large spring and summer salmon. At the time of writing, it is the subject of a drainage scheme which has badly affected the trout fishing and the general appearance of the river. Salmon fishing is hardly worthwhile. At present, the main tributary, the Kells Blackwater, is still untouched and is a first class trout river. It is a winding river running through rich pasture land. There are few rapids but most of the river is weedy glides and pools. The rapids are a haven for the smaller trout and there are a few good fish. The better trout live in the glides and deeps and provide excellent and very exacting fly fishing, especially on summer evenings.

Parts of the river are private fishing, and there is some association water. The associations are the Navan and District A.A., Mr Flanagan, Kentstown, Navan; the Kilbride A.C., T. O'Brien, 22 Dollymount Grove, Dublin 3, and the Kells A.A., Mr Fitzgerald, Bective Street, Kells, Co. Meath.

The other Boyne tributaries may provide some trout fishing but drainage work has badly affected most of them. A number of small rivers run into the Irish Sea between Drogheda and Dublin. The best of them are the Nanny, the Delvin and the Broadmeadow. They are association waters providing some trout fishing and some sea trout, but they are only of local interest.

This concludes the catalogue of Irish game fishing waters. At the time of writing, a licence for all anglers in the Republic is proposed and considerably more protection for runs of migratory fish and better regulation of angling. These measures, if carried out, should improve angling generally.

Angling reports are published in some periodicals which give the latest information on fishing in the major waters. Some of these are "The Shooting Times", "The Field" and "Trout and Salmon". Visiting anglers may refer to these reports before deciding on the venue of their visit. The casual angler may have a lot of enjoyment by just fishing around if he is experienced, but for more certain success, visitors are recommended to use hotels or guesthouses that cater especially for anglers and that are situated on or near good and well regulated waters. Game fishing is subject to peaks and declines and local knowledge may be important to make the best of a bad period.

The prices, etc. in this guide are approximate and as correct as is possible at the time of writing. More exact prices and addresses of Angling Club secretaries may be obtained from the annual supplement to Salmon and Sea Trout Fishing, and Trout Fishing in Ireland, published by Bord Failte, Baggot Street Bridge, Dublin 2. Free from Irish Tourist Board Offices.

Since completing this guide, new legislation has been introduced by the Irish Government to preserve runs of salmon. The information in this guide is still correct, but the salmon fishing season now finishes at the end of August.

The structure of Fishery Boards is being changed, but a visiting angler should still purchase a licence locally before fishing for salmon and sea trout. Latest information on charges and licences may be obtained free from Bord Failte.

LICENCES FOR SALMON AND SEA TROUT
and
ANGLING SEASONS

LICENCE FEES

In Ireland a state licence is required in order to fish for salmon and sea trout as follows:

All districts, full season	£10.00
Single district (specified) full season	£5.00
All districts, 21 days	£5.00
All districts, 7 days	£3.00

In most fishery districts late season licences (July to end of season) are available at £3.00 valid for district of issue only. In addition, late season licences valid for all districts can be obtained, costing £7.00.

Licences are obtainable from the Clerks to the Boards of Conservators for the various districts and also from various tackle shops, hoteliers and other agents. Holders of Foyle licences can obtain an extension licence valid for all fishery districts in this country for a full season for £7.00; or for a single (specified) district £2.00.

STATUTORY OPENING DATES FOR SALMON FISHING

January 1

Liffey
Garvogue River, Lough Gill, Bonet River
Bundrowes River (Lough Melvin, February 1)
Glenveagh System
Lennon System (including Lough Fern)

January 17

Waterville River and Kerry Inny
Behy River, Caragh River and Lake
River Laune, River Maine and Killarney Lakes

February 1

Rivers Glyde, Dee, Boyne, Dargle
Rivers Barrow, Nore, Suir, Cork Blackwater, Lee
River Ilen
River Shannon, south of Portumna and tributaries (except Feale) of Shannon below Portumna
Kilcolgan River
River Corrib, Lough Corrib, Owenboliska, Connemara Systems
Clifden and Cleggan waters, Dawros, Culfin, Erriff, Delphi, Belclare, Burrishoole*, Achill waters, Owenduff, Owenmore, Ballinglen, Moy System (except Palmerstown River), Easkey River, Ballysodare River, Drumcliffe River, Grange River, Bunduff River, Lough Melvin

February 2

Bracky River, Gweebarra River, Owenmarve River, Dungloe Waters, Gweedore River, Clady River, Crolly River, Bedlam River, Glenna River, Tullaghobegly River, Ray River, Swilly River, Mill River

February 15

Rivers Bandon, Argideen

February 26
River Slaney
March 1
Feale, Geale and Cashen Rivers
Shannon Systems above Portumna
Eske Systems (Donegal), Inver (Eany Water), Oily River, Stragar River, Glen River
Crana River
Finn River (Foyle)
Fane River
March 15
Owenvaragh (Courtown)
Kenmare Bay Rivers
March 17
Dunmanus Bay and Bantry Bay Rivers
Rivers Emlagh, Anascaul and Dingle and Ventry Harbour streams
April 1
Caherciveen Rivers (Carhan, Ferta, etc.)
Brandon Bay and Tralee Bay Rivers
Rivers Bunowen, Carrowniskey
Owenea, Owentocker
Culdaff River
May 1
Feoghanagh River
Owengarve River (Mulrany)
Glenamoy
June 1
Palmerstown River (Ballina)

STATUTORY CLOSING DATES FOR SALMON FISHING

Closing date for rod and line angling for salmon in all fishery districts is August 31.

STATUTORY CLOSING DATES FOR SEA TROUT FISHING

Sea trout which are regarded as salmon in law are exempt from the statutory closing date of August 31. The closing dates for sea trout fishing are as follows:
August 31
Slaney (above junction with and including R. Bann)
Barrow, Nore, Suir
September 15
Mattock, Nanny, Feale, Geale, Cashen, Smearlagh, Slaney (below junction with R. Bann), R. Finn (Foyle)
September 30
Owenvaragh (Courtown)
Waterford coastal streams (Colligan, Mahon, Tay, etc.)
Cork Blackwater
Brandon and Tralee Bay streams
Feoghanagh
Cullenagh (Inagh)
Newport River, Beltra L.
Owenmore
Owenea River, Owentocker River

Glenveagh System (Lackagh River, Glen L., etc.)
Glyde and Dee Rivers

October 9

Eske System
Inver (Eany Water)
Oily River, Stragar River, Glen River

October 10

Ballinglen River

October 12

Dargle System
Broadmeadow Ward
Argideen River
Bantry Bay, Dunmanus Bay and Kenmare Rivers (Roughty, etc.)
Meelagh, Owvane, Coomhola, Glengarriff
Waterville System, Kerry Inny, Clonee, Caragh
Caherciveen and Glenbeigh waters
Killarney Lakes, Maine River, Inch and Dingle area rivers
Kilcolgan River
Owenboliska River, Crumlin River
Screebe, Inver, Furnace, Cashla and Lettermuckoo Fisheries, Carraroe, Gorumna Rivers and Carna area
Gowla Fishery, Ballynahinch Fishery, Dohulla Fishery
Clifden and Cleggan areas
Dawros, Culfin, Owenglin and Erriff systems
Delphi, Carrowniskey, Bunowen, Belclare, Burrishoole, Owengarve, Achill waters, Owenduff, Glenamoy, Palmerstown, Easkey, Drumcliffe, Grange, Bracky, Gweebarra, Owenmarve, Dungloe Lakes (The Rosses), Gweedora, Clady, Crolly, Bedlam, Glenna, Tullaghobegly
Swilly, Fanad Peninsula waters, Mill River, Cranna River, Fane River

October 20

Culdaff River

BROWN TROUT ANGLING SEASON

Generally March 1 to September 30. Some western waters, notably Co. Clare Lakes, open February 15.
Boyne and tributaries close September 15, Lough Conn and some other western waters October 12.

Note

Anglers in the Republic are required by law to supply accurate statistics of catches. This information should be sent to: Dept. of Fisheries, Agriculture House, Kildare St, Dublin

(Source: Dept. of Fisheries)

APPENDIX

IRISH RECORD FISH
and
SCHEDULE OF SPECIMEN WEIGHTS

IRISH RECORD FISH

FRESHWATER FISH

Species	Weight lbs	Weight ozs	Date of Capture	Place of Capture	Captor
Salmon	57	0	1874	River Suir	M. Maher
Sea Trout	14	3	15.5.1973	Dooagh Beach, Achill	Dr Eoin Bresnihan
Brown Trout (river)	20	0	22.2.1957	River Shannon, Corbally	Major Hugh Place
Brown Trout (lake)	26	2	15.7.1894	Lough Ennell	Wm Meares
Bream	11	12	1882	River Blackwater (Monaghan)	A. Pike
Carp	18	12	6.6.1958	Abbey Lake	John Roberts
Dace	1	2	8.8.1966	River Blackwater, Cappoquin	John T. Henry
Perch	5	8	1946	Lough Erne	S. Drum
Pike (river)	42	0	22.3.1964	River Barrow	M. Watkins
Pike (lake)	38	2	25.2.1973	Lough Corrib	B. Hardiman
Roach	2	13½	11.8.1970	River Blackwater, Coppoquin	L. Robinson
Rudd	3	1	27.6.1959	Kilglass Lake	A. E. Biddlecombe
Rudd/Bream Hybrid	5	13½	12.4.1975	River Shannon Lanesboro	P. J. Dighton
Tench	7	13¼	25.5.1971	River Shannon, Lanesboro	R. Webb
River Eel	6	15	12.6.1979	L. Droumenisa, Bantry	J. Murnane

SEA FISH

Species	Weight lbs	Weight ozs	Date of Capture	Place of Capture	Captor
Angler Fish	71	8	5.7.1964	Cork Harbour	Ml. Fitzgerald
Bass	17	1¼	27.4.1977	Whiting Bay, Ardmore	M. Tucker
Black Sole	3	10	19.10.1970	Woodstown Strd., Waterford	R. W. Nicholson

Coalfish	24	7	26.8.1967	Kinsale	J. E. Hornibrook
Cod	42	0	1921	Ballycotton	I. L. Stewart
Conger	72	0	June 1914	Valentia	J. Green
Dab	1	13½	20.10.1979	Ballycotton	P. Curtin
Spur Dogfish	18	12	10.9.1977	Bantry	J. Murnane
Greater Spotted Dogfish	21	4	13.9.1975	Malin, Co. Donegal	D. Alexander
Lesser Spotted Dogfish	3	13	1.10.1978	Belfast Lough	E. Reid
Flounder	4	6½	21.8.1979	Ballyteigue, Co. Wexford	D. Gray
Garfish	3	10¼	16.9.1967	Kinsale	E. Bazzard
Tub Gurnard	12	3½	8.8.1973	Bullsmouth, Achill	R. Seaman
Grey Gurnard	3	1	21.9.1967	Rosslare Bay	B. Walsh
Red Gurnard	3	9½	17.7.1968	Belmullet	J. Prescott
Haddock	10	13½	15.7.1964	Kinsale	F. A. E. Bull
Hake	25	5½	28.4.1962	Belfast Lough	H. W. Steele
Halibut	156		23.7.1972	Belmullet	F. Brogan
Ling	46	8	26.7.1965	Kinsale	A. J. C. Bull
John Dory	7	1	6.9.1970	Tory Island, Donegal	S. Morrow
Mackerel	4	2	18.9.1979	Ballycotton Co. Cork	Ulrich Plassmann
Monkfish	69	0	1.7.1958	Clew Bay, Westport	M. Fuchs
Grey Mullet	7	12	7.9.1975	Brittas Bay	C. Quinn
Plaice	7	2½	27.5.1973	Youghal	C. Pratt
Pollack	19	3	1904	Ballycotton	J. N. Hearne
Pouting	4	10	1937	Ballycotton	W. G. Pales
Thornback Ray	37	0	28.5.1961	Ling Rocks, Kinsale	M. J. Fitzgerald
Blonde Ray	36	8	9.9.1964	Cork Harbour	D. Minchin
Sting Ray	51	0	8.8.1970	Fenit, Co. Kerry	J. White
Cuckoo Ray	5	11	3.8.1975	Causeway Coast	V. Morrison
Undulate Ray	18		11.6.1977	Fenit	A.-M. Liedecke
Homelyn Ray	7	7½	7.7.1976	Dunfanaghy, Co. Donegal	J. Kerr
Painted Ray	14	6	7.7.1979	Doughmore Bch., Co. Clare	W. Ryan
Ray's Bream	6	4¼	26.8.1978	Valentia	M. Sarney
Red Sea Bream	9	6	24.8.1963	Valentia	P. Maguire
Porbeagle Shark	365		1932	Keem Bay, Achill	Dr O'Donel Brown
Blue Shark	206		7.10.1959	Achill Head	J. McMonagle
Six Gilled Shark	154		28.8.1968	Kinsale	A. Bull
Common Skate	221		1913	Ballycotton	T. Tucker
White Skate	165		7.8.1966	Clew Bay Westport	J. Stack

Tope	66	8	15.7.1979	Carlingford Lough	Cyril Young
Turbot	26	8	1915	Valentia	J. F. Eldridge
Whiting	4	8½	4.8.1969	Kinsale	E. Boyle
Ballan Wrasse	7	8½	26.7.64	Killybegs	A. J. King
Cuckoo Wrasse	1	11½	23.9.1979	Larne	G. Denny

SCHEDULE OF SPECIMEN WEIGHTS

	Irish record		Specimen	Weight
FRESHWATER FISH	**lbs**	**ozs**	**lbs**	**kilos**
Salmon *(Salmo salar)*	57	0	25	11.339
Sea Trout *(Salmo trutta)*	14	3	6	2.721
Brown Trout *(Salmo trutta) (river)*	20	0	5	2.268
Brown Trout *(Salmo trutta) (lake)*	26	2	10	4.536
Slob Trout *(Salmo trutta)*	—		10	4.536
Bream *(Abramis brama)*	11	12	7½	3.402
Carp *(Cyprinus carpio)*	18	12	10	4.536
Dace *(Leucisus leucisus)*	1	2	1	0.454
Perch *(Perca fluviatilis)*	5	8	3	1.361
Pike *(Esox lucius) (lake)*	38	2	30	13.608
Pike *(Esox lucius) (river)*	42	0	20	9.072
Roach *(Rutilus rutilus)*	2	13½	2	1.021
Rudd *(Scardinius erythrophthalmus)*	3	1	2¼	1.021
Rudd/Bream hybrid	5	13½	3	1.361
Roach/Bream hybrid	—		3	1.361
Tench *(Tinca tinca)*	7	13¼	6	2,721
Eel *(Anguilla anguilla)*	6	15	3	1.361
SEA FISH				
Angler fish *(Lophius piscatorius)*	71	8	40	18.144
Bass *(Dicentrarchus labrax)*	17	1¼	10	4.536
Black sole *(Solea solea)*	3	10	2	0.907
Brill *(Scophthalmus Rhombus)*	—			3.629
Coalfish *(Pollachius virens)*	24	7	15	6.804
Cod *(Gadus morhus)*	42	0	25	11.340
Conger *(Conger conger)*	72	0	40	18.144
Dab *(Limanda limanda)*	1	13½	1½	0.680
Dogfish—Spur *(Squalus acanthias)*	18	0	12	5.443
—Lesser spotted *(Scyliorhinus Caniculus)*	3	13	3¼	1.475
—Greater spotted *(Scyliorhinus stellaris)*	21	4	16	7.257
Flounder *(Platchthys flesus)*	4	6½	2½	1.134
Garfish *(Belone bellone)*	3	10¼	2½	1.134
Gurnard—Tub *(Trigla lucerna)*	12	3½	5	2.268
—Grey *(Eutrigla gurnardus)*	3	1	1½	0.680
—Red *(Aspitrigla Cuculus)*	3	9½	2	0.907

Haddock *(Melanogrammus aeglifinus)*	10	13½	7	3.175
Hake *(Merluccius merluccius)*	25	5½	10	4.536
Halibut *(Hippoglossus hippoglossus)*	156	0	50	22.680
Herring *(Clupea harengus)*	—		¾	0.340
John Dory *(Zeus faber)*	7	1	4	1.814
Ling *(Molva Molva)*	46	8	25	11.340
Mackerel *(Scomber scombrus)*	4	2	2½	1.134
Megrim *(Lepidorhombus whiffiagonis)*	—		3	1.361
Monkfish *(Squatina squatina)*	69	0	50	22.680
Mullet—Grey, thick lipped, *(Crenimugil labrosus)*	7	12	5	2.268
—Red *(Mullus surmuletus)*	—		1	0.454
Plaice *(Pleuronectes platessa)*	7	2½	4	1.814
Pollack *(Pollachius pollachius)*	19	3	12	5.443
Pouting *(Trisopterus luscus)*	4	10	3	1.361
Ray—Thornback *(Raja clavata)*	37	0	20	9.072
—Blonde *(Raja brachyura)*	36	8	25	11.340
—Cuckoo *(Raja naevus)*	5	11	4½	2.041
—Electric *(Torpedo nobiliana)*	—		20	9.072
—Homelyn *(Raja montagui)*	7	7½	5	2.268
—Undulate *(Raja undulata)*	18		14	6.350
—Painted *(Raja microocellata)*	14	6	10	4.536
—Sting *(Dasyatis pastinaca)*	51		30	13.608
Ray's Bream *(Brama brama)*	6	0	5	2.268
Red Sea Bream *(Pagellus bogaraveo)*	9	6	4½	2.041
Scad *(Trachurus trachurus)*	—		2	0.907
Shad—Allis *(Alosa alosa)*	—		4	1.814
—Twaite *(Alosa fallax)*	—		1½	0.680
Shark—Porbeagle *(Lamna nasus)*	365	0	150	68.038
—Blue *(Prionace glauca)*	206	0	100	45.359
Thresher *(Alopias vulpinus)*	—		120	54.431
Mako *(Isurus oxyrinchus)*	—		200	90.718
Six-Gilled *(Hexanchus griseus)*	154		100	45.359
Skate—Common *(Raja batis)*	221	0	suspended	
—White *(Raja alba)*	165	0	120	54.431
—Long Nose *(Raja oxyrinchus)*	—		80	36.287
Stone Basse *(Polyprion americanus)*	—		8	3.628
Tope *(Galeorhinus galeus)*	66	8	40	18.144
Tunny *(Thunnus thynnus)*	—		100	45.359
Turbot *(Scophthalmus maximus)*	26	8	18	8.165
Whiting *(Merlangius merlangus)*	4	8½	3	1.361
Wrasse Ballan *(Labrus bergylta)*	7	6	4½	2.041
Wrasse Cuckoo *(Labras mixtus)*	1	11½	1¼	0.567

Scientific names in accordance with the *List of Irish Fishes,* third ed. 1976, by A. E. J. Went, D.Sc., M.R.I.A. and M. Kennedy, Ph.D. (Stationery Office for the National Museum, 1969).